FUSSBUSTERS
on the go

STRATEGIES AND GAMES

FOR STRESS-FREE OUTINGS,

ERRANDS, AND VACATIONS

WITH YOUR PRESCHOOLER

CAROL BAICKER-McKEE, Ph.D.

Ω
PEACHTREE
ATLANTA

Dedicated
to my father,
Mike McKee,
who gave me his wanderlust,
his appreciation of the written word,
and his silly sense of humor,
but fortunately not his hairline.
I love you.

Published by
PEACHTREE PUBLISHERS, LTD.
1700 Chattahoochee Avenue
Atlanta, Georgia 30318-2112

www.peachtree-online.com

Text © 2002 by Carol Baicker-McKee, Ph.D.

Book and cover design by Loraine M. Joyner
Composition by Robin Sherman

Manufactured in the United States of America
10 9 8 7 6 5 4 3 2 1
First Edition

Library of Congress Cataloging-in-Publication Data

Baicker-McKee, Carol, 1958-
    Fussbusters on the go : strategies and games for stress-free outings,
errands, and vacations with your preschooler / by Carol Baicker-McKee.–1st ed.
        p. cm.
    ISBN 1-56145-263-7
    1. Family recreation. 2. Preschool children–Recreation. I. Title.
    GV182.8 .B33 2002
    796–dc21
                            2002004830

Table of
Contents

CHAPTER TWO

Wait Gain 26

CHAPTER THREE

Surviving Doctors' Offices, Hairdressers, and Other Places Your Child Hates 56

CHAPTER FOUR
Going on Outings without Going out of Your Mind   82

CHAPTER FIVE
Don't You Hate It When the Kids in the Car
Go Whine, Whine, Whine?   110

CHAPTER SIX

Getting There Can Be at Least 10 Percent of the Fun

139

CHAPTER SEVEN

When You're Sentenced to Life on the Road   174

CHAPTER EIGHT

Because You Didn't Go All That Way Just to Listen to Incessant Whining, Did You?   205

CHAPTER NINE

Minor Disaster Management 239

Acknowledgments

I've noticed that the closer I get to a deadline, the more things in my life break or go wrong. (I'm sure this is some corollary to Murphy's Law.) And if you miss a deadline and get close to the new one, even bigger and more essential things start breaking. And what happens if you miss that deadline and have to set a third one? Let's just say it involves major appliances and X rays.

That's why for this book, I not only have to thank all those people I thanked the last time, like my husband Steve and kids, Eric, Sara, and Kyle. (See—I did the names out of order so that Kyle doesn't always go first. You're absolutely right that that's not fair.) I also have to thank all the people who kept fixing things or stepping in to hold things together for me so my family didn't come completely unraveled while I finished it.

So, thanks to the refrigerator repairman, the furnace guy, the plumber, and Ken the kitchen guy. And Dr. Scott Tyson and the other staff at Pediatrics South. And thanks to the Robbs who have chauffeured Eric to more than their share of camping trips and other scouting events, and to the Magalotti family (Roni, Mark, Paul, and Daniel) for filling in for me yesterday when I actually *forgot* to pick up the boys from Academic Games practice. My gratitude to Mary Lou Vanzin and family who always give me reminders of important forms and upcoming activity deadlines, as well as general moral support and bucking up. Thanks, too, to Brenda Nascone and family, because those morning corner chats helped me preserve my sanity when I was spending days as a computer hermit. I am grateful to my children's teachers and the support staff at Lincoln Elementary School and Jefferson Middle School in Mt. Lebanon, PA, for not saying anything about my kids' rumpled appearances or strange lunches the last month or so, and for being kind, stable influences in their lives. And to Koko the dog for looking over my shoulder while I worked and giving me encouraging licks.

I also need to thank all the people who help me support my writing habit, which includes my husband again, the librarians at the Mt. Lebanon Public Library, the members of my Monday night writers' group, and Judy Press, Andrea Perry, and Karen Baicker. And of course, I am deeply grateful to all the super people like Vicky Holifield at Peachtree Publishers, who give me boundless hope for the future of books and publishing, if they are any indication of the quality of folks running the business. Special, special thanks to Peachtree Associate Publisher Kathy Landwehr, without whom I could not have finished this project.

Introduction

About the Author
OR, HOW I CAME TO WRITE ANOTHER BOOK THAT MENTIONS BODILY FUNCTIONS ON NEARLY EVERY PAGE

The "About the Author" part of this book will answer the following questions:

1. I do not care to have lunch with this Carol Baicker-McKee lady, but what made her want to write this crazy book?
2. What makes her think *she's* qualified to write a book on going places with your kids and trying to keep them from being totally crabby?
3. Why the heck does she have to mention barf, pee, poop, boogers, and diarrhea on nearly every page?

I'll try to respond to the questions in the order they've been asked. (Legal Disclaimer: Notice I did *not* say I would really answer them.)

Answer to Question Number One This is an actual question that was submitted by a sharp student at a school where I did an author visit a couple years ago. It is one of the best questions I have ever been asked at a school visit, and I have the original piece of notebook paper framed and hanging in my office. The question was actually about a totally different book, but I think the question applies equally well to this one, so I'll answer it anyway.

I'm a mom, and I wanted to write this book so I would get out of doing the laundry for a while. It has sort of worked. I have not done any laundry in weeks. Unfortunately, neither has anyone else, not even the dog, and so we are all wearing dirty underwear except for the dog, who prefers to go au naturel. As for lunch, it's probably good that you don't want to have it with me. I have not been grocery shopping in quite some time either, and if you were to have lunch with me, you'd have to settle for licking some peanut butter off the knife since there's not really enough left to bother spreading it on a piece of bread. I'd advise you to ignore the dog's begging, while you're licking. You don't have to feel guilty and share with her, because there is plenty of her low-cal dog food left (I wisely bought the super-size bag last time.)—at least that's what I keep trying to tell myself when she stares at me with those big sad eyes.

Answer to Question Number Two If you look through my parents' family albums (*Author's aside: These are not, on the whole, actual albums, but rather shoe boxes and stacks of slides—I came by my own photo-shoebox storage "system" honestly.*), you will quickly understand why I am uniquely qualified to write a book about going places with crabby kids. There I am at three at the White House Easter Egg Roll, arms crossed and glaring. At seven or so, standing on a beach someplace looking utterly sad and miserable. And again at age nine at the Montreal Expo, huddled in my coat and scowling at the camera. Oh, and there at eleven, looking daggers at my sister next to a rickety bus in Banff, Canada. Probably there were few kids of my generation who were taken to as many places as I was while being as fussy, grumpy, crabby, irritable, and generally out of sorts as I was. And my parents never once *really* stopped the car and made me walk home. There were also many moments—documented in the family photo stacks as well—when I was pleasant, cheerful, cooperative, and a delight to be with, thanks in large part to my parents' expert management of me and their three other kids. Thus, I got to experience firsthand how to change lousy moods into reasonable ones while out and about.

I also have been on the parent side of the equation, which has given me opportunities to put my many theories to the test and see which ones work and which ones falter. I have been to the grocery store with kids in tow at least, oh, let's just say an infinite number of times, which means I've had a chance to find ways to make the whole experience less whiny. I've logged enough minivan kid hours to qualify me for a chauffeur's license. And with one child who was prone to ear infections (code for at the pediatrician's at least once a week) and two other kids with their share of strep throats, sinus infections, and big boo-boos, I learned ways to comfort kids in unpleasant circumstances. Finally, I've been brave enough to travel with my kids as far as Paris, France, and that says something, if you know what I mean.

I also have lots of those kinds of qualifications that look good on the back of the dust jacket, but aren't necessarily as useful for the actual writing of the book as they might seem. I'm a former teacher, from daycare and preschool classes to after school programs and community college. (In fact, the teaching qualification is helpful, particularly in the field trip expertise department.) I have a B.A. in psychology from Yale University and an M.A. and Ph.D. in clinical child psychology from the University of Virginia. I've worked as a child and family therapist in various outpatient and hospital settings, where I was privileged to learn from some very child-savvy folks as well as from some kids who taught me a lot about observing, being flexible, and the power of kindness in the face of strong emotions.

Does that answer your question?

Answer to Question Number Three Because I have spent so much time with young kids, I think they're good for a laugh. Plus, they are For Real Major Important Issues with young children; ignore them at your peril. And very few books on parenting or going places with young kids discuss barf, boogers, etc., in sufficient detail so that you really learn what to do about them.

About This Book

FussBusters on the Go is a sort of a twin to another book called *Fuss-Busters at Home.* You can certainly read one and not the other, just as you can invite one twin to your child's birthday party and not the other, but it might hurt the feelings of the one who is left out. And besides, they look kind of cute standing there together in their matching covers on your shelf.

During my therapy years I snagged one of my favorite quotes from a greeting card or something and pasted it on the wall of my office. It is attributed to Hodding Carter, who was a Pulitzer Prize–winning journalist, and who probably said lots of other poetic, slightly sappy, yet absolutely true things. Here's the quote:

> *There are only two lasting bequests we can hope to give our children. One of these is roots, the other, wings.*

Isn't that nice? Put it up on your wall or refrigerator too. In my mind, *FussBusters at Home* is sort of the *roots* book, since it's about helping your child have a settled, reasonably happy home life. This book, on the other hand, is the *wings* book, the one that looks at ways to help you start launching your child into the wider world. (Naturally when your child is this age, you'll be holding his hand and making sure he's buckled in safely, but it's still the beginning of his leaving the security of his nest.) Which is why you have a whole new crop of fusses to contend with.

I've divided the book into two main sections. The first five chapters are devoted to those short forays into the world around your town or community. The last four chapters address problems that arise as you venture farther afield on trips and vacations. Within chapters I have tried to group activities into subcategories where it seemed appropriate, such as ideas for car rides or strategies for trips on public transportation. And, as in the first book, I have tried to focus on suggestions that don't require an advanced degree in early childhood education or Styrofoam trays.

Each chapter opens with a short introduction that highlights the content of the chapter, and sometimes relates real-life anecdotes designed to help you feel like you're at least a better parent than I am. The individual activities or tips are described in easy-to-follow directions, and I've occasionally included safety tips or references to other helpful resources like books or websites.

Preschooler Principles

The following are some characteristics of young children that have guided the development and selection of the activities in both *FussBusters* books. Understanding these principles may help you interpret your child's responses and guide you in choosing activities to suit your child's needs. Plus, this section gives me a chance to use that expensive education I spent years pursuing.

- *Preschoolers like consistency, rituals, predictability.* Life is full of surprises for young children. Anything that makes the world more predictable or that lets them know what to expect makes them feel safer and braver. Repetition helps them master new skills, ideas, and language. Finally, routines help them develop responsibility—they learn *what* they should do *when.* "Do it again" is the credo of the young child. That's why they want to have peanut butter and banana sandwiches on white bread with the crusts removed and cut into perfect triangles for lunch. Every day. For the next four years.
- *As inconsistent as it seems, preschoolers like novelty and variety.* They like novelty and variety—within a framework of predictability. Serve that perfect peanut butter and banana sandwich on a doll's plate inside a cardboard box,

and you'll be a hero! On other occasions, your support and encouragement will help your child to welcome the new and accept changes.

Young children also have short attention spans and may need more frequent shifts of activities, with a balance of quiet and active things to do. That's why they alternate between teasing their little sister in whispers and tackling her with Tarzan yells.

• *Preschoolers need to move their bodies.* Young children are developing their muscles and the neurological connections that control them. They need space and permission to be active and use their large muscles. They'll use them in the dining room on the chandelier if you don't send them outside. And don't forget opportunities to use the small muscles in their hands and eyes as they do art projects, manipulate small toys, look at books, and disassemble the VCR.

• *Preschoolers use all their senses.* They learn with their whole selves. Sensory activities will capture their attention, and many, such as water play, have a wonderfully calming effect.

Preschoolers' drive to use their senses can still cause trouble, though. Even though their emerging self-control helps them to refrain from touching things they shouldn't or putting everything in their mouths, temptation may sometimes override their better sense, leading them try out your best makeup on the dog. Supervise and continue to childproof their play areas. Pay attention to the safety notes included with some *FussBusters* activities.

• *Preschoolers' temperaments continue to shape their actions and reactions.* Individual differences can be quite striking—and perfectly normal. Be flexible and respect your child's special needs, interests, and tastes. Even if they run more strongly in favor of slugs and superheroes than yours do.

- *Gender rules.* Gender identification is quite strong during this period. Young girls may reject seemingly neutral activities as "just for boys," and boys may refuse to do anything they see as "girl stuff." If you have a little girl, odds are good that she will spend hours enveloped in tulle waiting for Prince Charming, and if you have boys, expect to spend a great deal of time discussing the relative merits of various dinosaurs and arguing about whether he is allowed to pretend the hose nozzle is a ray gun that can annihilate his sister. These sexist attitudes will make you want to gag, but don't get too worked up. By first grade, most will have faded dramatically, even if you skip the equal rights lectures.

Preschooler Management 101

Ever wonder why your child is more cooperative with his teacher or grandparents? The main reason is security—he feels comfortable enough with you to risk making mistakes or even misbehaving. You can't (and wouldn't want to) change that. But another reason may be that teachers and grandparents have acquired skills from long and repeated experience with young children. Adopting these attitudes and strategies can make your life with your child easier—and more fun.

Anticipate—Remember both senses of this word:

- *Be prepared.* Thinking ahead will help you avoid problems and set the stage for success. For example, buy clothes your child can fasten himself or place dishes where he can reach them easily. You can also help prepare your child, whose sense of the future, recall of the past, and awareness of time is just developing, for events on the horizon. As much as possible, tell him what to expect, warn him of upcoming transitions, and remind him of important rules, like "Don't say 'poo-poo butt' to Great-uncle Walter."

- **_Look forward to._** It's easy to get bogged down in the drudgery of everyday life with a preschool child. But changing your mindset to expect pleasure can improve both your mood and your child's behavior. Take advantage of the opportunities young children offer you to slow down, to live in the here and now, to notice and marvel at all the small miracles in the world.

Communicate clearly.

Language is still a new skill for small children, so you have to make it easy for them to understand you. What works:

- Make sure you have their attention.
- Exaggerate your facial expressions, tone of voice, body language.
- Give only one or two directions at a time.
- Be specific.
- Don't offer choices unless you mean them.
- Make sure you understand their messages.
- Give them the words they need.
- Use the word "poop" when you really need them to hear you.

Invoke imagination and humor.

Making believe is an important and emerging skill during the preschool years. _And_ it's probably the easiest route to securing your child's cooperation. He might balk at dressing for church, but he'll cheerfully don his Sunday-best space suit! A good dose of silliness helps too.

Reset your clock.

Preschoolers have short legs, and most of the time we remember to adjust our strides to match their slower pace. But we also need to remember that *many* tasks take young children longer. Allowing enough time will reduce stress for everyone and boost your child's emerging competence.

Conversely, we sometimes need to speed things up, to adjust for children's shorter attention spans and smaller energy reserves. Two hours at the art museum is probably an hour and a half too long for most young children. Accept that, for a few years, you'll need to be flexible and accommodating.

Refocus and reframe.

Distraction, so effective with toddlers, is also a useful tool with preschoolers. Finding an element of challenge may be the best way to keep a child this age from noticing how much he dislikes something. For example, "I'll bet I can scrub my hands longer than you can!" can produce some impressively clean hands for both of you.

Just as reframing an old picture can bring out its beauty, so can describing an event differently change its impact. If your child was scared by a thunderstorm, you may be able to influence her perception of the experience by helping her notice how well she coped by closing her eyes and covering her ears.

Put yourself in your child's shoes.

Stooping down to your child's size, sometimes literally, will help you make sense of his behavior and remind you of ways to structure his environment so he can succeed. It's good to remind yourself that he may not be able to see what's on the countertop, reach the rack to rehang his towel, or carry that heavy plate.

Take Care:

- ***Of your child*** Your child may loudly assert her competence and independence, but the next minute she may beg for you to help take off her socks. You should expect her to need you especially when she is tired, ill, or stressed by new experiences or problems with her friends or at home. And, no matter how capable she seems, she will need frequent encouragement and reassurance, as well as regular physical contact and demonstrations of your love and affection.

- *Of yourself* On airlines, flight attendants instruct you to fit your own oxygen mask before you help your child—if you pass out, you'll be no use to your child, and she may not be able to help you. The same principle holds true in everyday life. So don't feel guilty about using activities just to give yourself a half-hour to read a magazine. And feel free to skip suggestions that you find unappealing.

CHAPTER ONE

Un-Erring Those Errands

Okay, let's see a show of hands. How many of you would rather have a root canal than go to the post office, the dry cleaners, and the supermarket with a couple of kids under the age of six? Well, me neither. Even though I have the nicest, gentlest dentist in the world, high-stakes dentistry has never been my cup of tea. Still, it's a closer call than it ought to be.

Running errands involves a whole slew of things that preschoolers hate: adult-oriented activities, transitions, temptations that must be resisted, and time away from their friends and action figures. This means that running errands requires you to have the patience of seven preschool teachers, the ingenuity of a four year old stalking the Kit Kat bars you've hidden on the top shelf of the hall closet, and the energy level of said four year old after he reaches the candy cache. Or at least the forbearance of fellow shoppers who'll look the other way when you turn into a ranting, raving maniac. It's also helpful to have a child who has not yet learned the phone number for Child Protective Services.

I can't give you the patience, especially since I tend to run a bit short of it myself when I'm shopping with the kids, nor can I tell you for sure how to find the energy. (Some people swear by herbal extracts like ginseng, but I've noticed that the Kit Kat bars will work at least short-term. Although with that approach, you're putting yourself at risk of spending time in the dentist's chair and *still* having to run errands with the kids.) I *can* give you a bit of the ingenuity, in the form of activities that will trick kids into thinking that they're having, if not a good time, at least not such a miserable one. And that can be a Very Good Thing. I'll tell you why momentarily.

This chapter contains a variety of activities for the various shopping experiences you're likely to encounter frequently if you're an urban or suburban parent. (I didn't really come up with great ideas for when you're hauling the garbage to the dump or picking up a dozen bales of hay—I don't have the expertise for those situations, so if you need some ideas for them, all I can say is good luck.) The chapter opens with ideas for stocking the supplies that will grease the wheels of your shopping cart–bound experience, then tosses in ideas for preventing or handling problems when you're dragging the gang through the supermarket or mall. The last few activities will help when you encounter major difficulties, like kids doing the pee dance in the checkout line or visits to the (shudder) toy store.

Now, back to why it's good to distract the kids and keep them in good humor. You might have a kid like I was—one who turns into a temperamental terror when stressed by too much shopping. One day when I was about four or five, my mom stopped to drop something off at someone's house after we'd spent a long afternoon of running one errand after another. She left me waiting in the car, and then got to chitchatting with her friend while I fumed. Several minutes later, when she showed no signs of coming back to whisk me home, I locked all the car doors. And when my mom returned and tried to use the key to open the doors, I just kept locking them as fast as she could unlock them. I don't remember how our standoff ended (probably my memory loss is due to posttraumatic stress disorder), but I do know that after that day, my mom respected my Errand Quota and was careful not to exceed it. And you should keep that in mind, too, even with these ideas to help you stretch your kid's shopping toler-ance. Or pretty soon you might find yourself preferring the root canal.

Make Like a Boy Scout
AND VENTURE OUT PREPARED

When you have a baby, it's a bad idea to leave the house without a spare diaper. And with a preschooler, it's almost as bad an idea to leave the house without a backup action figure or two for emergencies. The good thing about preschoolers is that you won't *have* to have as much junk as you absolutely must have with the tiny guys, but errands and outings will still go much more smoothly if you're prepared for the usual contingen-cies, from queasy stomachs to teasing siblings.

The Well-Stocked Car In addition to all the usual supplies you prob-ably keep in your car (like change, your sunglasses, and a cell phone) if you are lugging kids with you, you'll be prepared for most everyday kid "emergencies" if you have the following:

- First aid kit, with *lots* of adhesive bandages, Dramamine (if car sickness is a problem), children's acetaminophen or ibuprofen
- Chemical hand warmers/ice bags (good for bigger boo-boos)
- Blanket and towels (many uses)
- Plastic bags (for garbage or finds)
- Tissues, paper towels, napkins
- Hand wipes and/or Purell-style hand-sanitizing lotion
- Stacking plastic containers, like those used for Cool Whip, or coffee cans, with lids (for food messes or as emergency barf/ pee containers)
- Sunscreen, skin lotion (good for distraction, as well as for intended use)
- Gallon milk jug filled with water (replace frequently) and spray mister bottle (for wash-ups, stain treatment, cooling mist, cleaning boo-boos)

- Change of clothing for all kids, including underwear
- Small toys, rotated periodically, inflatable ball
- Children's books and tapes, also rotated
- Small individually packaged snacks (I recommend lollipops and raisins, both of which keep well.) and drinks (Sports bottles are great, preferably filled with water, as well as shelf-stable chocolate milk found in packages similar to "juice boxes.")
- Paper, pen or pencil, clipboard, roll of tape, stickers
- Eye mask, small pillow

TRY THIS!

For kids who no longer put small things in their mouths, a great, easy car toy is a margarine tub with a slit in the lid and a bag of pennies. Most preschoolers will spend long periods plonking the pennies through the slit. You can also hand out pennies as tokens or rewards. Some kids use them to tally things they're counting like red cars, stop signs, etc.

You might also want to stock a laundry stain stick or spray, car shades, and individual tape player with earphones if you can't bear to listen to Raffi one more time. It's also a good idea to keep a laminated card in the glove compartment with emergency numbers, insurance information, allergies, etc. Remember to update it as needed.

The Well-Stocked Tote

If your diaper bag days are over, you'll be able to get by lugging a lot less stuff. Yes, I know some of these items overlap with the car supplies, but you won't want to take the time to hunt down and transfer what you need to carry along. Here's the good news: Most threes can carry their stuff themselves! A small backpack is best, but some prefer a pocketbook or briefcase (an old backgammon case works well). If you make a picture list of the necessary items, you can laminate it and attach it to the bag. Then your child can be in charge of making sure he has everything. Suggested supplies:

- Snack, including drink
- A few small toys (miniature cars, figures, animals) and/or book
- Small notebook and pen or pencil
- "Lookers"—magnifying glass, compact mirror, mini-binoculars
- Purell (available in tiny bottles) or hand wipes, small package of tissues
- Band-Aids
- Stickers or tape
- A couple of plastic bags, including a zipper-style one

Grocery Store Games
SHOP 'N' PLAY

Playing a few games each time you shop will make the experience more enjoyable for both you and your child. It may even speed things up, since your child will want to hurry along to the next "play station." Here are a few of my kids' favorite supermarket games:

Mine, Mine!

Choose some produce that you are buying in quantity, like peaches. Show your child that there are small differences between the items. Like snowflakes and children, no two peaches are exactly alike. Have your child choose a "favorite" that she would like to eat later. Examine it carefully for blemishes, color markings, shape variations, and so on that will enable her to recognize it. At home or in the checkout lane, see if she can find "hers." Let her eat her one-of-a-kind treat once it's paid for.

Weighty Matters

My kids' eyes light up at the scales. We have estimating contests for items we're going to weigh, offering a small prize, like picking what kind of ice cream we buy, for the closest guess. Obviously, this game takes experience. Younger kids may be able to join in if you provide them with a range of choices. Or play a junior weight game: Let them hold two objects and decide which feels heavier. Use the scales to check their answer.

What's What?

Have your child close his eyes. Pull something off the shelf and let him examine it without looking. Help him notice shape, weight, temperature, scent, and any other characteristics that seem appropriate. Then have him guess what it might be. You can adjust the difficulty level of this game in many ways. For example, an easier game for a young child is to try to distinguish between two wildly different items, like a package of cheese versus a carton of yogurt.

A Doaf of Dread

Fetching is one of the best jobs for a preschooler in the store. Make it more interesting with silly language that he has to puzzle out. For example, change the first letter of each word like "a pox of pereal," use the same vowel sounds ("a boonch of boo-noo-noos"), or use pig latin, gibberish, or a different language. Once your child has figured out what he's supposed to find, you can direct him to the specific brand and size you want. Make sure it's something he can reach easily. And, keep in mind that preschoolers are not the most discriminating shoppers. You'll want to avoid having them choose things like the cut of meat you're serving at the dinner party for your boss. Okay, don't even let them choose the strawberries for your morning cereal, unless you don't mind bruised and moldy ones. I know, I know—how can the same preschooler who has a shrieking fit if you try to serve him a banana with a microscopic bruise be completely blind to massive rot when he's in the grocery store? I don't know—but he can be. So, *always* reserve veto power for his selections.

Paper Towel Balancing Act

Be prepared for frowns from crabby sorts who don't approve of kids having fun, but this game is good for high energy kids. Paper towel rolls are a great material, because they won't break or hurt anything if dropped. You can play several ways, such as pitting a kid against a standard (e.g., balance it until I count to five, until you walk to the end of the aisle, etc.) or against another person (though this may prove too frustrating). Other items to balance include small packages of paper napkins (on his head) or boxes of plastic bags (on his outstretched arms). But don't let him try the carton of eggs, even if he swears he's a balance pro.

Checkout Challenges

Estimate the total for the groceries, giving younger kids the option of choices you specify. Kids are often amazed at how much groceries cost. Other fun guesses: how many bags will be needed, which two items will end up in the same bag, which line will win (hint: not the one I'm in), whether there will be a price check or other problem. Naturally, a quarter for the machines will be a coveted prize for the winner.

Shopping Stickum
STAY TOGETHER STRATEGIES

Keeping the kids within arm's reach or at least eyesight is one of the most aggravating parts of shopping. If you let them roam, you'll invariably spend a lot of time scolding and threatening. On the other hand, if you let them *push* the cart, they'll manage to ram it into a precarious display or a senior citizen. And getting them to ride in the cart is even worse. These strategies, while not nearly as good as a sitter, worked *much* of the time for me and cut way down on the squabbles.

A Cart of His Own

Some supermarkets actually provide pint-sized carts for young shoppers. Ours didn't, so we just brought our own. An umbrella stroller equipped with a bag in the seat (hook it over the handles) will do in a pinch. Your child will stick with his own shopping longer if you give him his own list. You can have him memorize a list of items as long as his age on the way to the store, tell him items to look for aisle by aisle, or make a picture list for him to use. Coupons can also act as a list, but you risk losing them. It's a good idea to make sure the items are distributed throughout the store and that at least some are things he likes. Obviously, avoid anything breakable, heavy, or that requires skill to select (like most produce).

Pet Carts

This is a bit goofy, and it slows you down on entry, but it works well with some kids. Buy a cheap, short nylon leash. When you get to the store, let your child select a cart to be her pet. Give it a name and discuss its characteristics. Then attach the leash to it and let your kid "walk" her pet through the store (while you push). We always got stuck buying cart biscuits (animal crackers) and cart food (usually junky cereal) to feed it, but somehow it felt better to have her begging for her pet instead of herself.

Scavenger Shopper

This is good for high-energy kids. At the start of each aisle, pick something they'll have to hunt for, but that they'll be able to recognize. (It doesn't have to be something you're buying.) I often chose something not right at eye level, so the hunt was a little more challenging. If they found the item by the time I reached that point, they won. Winning was reward enough. Speedy, experienced shopper-hunters can be given several items to locate before you finish the aisle, like rice, chicken noodle soup, and SpaghettiOs.

Cart We'lls

My boys were both booted out of the cart at early ages to make room for the next baby, and my daughter preferred to walk (clamped to my leg), so I can't claim much success in getting preschoolers to ride nicely. But here are ideas my friends claim worked for them:

- Bring along a normally off-limits small toy like a handheld electronic game that can only be used while the kid is sitting quietly.

- Put a bigger preschooler in the back of the main part of the cart, with a firm rule that he must remain seated or lose his ride. (This technique is definitely not recommended by the safety folks, but I see people doing it all the time.) You can take two carts, one for groceries and one for kid(s), if you don't have enough room for the food. (It also helps to have two grown-ups for this system. And then you can divide and conquer, which has its advantages too.)

- Promise a zooooooom ride down a deserted aisle if the kid cooperates while you shop. Obviously best for off-peak hours shopping. Can be fun for everyone—just take care to avoid collisions.

Shopping on the Incentive Plan
ENTICEMENTS AND REWARDS

When I was a kid, I loved going grocery shopping with my mother and sisters. Really. This was because every time when we got to the bakery section, my mom got herself a cup of coffee and we kids got doughnuts. My mom says she did it for herself—a little pleasure to look forward to in a busy day—not to bribe us into being good. I tell this story because this treat has the elements you want in your incentive plan:

- *ritual in nature* (something you do each time, not as a reward or bribe, but just as a pleasure)
- *modest investment* (of both money and time)
- *enjoyable to you too* (not something you'll cringe at doing or giving to your kids)

You can arrange whatever treats you like, but here are some ideas (besides the good doughnut one) that have worked for people I know.

Quartermaster

You cannot get out of the store without passing through the gumball gauntlet. One way to structure the gumball issue is to give your child a small weekly allowance of slightly more than a quarter (a dime per year of age was what we used). Your child can then *choose* whether to bring her quarter to spend in the machines. I also used to let the kids occasionally win quarters (one max per child) for playing our shopping games. Finally, our grocery store refunds five cents on each bag you reuse. If the kids reminded me and toted the empties, I let them have the money, up to twenty-five cents each.

TALES FROM THE TRENCHES

For a few years around the holidays, I handed out quarters in the checkout line and told the kids they could choose something from the machines or put their coins in the Salvation Army kettle. We talked about poor children and hungry people, so they would know what was at stake, but I didn't pressure them if they chose the machines. But I was pleasantly surprised at how often they put their money in the kettle. And it meant more to me—and to them—that it was their choice to do so. (It was only later that I discovered that altruism was not their only motivation—they were competing *bitterly* to collect sets of the little cards the Salvation Army guy gave as thanks.)

Chooser

Because getting to be in charge of selecting something—cereal, snacks, Wednesday night's dinner—is very powerful and appealing to preschoolers, you can hand out the privilege as a reward for acceptable behavior. (Reserve veto power, though, or you'll eat nothing but macaroni and cheese and french fries for dinner on Wednesdays.) Want to make this privilege even more exciting? Give your kid cash to pay for his choice himself. Maybe you'll be really nice and let him carry the bag too.

After Outings

This is one of the best. Promise a trip to the park or other fun place if you get your shopping (and putting away) done in the allotted time. One friend who passed a playground on the way home used to stop and let everyone out for five trips down the slide, then back in the car quick, before the ice cream melted.

MORE TO KNOW

Certain child expert types would firmly oppose shopping on the incentive plan, accusing you of bribing your kids to have good behavior or of creating materialistic, reward-oriented brats completely lacking in moral fiber and responsibility. I disagree with them. Used properly, built-in treats—and even explicit rewards—encourage not only good behavior, but also a warm relationship you'll cherish.

Shopper, May I?
AND OTHER FOOT UN-DRAGGING REMEDIES

These are good games for distracting your child from his professional whining practice and sometimes for getting him to pick up the pace.

Shopper, May I?

Have your kid ask questions à la "Mother, May I?" about how he can move toward your destination. For example, he might say, "Shopper, may I take six giant steps?" or "Shopper, may I take scissors steps all the way to the fountain?" If he asks about something you don't want him to do, respond, "No you may not. But you may…." In case you need a refresher course for Mother, May I, here are some of the kinds of steps: umbrella steps (Twirly—save them for open areas.), baby steps, slide steps (We called them banana steps.), bunny hops, backwards steps (avoid in crowds), heel-to-toe steps, horse steps (gallops), skip steps, grapevines, and leg crossers. Preschoolers also love it when you just grab their hands and skip with them—sing "Skip to My Lou" substituting your destination for "My Lou."

Simon Says Hold Hands in the Parking Lot

Thank goodness for that Simon guy—commands issued by him are obeyed cheerfully and quickly. This, naturally, is not the time to try to trick your kid by mixing in non-Simon commands. But it is a good idea to throw in a few silly or fun commands, like "Simon says croak like a frog," or "Simon says pick what kind of cookies we'll buy." And now and then, you might go along with a reasonable Simon demand from your kid, like "Simon says let me have a penny to make a wish," just to build the spirit of cooperation.

Eye Spy to Buy

This game gives kids permission to move around (since they dash over to point out their guesses rather than simply naming them), but keeps them by definition within your sight. From your point of view, it's a good idea either to give such specific hints that they can't go wrong, like, "I spy to buy something orange and long and skinny. They grow under the ground, and rabbits like to eat them." (carrots)—or something so general that you can sort-of cheat and let them win (or keep them from winning too quickly, as it suits you), like, "I spy something green."

A variation is to have your child hunt for unusual items, like alligator pears. We found the game worked well in the produce aisle, where there were often exotic fruits and veggies we didn't know already, and in places like hardware stores where there are bewildering varieties of cool tools and other objects. Sometimes we just have to buy whatever weird thing the kid identifies correctly. By the way, an alligator pear is an avocado.

Raceways

"Beat you to the candle shop—I'll walk and you trot like a pony." Three and four year olds fall for this trick pretty much every time. Fives and sixes may be onto you, and that's when you sing, "I've heard of Chicken Little, I've heard of chicken stew! I've heard of chicken chow mein, but now there's something new! Chicken (*child's name*)! Chicken (*child's name*)! Bock, bock, bock!" If necessary a little trash talking will usually lure the most skeptical kid into going along.

Speed Shopping Strategies
WHIPPING THROUGH WITHOUT WHINING

I think this is a corollary to Murphy's Law ("If something can go wrong, it will."): the bigger the rush you're in, the slower your kids will move. That's why it's a good idea to summon a little energy at the outset, and use a strategy like one of these to shift your kid into racecar mentality.

The Buckle Brigade

Getting in and out of the car at a speed faster than a glacier moves is often the biggest hurdle. I found it helped to get the kids ready to move quickly well before we reached our destination. I'd tell them to start unbuckling (or whatever they could do to help be ready) as soon as I put the car in park, and see if they could be done before I got their door open. Then I'd start narrating the approach: "Oh, I've spotted an empty parking space. I'm pulling in . . . braking . . . got the gearshift. . . . Parked!" This simple game worked over and over, but sometimes I'd dress it up a bit. You can do the same kind of thing getting back in: "Let's see if you can climb up in your seat before I can get the packages stowed," or something similar.

Surgical Strike

The old imagination strategy. You have lots of options, but my kids loved it when I pretended we were surgeons who'd been shrunk to enter the patient's body and remove some diseased organ (which was whatever we had to buy). Usually there was some terrible outcome, like a deadly fart explosion, that would occur if we didn't succeed in performing the operation by the specified time. I'd talk up the whole mission while we zipped around the store, making sure that we were constantly flirting with disaster. People will give you strange looks, but don't mind them. This game not only speeds up the process, but it also makes the kids giggly and cooperative, and that's worth a strange look any day, isn't it?

Other good pretending themes can include whatever your child's current passion is—dinosaurs, horses, fire trucks, fairy princesses, etc. Just make sure to narrate a theme of impending disaster and a need for speed. My kids were also fond of playing Mission Impossible (They loved being secret agents disguised as regular kids and retrieving the plans or codes cleverly hidden in a seemingly ordinary carton of low-fat milk.); being racecars (Naturally they were traveling under a yellow caution flag so they had to zoom without flat-out running.); impersonating astronauts avoiding space aliens and asteroids; and portraying ants saving the baby larvae from the attacking anteater.

Beat That Song!

Another strategy that requires you to sacrifice your dignity, especially if you sing as badly as I do. Sometimes I'd enlist one of the kids to sing instead, because even though they inherited my tin ear, at least they were a bit cuter. The point would be to get out of the store by the time we finished singing some longish, annoying song, a specified number of repetitions of a shorter one, or a medley. Probably the kids just rushed because they were embarrassed to be seen with their off-key and weird mother, but it was effective. Plus, people let you cut in front of them in the checkout line. You can also simply race the clock, but that's kind of boring, don't you think?

"Look with Your Eyes, Not with Your Hands"
AND OTHER ENTRIES IN THE PARENTS' ESSENTIAL SHOPPING PHRASEBOOK

Probably you are already familiar with that glassy look that comes in your child's eyes whenever you start to give those lectures about how the store is full of breakies, and if something gets broken, then blah, blah, blah. That's why it's better to have a repertoire of shorthand phrases that you can insert at the perfect moment. Here are some of my favorite and most used one-liners.

"Look with Your Eyes, Not with Your Hands"

I scolded one of my kids one day for picking up some fragile item in a gift shop right after I'd just told her not to touch anything. She looked up at me with those big, innocent eyes that preschoolers know how to use so effectively and said, "But I wasn't touching it; I was just looking at it!" Preschoolers "look" with all their senses, hence the need to be very specific. I still use this reminder when roaming crafts fairs and art galleries with my tactile kids.

"Hands in Your Pockets, Please"

Ever notice how department stores always locate the crystal and china department between the entrance and the kids' clothing department? I suspect it's the store equivalent of a speed trap. Rather than telling kids not to touch, I found it more effective simply to have everyone thrust his hands deeply into his pockets. Sometimes I'd slip a coin or other goody in first—and if it was still there along with all the required fingers once we navigated the treacherous waters, the kid could keep it.

"Red Alert! Glue Zone!"

Big crowds, lots of commotion—in these circumstances you need your kid to stick to you like glue. Sometimes we called those places "hand-holders" too. Either way, the kids knew the shtick, attached their little bodies to ours, and most of the time got to skip the whole getting-lost lecture.

"This Is a List Trip"

In other words, your kid can skip the begging and whining—you're absolutely, positively not buying anything extra this time. Just make sure you mean it; slip up even once and this phrase will never work again. (It's also not a bad idea to dispense a small reward occasionally at the end of a list trip—like stopping at the park to play or handing out a snack you've brought with you).

"RYM"

Code for "Remember Your Manners." Say it to prompt your child to say thank you without embarrassing him with the standard, "What do you say?" (Especially since that phrase may prompt him to say something charming like "This is stupid.") RYM works to remind your child to use a wide variety of manners as he learns them and is especially useful for shy kids who are easily embarrassed.

It's Done with Mirrors
THE MAGIC TRICK OF DISTRACTING KIDS IN THE DRESSING ROOM

Personally, I prefer not to spend much time in dressing rooms with kids. Partly it's because preschoolers have a small reservoir of dressing room tolerance, no matter what amusements you provide. But mostly it's because I really prefer not to listen to the kids' blunt commentary on my stretch marks and spider veins, which always seem to glow like neon under the fluorescent lights. But if you're thicker-skinned—or lucky enough not to have VSOA's (Visible Signs of Aging)—these ideas may make the dressing room into less of a torture chamber.

Mirror, Mirror on the Wall

Most kids will happily twist and turn and check themselves out in front of a mirror, especially if you get them started making silly faces and funny poses. For an extra dose of fun, you can tote a hand mirror in your purse and show kids how to turn their backs to the big mirror and look into the little mirror, adjusting the angle until they can see the backs of their heads and other interesting sights. And there's always the classic amusement of breathing on the glass and wiping off the condensation with a tissue.

Naked Barbies

Actually, you want to start with them clothed, as most preschoolers are much better at undressing dolls than dressing them. But many kids will enjoy playing dressing room with their dolls while you try on your own clothes. My kids liked finding assorted gross things on the floor to use as outfit accessories too. Then they'd have the dolls parade in front of the mirror. (I think that Mattel should make a Mommy Barbie complete with stretch marks and spider veins, don't you?) Boys who shun Barbies as disgusting girl toys may be content to undress G.I. Joes. Other small pretending toys will keep kids occupied too—just be sure to bring a stash of novel ones.

In a pinch, snag an extra outfit or two with large, easy fasteners (like big buttons with stretchy holes or oversized zippers)—and your child can pretend to dress an invisible person while you try on your clothes.

Hide 'n' Dress

Let's say you want to try on something like bathing suits without the scrutiny of your five-year-old son and there's no sitter available and you don't have time for mail order. I've found that hand-held electronic games will captivate boys so thoroughly that they wouldn't notice if Batman were changing in there. (Keep a game in your purse that's only available for these kinds of emergencies.)

But if you don't have such a perfect toy handy, (*and* you have a kid who isn't going to wander off and either annoy the heck out of other bashful folks trying on bathing suits or get you arrested for neglect), play one of these no-peek games:

- *Under the Door Tennis* Those little plastic size markers that go on hangers slide or roll back and forth pretty nicely. Give the kid a hanger for a racket or you can both play with your feet. Let the kid win.

- ***Next-Door Neighbors*** Find adjoining dressing rooms, and park your kid in the one next to yours. Use conversation to occupy your child and keep tabs on him. Of course, you'll need an especially captivating topic to be sure your child stays put and happy. Try one of these:

  - A discussion of things people can do with worms (I actually spent twenty-five minutes once on this topic, and discovered as a bonus that it's a powerful appetite suppressant and helpful for shedding those extra pounds that are so unattractive in the suits you're trying on.)

  - Pretend you're prisoners in adjoining cells. You can discuss your wrongful convictions and share methods for taming the rats that visit your cells. Make plans for a jailbreak and a rendezvous at the fast food restaurant on the home, reminding yourself to order the salad and Diet Coke instead of the cheeseburger and fries.

  - Do some make-believe interior design of your respective dressing room "homes." Most kids are more than happy to pretend that their dressing room is a playhouse and make plans for equipping it to suit their tastes. We always liked to plan super cool features, like automatic cookie dispensers, twisty slides into the bed, indoor swimming pools with sprinkler attachments instead of boring tubs or showers, and other kid-fantasy features.

Can't You Hold It Until We Get Home?
VISITING THE POTTY WHEREVER YOU GO

"We go before we go." That's a firm rule in my house, especially before shopping outings. Nonetheless, you will probably visit potties in some interesting places when out and about with your young child. The following ideas may help with common problems.

Advance Scouts

Especially if your child is newly potty trained, get in the habit of scoping out the location of the rest room before you need it. Stop at the checkout counter or service desk as you enter a store (especially if you'll be there for a bit) and ask where it is. Keep an eye on the time and schedule pit stops before you need them.

Adjusting the Fit

Graco makes a portable potty seat (available from the Right Start catalog at www.rightstart.com under health and safety products, as well as from larger baby supply stores). Boys can be boosted to pee-height by standing on your feet or bracing themselves on your bent knees. Many malls and airports now have family rest rooms with small potties—and privacy, so you don't have to fret about the six-year-old-boy-in-the-ladies-room dilemma. Some chain department stores, like IKEA, do too—and I make sure to give them my business. (By the way, I always take the six-year-old boy in the ladies' room with me—I'm sorry if it makes some women uncomfortable, but public rest rooms are not safe for young kids alone.)

Dealing with the Gross Factor

Most of the time, you really don't have to sweat it—kids are more likely to pick up germs in the Food Court than in the bathroom. (I still make my kids put the strips of toilet paper on the seat before they sit down, though, because my mom made me and now it's a Family Tradition.) What's more effective, though, is to carry Purell, squirt a little on a wad of toilet paper, and wipe the seat—and the flush handle—first. (You can also buy disinfecting towelettes, but they're expensive.) The sink area and doors often have more disgusting germs than the toilets do, so show your child how you turn faucets on and off with your elbows if possible, discard paper towels without touching the can directly, and use your body, not your hands, to open the door when you're done. (If the door pulls open, use a paper towel to open it and discard the towel in the nearest waste bin.)

Desperate Measures

- *Finding a Toilet* There are toilets for the employees in most businesses. Given the right persuasion (such as turning to your child and saying something like, "Try not to pee right on the carpet, dear."), you can probably gain access. If the clerk insists there is no toilet, ask where she goes—it's probably the nearest option.
- *The Squeeze Play* Have your child sit on a bench with her legs tightly crossed, while you tell her a short story. (Nothing with water or humor, please.) When she stands up, the urge may have temporarily passed, giving you enough time to locate a rest room.
- *Isn't That What Landscaping's For?* I never got that desperate, but I've caught more than one parent crouched behind the yews with a relieving tot. I also recommend carrying an empty plastic container (with a tight lid) in your car for emergencies.

Accidents Will Happen

Your child's comfort is your first priority. Keep telling yourself that. Tend to her first, being sympathetic—she's probably embarrassed and upset. Reassure her that it's no big deal and it's happened to plenty of other kids. Notify store personnel that you need a cleanup in aisle X, scoot your child to someplace private, and remove her pants altogether if you have dry ones or she's wearing a dress or long T-shirt. (I once bought inexpensive replacement clothes, when I really needed to finish my errands.)

High Anxiety
ELEVATOR/ESCALATOR ISSUES

Fortunately, serious accidents are rare, but small children are certainly at risk on people movers because of their ignorance of safety rules, their desire to touch and investigate, and their size. You need to make kids aware of the dangers without scaring them so much that they refuse to ride.

Escalator Safety Deputies

- Young children like being in charge of safety rules, so you might as well make it official. Then they can be the ones to nag about holding your hand, instead of the other way around. (Of course, then you won't be able to break the rules by toting the stroller up the escalator.)
- Before you get on, do a quick shoelace check—kids have been badly hurt when their laces got caught between steps or along the sides. Remind your child never to touch the steps; if something drops, you'll pick it up.
- Getting on and off the moving steps is daunting to many novices. I had good success by chanting a rhyme as we walked on—it distracted from their fear and helped them take smooth, even steps. Try reciting these lines and having the child walk forward on the word "stepping."

> *One, two, three, four,*
> *Stepping on this moving floor.*
> *Five, six, seven, eight,*
> *Riding up* (or *down) is really great!*

Have your child face front as you near the end. To exit smoothly, try a countdown or a traditional get-set rhyme like:

One for the money, two for the show,
Three to get ready, and four—let's go.

Elevator Operators

- Teach your child elevator etiquette: wait for all the people to exit before getting on, step to the back so everyone will fit, and face forward while riding. Preschoolers who know their numbers (and can reach the buttons) may ask, "Floor, please?" but they must share the job with any other young riders.

- The biggest problems with preschoolers and elevators occur with the doors. We required an adult to get the door (with body or door open button) before kids got on or off. Be especially wary of older elevators, whose doors may not open automatically when they hit something.

- The other big problem is the possibility of separation. A good safety rule is that if a child somehow gets stranded on the elevator alone, he should *stay on until he returns to you. He should not get off, even if someone offers to help!* Let your child know that you will push the button for the elevator again and wait right there for him until the car comes back, even though it may take a while. He can sing a song or say his ABC's until he returns to keep from feeling scared.

- Okay, this isn't a safety thing, but it's a ritual my kids love when we have the elevator to ourselves. They jog in place and then try to time a jump for the moment the elevator stops—it gives them a momentary feeling of weightlessness.

The Toy Store Tango
TIPS FOR THOSE DIFFICULT SHOPPING EXPERIENCES

You'd think that wandering around a toy or candy store would be a treat for a young kid—but those kinds of shopping outings are the ones most likely to cause complete meltdowns. There is simply too much stimulation, temptation, and frustration. Try these ideas to shorten the trip and cope with strong feelings.

Pre-shop

Try to make, or at least narrow, decisions before you enter the store. The internet makes this much easier. In addition to the well-known www.etoys.com, there are many other toy shopping sites, like www.toysrus.com and www.imaginarium.com, as well as homes for specific brands, like www.playmobil.com, where you and your child can browse without crowds or other distractions. I'm also a big fan of letting my fingers do the walking and calling to make sure the store has the item I'm looking to buy. If nothing else, help your child narrow the choices of what to purchase, so you don't have to roam through the whole store.

Prepare and Predict

Ahead of time tell your child why you are going to the store, how long you'll be spending there, and whether you will be buying anything for him. If he has a tendency to melt down, help him by predicting his reactions. You can say something like this: "Today we are buying a present for your friend Jake. Sometimes when we shop for a gift, you feel frustrated and wish we were buying something for you. Instead of crying or whining, I need you to squeeze my hand, take a deep breath, and use your words. Soon it will be your birthday, and then you will get presents."

Put Blinders On

I wish I could do it literally.

- Reduce stimulation by giving your child something to hold and focus his attention on. One of my kids liked to choose an unbreakable "look at" toy as we entered to examine while we shopped and to return when we checked out. Since we did this every time, it was a routine and rarely turned into a buy-it-for-me struggle.

- Avoid aisles with lots of electronic toys and noises.
- If possible, shop during off-hours when the store is less crowded and when your child's energy level is higher.
- Sing, call his attention to a non-merchandise sight (e.g., "I wonder how many squares of tile there are in this aisle?"), or play a game (e.g., "Can you hop all the way over to the Barbie display?").

The Birthday List

I carry a pretty blank book (from the dollar store) with pages for each child. Whenever someone begs for something, I just ask, "Shall I put it on your list?" This technique isn't foolproof, but it's effective more often than I'd have guessed—especially if I make writing the entry into a solemn production. (And if you include useful information like store, date, and price, it can make later birthday shopping and suggestions to relatives much easier.)

The Ins and Outs of In and Out
SURVIVING A SERIES OF SHORT ERRANDS

After the toy store, the worst shopping trips with young kids are those where you have to make a number of stops—too many transitions and too much getting in and out of the car seat. The following ideas can ease the stress on everyone and prevent some of the whining.

Schedule Sanity

Try to avoid these trips in the afternoon, especially with a child who is giving up naps (too much chance he'll fall soundly asleep on one of the short hops). I used to try to save a relatively fun errand (like the dollar store) for last, until I realized that everyone was so worn out by the end that they didn't even enjoy the reward. I switched the fun activity to the middle, and it worked much better. Also, pay attention to the total time of the outing, and be sure to schedule breaks to eat, pee, or dash about a bit if necessary.

Lists You Can Touch—or Eat

Probably you get a feeling of satisfaction from crossing finished tasks off your to-do list. Preschoolers do too, but they prefer lists that they can get their hands on—or sink their teeth into. Try hanging a chain of plastic links, paper clips, or paper from the car seat or rearview mirror, with a link for each errand to run. As you finish each task, your child can remove another link. This activity will distract him as he gets in the car again, and it provides a visual picture of how many errands remain. One mom I know makes her kids "necklaces" from LifeSavers or other round candy, with beads for each leg of the journey. Another gives the kids coins to deposit in a tube—when it's full, they stop for ice cream.

Imagination can also make the errand list more appealing. Pretend each stop is a different country (or continent) on an around-the-world trip, or a new planet with interesting aliens and landmarks.

You Can Bet on It

Which errand will take the least time? Which one the most? Have your kids make bets on various categories, and check your performance. This activity also focuses your child's attention on something positive. You can hand out small rewards, like a piggyback ride across the parking lot or a quick treat.

Ritualize It

One dad I know always gives his kids money to buy a single "pretty" stamp of their choice when he takes them to the post office. They add them to the kids' stamp collections, but you could also have a ritual of mailing a letter or postcard to your child with it. Another family I know puts the kids in charge of collecting wire hangers to take back to the dry cleaners (who gives them lollipops in exchange). These little habits make the kids look forward to otherwise dull errands.

CHAPTER TWO

Wait
Gain

Preschoolers are not fond of waiting." This sentence is an example of the literary device called "understatement." "Preschoolers detest, loathe, abominate, scorn, object to, despise, abhor, are repelled by, feel malice toward, view with horror, anathematize, curse, dislike intensely, and resent waiting." This sentence is an example of a literary technique called "using a thesaurus." It comes much closer to conveying how preschoolers really feel about waiting, but it is not quite strong enough because I got tired of copying all the words and phrases that mean "hate" out of my thesaurus. At any rate, the second sentence gives you some idea of why you will need this chapter, in case you've been in a coma for the last couple of years and haven't noticed that you do.

Not to depress or frighten you, but I feel obligated to warn you that you'll need waiting games not just for the preschool years, but for the rest of the time that you have children living at home. Maybe longer. All kids loathe waiting, even if it's for something they want. Or maybe especially then. Either way, keep in mind that you'll need an incredibly huge supply of distractions over the next years. In fact, I strongly recommend that whenever you see a book or a magazine with the phrase "waiting games" on the cover, you buy it and add it to the stack that you lug around in the trunk of your car so you'll be prepared for delays at restaurants, doctor's offices, or the post office during the holidays.

Wait! Sorry—there's that bad word again—but I meant to add this important phrase: leave most, if not all, of those books in the car for later. The majority of books on waiting games I've found are intended for school-aged kids (even though kids that age have an easier time waiting to begin with). Your preschooler is not going to enjoy activities like making as many words as he can out of the letters in the word "spaghetti." All kids anathematize (can you believe that's a legitimate word?) any game in which their score is zero. On the plus side, what preschoolers lack in dexterity, reading skills, and thinking power, they often make up in imagination and willingness to be silly. Although an older child would disdain pretending play like "You be Mister Salt and I'll be Mrs. Pepper, and these pink things will be our twins Sweet and Low," a preschooler will be delighted by it.

This chapter has ideas for distracting your child based on different kinds of waiting situations, like sitting at a table (such as in a restaurant), hanging out in a waiting room or area where your kid can move around a bit, and, *shudder*, for waiting situations where he'll have to be quiet as well as relatively still. No kid (or adult) will enjoy all of the suggestions, but everyone should find something to like. If your kids are like mine, they'll pick up some favorite games and activities that they want to do *every single time you have to wait.* So, don't introduce anything you abominate as much as I detest the card game War. Good luck! And please don't curse me if your child still doesn't like waiting—that's just normal.

Just Seeing Half the Picture
AND OTHER PAPER AND PENCIL PLAY

A pen or crayon and the back of a placemat can keep a preschooler occupied for a good chunk of the time that you're waiting for food in a restaurant. Try some of these keep-busy-on-paper games.

Just Seeing Half the Picture

Out of your child's sight, draw a simple picture on a piece of paper, then fold the paper in half and show your child half the picture. Can he guess what the whole picture would be? Unfold and show him to check his answer.

Begin with easy, symmetrical pictures and move to more challenging ones as your child becomes skilled. Guess alphabet letters or numbers instead of drawings. Or write simple words that your child knows (like his name). Try folding the paper different ways. Have your child test you.

TRY THIS!

Not an artist and can't think what to draw? Try some of these easy figures: a face, a stick figure, a snowman, a cat's face, a flower, a sailboat, a house, an evergreen tree, a teddy bear, a star, a heart, a butterfly, a package, an apple, balloons.

What Did I Forget?

Draw a simple picture, like a stick figure, but leave out a significant detail, such as one foot. See if your child can figure out what *important* thing is missing. You can do many variations on the same basic drawing, gradually being subtler in what you omit (e.g., an eyebrow).

Hangman, Jr.

The easiest variation is "Draw-a-Picture Hangman." Start with a simple geometric shape, like a square. Your kid tries to guess what it might be, like a present. Then you add another feature to the picture, like a small rectangle at the bottom (to be a door, if you're making a house). Kid guesses again. He tries to figure out what you're making before you complete the drawing.

For an older child, set up the traditional layout for a three- or four-letter word (Draw a gallows and use dashes for each letter.) Write all the vowels and have the child point to them one at a time, until she has filled in all the vowel spaces. Then give her a choice of all the consonants in the word plus five to ten "red herrings." Talk through the play, helping with the sounds and offering suggestions about letters that might work. Or, supply a word bank—the chosen word must be one of the ten or so written next to the board. Played this way, the game is a visual matching exercise.

Tic-Tac-Toesy

Even preschoolers tire of the basic game pretty quickly. We have more fun playing "try *not* to get three in a row." Or play "Connect Three." Draw a grid of five squares by five squares. Players use circles and X's to fill in squares, alternating turns. The catch is that squares have to be filled in from the bottom up, as in the commercial game "Connect Four." Players can win horizontally, vertically, or diagonally. This takes more strategy than simple tic-tac-toe.

Blindfolded Auto Racing
MORE PAPER AND PENCIL GAMES

This first activity is one of my favorites—and the kids' too. It can be played by any kid old enough to hold a pencil and manipulate it with some control. We've been playing for years, and it's still fresh and fun.

Blindfolded Auto Racing

Don't hand your child the car keys! But do let him choose a crayon to be his car and gas it up for the big race. You and any other players should choose a crayon-race-car too.

On a blank piece of paper or the back of a paper place mat, draw a wiggly, oval racetrack (for new drivers, make it wide and relatively smooth). Mark the start and finish lines and put a checkered flag at the finish. Then, ladies and gentlemen, start your engines! The first racer places her crayon on the start line, takes a minute to study the course, closes her eyes tightly (no peeking!) and starts driving. When she veers off the course (and she will), the other racer calls "Crash!" and Racer One stops. Now Racer Two takes a turn, stopping when he crashes. Drivers alternate turns, beginning at their crash sites and continuing until a winner crosses the finish line. We allow equal turns, making ties possible. Drive carefully!

You can adapt this game for many sports. For example, to play blindfolded bowling, draw an alley and make a pyramid of ten X's at the end to represent the pins. The bowler has to draw a line down the alley, being careful not to end up in the gutter, and hit as many pins as possible by scribbling at the end. Keep score bowling style, allowing two "rolls" per turn.

Roller Coaster

This is a good starter version for children who don't want to draw with their eyes closed. Make an X to show a starting point. Draw a long, wiggly, swooping, curling line to represent a crazy roller coaster. Narrate the "construction" of this amazing ride as you draw. Finish with a star to indicate the end of the ride. Your child chooses a different color crayon to "ride" the roller coaster, trying to be careful not to jump the track.

Shape "Braille"

Explain to your child how blind people read special letters made from bumps on the page. Then play this game to show him how well fingers can "see." Have your child close his eyes. Using heavy pressure, draw a simple shape (like a square or triangle) in crayon. Place your child's fingers on part of the line and let him trace it with his fingers. Can he tell what it is?

Name That Clink!
AND OTHER GUESSING GAMES

Guessing games are great because they require no props, they allow everyone to play, they can be played in many ways, and they're just plain fun, whatever your age.

Name That Clink!

Gather several objects from the table, like glasses filled to different heights, a pepper shaker, and the sugar packet holder. While your child watches, tap each one with a spoon or the flat side of a knife. Comment on the different tones. Then have your child close her eyes while you tap one of them. Can she identify the one you hit? Take turns tapping and guessing.

Twenty Hints

Go ahead and play the traditional Twenty Questions if your preschooler can. (We started our kids young—just gave them lots of help with what questions to ask.) Otherwise, try this junior version. Pick a category that your child is knowledgeable about (and you are too) like dinosaurs, animals, vehicles, or book or cartoon characters. Give your child hints, one at a time, about the item you've chosen and see if your child can guess what it is before you've given twenty hints. When it's your turn to guess, your child can either give you hints or you can ask him questions.

Which Hand?

Most preschoolers will happily play this simple game over and over. Take a small object, like a coin. Hide the object in one of your hands, keeping them beneath the table and out of sight. Then bring your hands up, and let your child guess which hand has the object. If she guesses correctly, she becomes the hider. Otherwise, you hide it again.

A variation of this game is called "Up, Jenkins!" Hide the coin in one fist beneath the table. The guesser says, "Up, Jenkins." The hider then brings his fists up, elbows resting on the table. The guesser says, "Down, Jenkins" and the hider quickly slaps his hands down onto the tabletop, palms open. The guesser, guided by the "clink," tries to tell which hand is hiding the coin. (Preschoolers find it challenging to do the quick slap down, so they may need to be the guesser each time.)

The Shell Game

You need two or three empty coffee cups to play this game. In front of your child, place a coin or other small object under one of the cups. Tell him to keep an eye on the cup with the coin. While he watches, switch the cups around. After a while, stop and see if he knows where the coin is. As he becomes skilled, do the switching faster and trickier.

Measure Up

How many straws long is the table? How many sugar packets will fit on the place mat? You'll find there is no shortage of items to measure (or nonstandard units to use). This activity is good for giving a restless child a chance to move around, while still keeping his behavior in bounds—let him measure the circumference of the table or count paces to the salad bar.

Penny Pile
COINED GAMES

It's great to have a few coin games in your repertoire, since you'll seldom be without at least a small amount of money. Many of these games can also be played by making marks on a piece of paper, though preschoolers find them easier to play when they have actual objects to handle.

Penny Pile

You need two players for this game. Make a pile of ten pennies or other small objects. Tell your child that you will take turns subtracting or taking away the pennies. Each time, the player may choose to take one penny or two. Try to be the one who takes the *last* penny.

Narrate the subtraction process. "There were six pennies in the pile. I took one. Now there are just five left." In time, your child can take over the narrator's (and subtracter's) job. After playing a few times, your child may begin to notice that strategy can improve her chances of winning.

For example, if there are four pennies left, she should take only one. Then, however many you take, she will still win.

You can try some variations too. For example, you can take turns *adding* pennies, trying to be the one who adds the tenth. The strategy is the same, but the arithmetic is different. Or, you can play regular penny pile, but try *not* to take the last penny. This changes the strategy while keeping the arithmetic the same. You can also change the number of pennies in the initial pile and/or include more players (which makes the strategy *much* more complicated).

Penny Guessers

I have my nephew Jake to thank for this game. The beginner version is for two players. Each player needs three pennies. Players put their pennies in their laps and decide on a number of pennies—between zero and three—to hide in their hands. When they're ready, players chant, "Yes, yes, Penny guess!" and put their fists on the table. Each player then guesses at the total number of pennies in everyone's hands combined (zero to six). The player who is closest wins the round. Players alternate guessing first. Kids will soon realize that going second is an advantage. It may take them a little longer to figure out that bluffing and strategy play a role too. This is a nice game for players of mixed ages and abilities, because each can get something different out of it and because chance plays a big enough role to keep the win-loss records reasonably even. Adding more players will increase the challenge for skilled players.

LITERATURE LINKS

Math for young children is more than counting. Want to learn more math games to play with your young child? Try these books: *One, Two, Buckle My Shoe: Math Activities for Young Children* by Sam Ed Brown; *More Than Counting* and *Much More Than Counting* by Sally Moomaw and Brenda Hieronymus. Or, try these websites: www.learningplanet.com and www.funschool.com.

Turtle Relay

This game is for any number of players. To get started, you need two coins of the same combination (such as a penny and a nickel) per player, plus one extra coin for players to flip. Each player lines up her coins so that they touch. On her turn, the player shakes the extra coin in her hands or a cup, then slaps or dumps it down on the table. If it's heads up, she gets to jump the back coin over the front one. Tails, she stays put. Players move their coin turtles this way toward a specified finish line.

Coinstructions

If you have a nice handful of coins, your child can use them as building supplies. My kids liked to stack up pyramids of pennies, placing each succeeding layer bricklayer-style over the "joint" between two coins. (You can also build a circular tower this way.) Or, simply lay out repeating patterns of different coins (quarter, nickel, nickel, penny) or use them to make mosaic pictures (flowers, faces, etc.).

Straw Votes
THINGS TO DO WITH STUFF ON THE TABLE

These are not things to do in a four-star restaurant—but since I wouldn't visit one with a preschooler, I don't worry about that. Hope you don't either.

Straw Stuff

Preschoolers love straws and you will too once you realize what great entertainment value they have. Our favorite straw activity is "Snake." Scrunch up the paper when you remove it from the straw, leaving a squat spring-like wad. Use a spoon (or better yet, the vacuum straw method described in the next paragraph) to drip a *tiny* drop of liquid onto the paper in a couple spots. As the paper gets wet, it will uncoil and "writhe" like a real snake.

Straws as vacuums are also fascinating. Show your child how to clamp her finger tightly over the top of the straw when it's submerged in her drink (or when she's sucked liquid up to the top). She can then lift the straw out of the liquid, but the liquid inside the straw will stay put—until she removes her finger. The polite restaurant behavior thing to do is just to let the liquid run back into the glass, but in fast food or family-style places, we let kids drip a little of their drinks into their mouths that way. If you can finagle an extra glass or coffee cup, your child can transfer her beverage from one container to the next (and this may also keep her from finishing it before the food comes).

Finally, straws make great hockey sticks. (Use the straw paper as a puck and shoot it at a goal made from a paper place mat folded like a tent.)

Saltshaker Magic

I still remember being amazed at this trick as a child. You need an old-fashioned saltshaker with straight sides. Let your child try to balance it tipped, like the Leaning Tower of Pisa. Can't do it. Bet him that you can. Pour out some salt; it's possible to do this trick with just a few grains, so go easy. Push some grains into a row, then lean the shaker against the row. It takes some skill, but with a little practice (and no one bumping the table) you should be able to do it almost every time. This trick works because salt crystals are shaped like little cubes; sugar crystals aren't and won't work. Afterwards, everyone can take a close look at the little box-shaped crystals.

Napkin-Gami

Folding neatly is a challenging activity for most preschoolers, so I wouldn't attempt any intricate origami projects with them. But most will enjoy folding and refolding their napkins. We don't try to make real proj-ects, but the kids will often examine their finished products and decide what they've made. Show them how to match edges and make sharp creases. You can also show them how to fold their napkins lengthwise or on the diagonal, then how to fold the edges or corners into the creases, and then how to turn the project over and do additional folds on the other side. On occasion, we've lured skilled wait people into demon-strating some very fancy napkin styles, and that's fun too.

Memorabilia
RECALL FOR FUN

There is an endless variety of these activities—which is good, because my kids love them.

What's Missing?

This is just that standard party game. Arrange five to ten objects on a place mat and have your child spend fifteen seconds or so examining them. Have her close her eyes while you remove one or more items. Then she opens her eyes and tries to guess what's missing. Make the game easier by letting your child handle and name each object during the study period. Make it more challenging by rearranging the remaining items or using more to start. Another variation is to have your child keep his eyes closed, and recite as many items as he can recall.

What's Different?

Similar to the game above. Let your child study the table setting carefully. Then while she hides her eyes, change something around. Silly changes, like turning things upside down, are usually enjoyed (and spotted) the most by preschoolers. For younger children, we often change several things and count it as a

MORE TO KNOW

Photographic memory is rare in adults, but one type, called eidetic imagery, is more common in young children. Some kids can clearly see pictures in their heads with their eyes closed after they've viewed the images. Others do better if they study a picture carefully, and then stare at a blank piece of paper. They may be able to "see" the previous image as if it were a ghostly reprint. These memories are vivid, but short-lived, so don't wait too long before testing recall. A detail-laden placemat is a perfect tool for seeing if your child has this ability.

"win" if they notice any of the changes (and we point out the ones they missed too). Your child will also enjoy a chance to be the quick-change artist. You can change clothing or hair on yourself, as well as items in the environment.

Pig, Car, Clown Hat

My kids loved trying to recall short sentences or lists of three to seven words or numbers. We taught our kids mnemonic tricks, like making vivid mental pictures of the items on a list. For example, help your child remember the title list by "seeing" a huge purple pig riding around in a tiny yellow car topped by a spotted clown hat. With this trick, my kids could often recite the list many minutes, hours, or even days later. Another technique is to have your child picture the items being placed around a familiar place, such as on pieces of furniture in his room or on equipment at his favorite playground. Older preschoolers may enjoy trying to recite a *short* list (two to five items) *backwards*—this task is very challenging for young kids, and many cannot do even two items backwards.

"I Never Saw a Purple Cow"

Since you have your kids captive, use the chance to teach them to recite short rhymes, poems, limericks, jokes, riddles, or tongue twisters. My kids particularly enjoyed learning silly poems, anything involving potty humor, and tongue twisters. Here are a couple of tongue twisters to get you started:

Three fleas flew through these trees.

She sells seashells by the seashore.

Bubba's baby bumped the bottom bottle.

Penny School
AND OTHER MOVING WAITING GAMES

Restless preschoolers will wait more patiently if they're not only distracted, but also mobile. The following games are good for spacious or relatively empty waiting rooms.

Penny School

For two or more players. This is a recess game from my mom's childhood. It is ideally played in an area with several empty seats in a row, though if they're not available, players can stand and take steps forward instead. Pick one person to be the teacher. Everyone else piles onto (or stands near) one chair or stands together if chairs aren't available. The teacher hides a coin or other small object in one hand and puts both hands behind her back; then she brings her closed fists forward to give the first student an "examination." If the student "passes" (picks the hand with the coin), he gets to move to the next "grade" (seat). You can alternate turns, but to minimize pile-ups, we played that a student's turn continued until he missed and could no longer graduate to the next grade. Two players can take turns being teacher and student.

For added interest, we usually spent a lot of time discussing the school issues (like how "old" we were in each grade, and what we were now big enough to do). You can also play this game with different themes, like "Around the World" (Pretend to visit each continent or sail every ocean.) or "Who Wants To Be A Millionaire?" (Pretend to move up the money ladder, deciding after each turn whether to keep playing or stop. See who wins the most money—that is, gets the longest string of right answers— by the time your wait is done.)

Doctor Says

For two or more players. Play "Simon Says" with a twist appropriate to your setting. This can help prepare your child for the coming experience, as well as providing fun while you wait. Give commands like, "Doctor says,

'Stick out your tongue!'" or "Pretend to brush your teeth." (We mix in regular "Simon Says" orders too, for variety.) Stick to nonthreatening activities—it's usually better to avoid raising anxiety about shots, cavities, or other unpleasant prospects.

Rock, Paper, Scissors Race

For two players. Add a movement component to this classic game to make it more fun. Two players face each other an equal distance from a target (like a chair or the wall). Players each wave a fist back and forth while chanting, "Rock, paper, scissors. One, two, three!" On three, both players "shoot" their hand forward, in a fist (rock), flat hand (paper) or peace sign (scissors). Rock beats scissors, paper beats rock, and scissors beats paper, in case you've forgotten. (The same choice is a tie.) The winner stays where he is, but the loser must take a step closer to the target. The game repeats with the players standing in their new positions until one player—the loser—reaches the target.

Charades, Jr.
FIGURE-IT-OUT-WHILE-YOU-MOVE GAMES

Most adults have been brainwashed into believing that you have to choose a seat and sit there in the waiting room until it's your turn. But there's no rule about that, and even etiquette permits young children to move around a bit, so long as they're not being excessively rowdy or destructive. These games are likely to bring smiles not only to the faces of your young charges, but also of fellow waiters, especially if you invite them to join in too.

Charades, Jr.

For two or more players—the more the merrier. The easiest beginner charades are "Animals" or "Actions." For younger kids, limit the categories even more, like "Farm Animals" or "Things We Do in the Morning." Advanced players may be able to act out nursery rhymes, especially if you specify a handful of possibilities. Play this as a noncompetitive game—everyone cheers when someone guesses the charade correctly.

If more than one child is participating, ask the player to think up something for you and the other children to guess, offering a few suggestions first if necessary. Or you can whisper something for the player to act out, like "chicken" or "brushing teeth." Offer ideas if the player can't think of how to show something. Remind him to try not to use any sounds or words, but be tolerant, because preschoolers have a hard time following that rule. If the young guessers are way off the mark, help nudge them closer to the answer by talking out what the actor is doing.

Acting School

For any number of players. This simple, noncompetitive game challenges kids to identify emotions. You pretend to be a caricatured movie director (with an interesting accent) trying to get his actors to show an emotion using the Method approach. (Instead of labeling the feeling, the director has them imagine and act out a situation, experiencing the feeling in a "real" way.) For example, if the target emotion is surprise, the director might say things like, "You walk into your house. Strange—all the lights are off. It's very dark. You trip over something on the floor. Suddenly the lights come on! All your friends are there, wearing funny hats and blowing on horns. Oh! It's your birthday party! Now, *show* me what you are *feeling!*" Have the kid show, then name, the emotion if he can.

Write Back

Can be adapted to any number of players, but fewer is better. "Writing" with your finger on a child's back is soothing as well as distracting. Start with a demonstration. "I'm making a heart on your back. Can you feel it?" Then offer a choice of two simple pictures, letters, or numbers. "Am I drawing a circle or a square?" "A snowman or a sailboat?" "A *B* or a *W?*" Trade places and let your child write on your back. You can also write on palms (the guesser can watch or close his eyes, depending on his skill) or draw in the air with big sweeping motions (either with your hand or by moving his). We always wrapped up this game by writing "I love you!" to each other.

Mirror, Mirror in the Chair
QUIET IMITATION GAMES

These movement activities for two players are good for crowded waiting rooms, since you remain seated while you play. And they're almost as much fun as some of the rowdier games, especially if you let yourself do silly motions like making fish faces or flapping chicken wings.

Mirror, Mirror in the Chair

Arrange your chairs so that you and your child are facing each other. Tell your child that you have turned into his mirror. You will do whatever he does, but he needs to move slowly because you are a beginner mirror, and you can't work quickly. Have your child perform a series of actions, such as crossing his legs, raising his hands, or opening his mouth wide, while you try to keep up, doing just what he does. After a couple of minutes, trade roles.

MORE TO KNOW

Moving slowly is challenging for most preschoolers. Be sure to model slow, smooth movements when it's your turn. Some children may need to be the mirror first in order to grasp the concept.

Monkey See, Monkey Do

Wave your magic finger wand and turn your child into a monkey. Remind her that monkeys love to copy people. Perform simple actions, such as clapping hands, rubbing your tummy, or shaking your head. (If space and place permit, you can try more vigorous actions, such as hopping on one foot.) Once you finish, your child can repeat your actions.

After she masters one-step actions, try two- and three-step combinations for her to copy. Later, read the classic book *Caps for Sale* by Esphyr Slobodkina for more monkey business.

Funny Faces

Play the mirror or monkey game, sticking to funny faces. And to make it harder, try not to laugh. First one to laugh is the mirror or monkey in the next round.

Follow My Finger

Remember how delightful it was when your infant learned to track your moving finger? Your preschooler does that trick with a charm all her own. Have her hold her head still. (She can prop her chin in her hands if necessary and feasible.) Point your finger and hold it about 12 inches from her face. Slowly move it side to side, up and down, and around in circles as she follows with just her eyes. Finish off with some crazy, zippy moves or zero in on her nose as she goes cross-eyed. Then let her do it for you!

Bouncers
AND TICKLERS TOO

Stressful waiting situations, like the doctor's office, may cause children to need physical reassurance and even a little babying. I think that's why my kids always insisted on playing these games when we went for checkups—that, and the fact that as soon as you've done something *once* with a young child, it's a tradition.

Knee Bouncers

Here are a couple of our favorite traditional rhymes. Smaller children can sit on your lap facing you; bigger kids can face outward.

Father, Mother, and Uncle John,	(Bounce child on both knees.)
Rode to market, one by one.	(Keep bouncing vigorously.)
Father fell off,	(Tip child to one side.)
And Mother fell off,	(Tip to the other.)
But Uncle John rode on,	(Bounce, then straighten legs
and on, and ON!	like a slide.)
Trot, trot to Boston,	(Bounce child, tipping to one
	side.)
Trot, trot to Lynn,	(Bounce tipping to the other.)
Watch out for little boys (or *girls*)	(Bounce.)
Who might fall . . .	(Bounce and pause.)
Might fall . . . (repeat as desired)	(Bounce and pause.)
IN!	(Open legs so child falls
	through.)

Ticklers

I enjoy these traditional touch-me rhymes as much as my kids do, so make sure you get your kids to reciprocate on you.

Treasure Hunt

Going on a treasure hunt,	(Pat palms rhythmically on upper back.)
Going on a treasure hunt!	
X *marks the spot.*	(Make an X somewhere on the back.)
Four big boulders	(Tap fist four times in a square.)
And a little tiny dot!	(Dig fingertip in.)
Spiders climbing up your back,	(Creepy-crawl fingers up.)
Bite you, bite you!	(Gentle pinches by shoulders.)
Blo-o-o-o-o-d dripping down.	(Lightly run fingers down back.)
Tight squeeze!	(Squeeze shoulders suddenly.)
Cool breeze.	(Blow on back of neck.)
Shivers all around.	(Lightly shake fingers from scalp down.)

The Sea

Here is the sea, the wavy sea.	(Wave fingers across the middle of the back.)
Here is my boat—	(Draw a sailboat with your fingers.)
And here is me!	(Poke a finger above the boat.)
All of the fishes down below	(Lightly tap fingers on lower back.)
Wiggle their tails . . .	(Jiggle fingers vigorously.)
And AWAY they go!	(Suddenly move fingers to sides and tickle)

Reading Rooms
MARIAN LIBRARIAN TO GO

Reading is one of the best ways to pass otherwise dull or anxious moments. Because you can't always rely on waiting rooms to provide interesting, age-appropriate reading material, get in the habit of toting a few books in your car or carryall. (See below for suggestions.) But, if you do find yourself stranded with only waiting room magazines and half-chewed board books, try these literary activities to keep your child contented.

Magazine Scavenger Hunt

Here is a checklist of ten items to find in pretty much any parenting magazine. You can also make up your own list.

- A crying baby
- A sleeping child
- A high chair
- A stroller
- Two children together
- An animal
- Someone wearing red (or whatever your child's favorite color is)

- The letters in your child's name (They don't have to be in order.)
- A car, minivan, or SUV
- The number that equals your child's age

Dole out items two or three at a time.

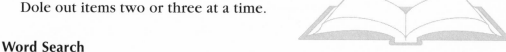

Word Search

Turn to a page in an easy reader. Pick one word and write it in large print on a piece of scratch paper. See if your child can find it in the book. Talk her through the search process if necessary, noticing features like beginning and ending letters and the length and shape of the word. Praise any reasonable attempts to find a match. You can also play simpler search games, like counting all the letter *T*s on the page, or how many periods there are in a given section. Beginning readers can be given more challenging tasks, like finding words that end in "ing" or rhyme with cat.

Recommended Wait-and-Read Materials

- ***Search Books*** Children are captivated by the visual hunt books like the *Where's Waldo?* series by Martin Handford, the *I Spy* series by Jean Marzollo and Walter Wick, *Animalia* by Graeme Base, and my favorites, Joan Steiner's incredible *Look-Alikes* books.
- ***Get Ready Books*** Mr. Rogers's classic *First Experiences* books on visiting the doctor, dentist, hospital, and so on, continue to ease children's fears and help them understand what's coming up.
- ***Teeny, Tiny Books*** These are increasingly popular—and easy to tote around. Look for the interactive *Mouse* series by Michelle Cartlidge and the miniature reprints of old Golden Books.
- ***Short Chapter Books*** For a start, try the heavily illustrated *My Father's Dragon* series by Ruth Stiles Gannett, or the hilarious *Captain Underpants* books by Dav Pilkey.

- *Nonfiction* Enjoy the detailed illustrations of the Eyewitness series books published by Dorling-Kindersley or the Cross-Section books by Stephen Biesty. Aim for books on your child's current passion.
- *Joke, Riddle, and Funny Poem Books* We liked any of the poetry books by Shel Silverstein or Jack Prelutsky, as well as joke collections from the library (especially knock-knock and elephant jokes).
- *Puzzle Books* The British publisher Usborne has appealing series at different levels of difficulty, including the *Puzzle Adventures* books. *Highlights for Children* magazine also publishes a subscription series called *Puzzlemania*.
- *Magazines and Comics* Stock up at yard sales, book sales, and flea markets on back issues of quality children's magazines like *Ladybug, Highlights for Children, National Geographic World,* and *Nick, Jr.* Most kids also enjoy comic strip collections (*Peanuts* books by Charles Schulz are favorites) and the comics pages from the newspaper.

Zoomers
CHOREOGRAPHED MOVEMENT

These activities will enable you to direct your child's movements—and, with luck, thereby keep it in bounds.

Zoomers

For two or more players. Turn your child's hand into a jet and yourself into an air traffic controller. Use the arm of the chair for a runway and direct the hand-y aircraft to various airports around the room. Your child can radio the tower for permission to land and take off, as well as receive reports on traffic, weather, and changes of flight plan.

Moving Day

For you and one child. Have your child stand next to her seat and turn her into a mover. Then narrate items (preferably silly or exciting ones, like a green elephant or a bag of jewels) for her to remove from her house (chair) and load in her imaginary moving van. Start with as many items as her age. Then narrate her drive to her new house (a different chair). Give precise directions, but let her back up or make unnecessary turns to get her wiggles out while she drives. Once she pulls up to her new home, see if she can remember all of the items in her truck as she unloads them. Still feeling squirmy? How about *another* move?

Treasure Trail

Best for two players; otherwise it gets too pushy and competitive. While your child has her eyes closed, hide a small toy or other object somewhere in the room. Then give your child step-by-step directions until she finds it. (Have children who don't yet know right from left hold a penny in one hand, and tell them to turn "to the penny hand" or "to the empty hand.") Give commands like these: "Take three steps forward and stop," "Turn so you're facing the door," "Hop two times like a bunny," and so on. Advanced players can take turns being the director. You can also spice up this game with some imagination. My kids liked to pretend to look for pirate treasure with a map, to be remote-control robots, or to be assistant detectives searching for a kidnapped teddy bear.

Moving Music

Songs and finger plays give preschoolers acceptable outlets for their wigglies. Anything that requires motions will do, but here are some suggestions of adaptable, expandable classics to get you started:

- ***Shake Your Sillies Out*** And clap your crazies, stomp your squigglies, waggle your wigglies, flap your flutteries, jump your jigglies, march your maddies, and so on. If you don't know this song, you can hear it on *More Singable Songs for the Very Young* by Raffi. (There's also a sample of it on the

Amazon.com page for this album).

- *This Is the Way We...* The traditional version is "bake our bread," etc., but we like to play different musical instruments, use tools, or move various body parts in different ways too.
- *If You're Happy and You Know It* Clap your hands, of course, and yawn and stretch if you're sleepy, cry if you're sad, stomp your feet if you're mad, etc.

Whispering 101
VOLUME CONTROL AND LIPPER ZIPPERS

From time to time, you may find you need to take your child places where Quiet is a must. And this is a problem, since most preschoolers prefer Ear-Shattering Loud. Short of using duct tape (not recommended by most parenting experts), you probably can't keep your child silent for an extended period of time. These metaphors, though, may help young children fully grasp what they're supposed to do, and make quick, non-verbal reminders when needed.

Volume Control

Before you enter the Quiet Zone, tell your child to turn her volume down. My kids pretended to turn ear or nose knobs, push belly buttons, or program a series of controls. It's best to have your child perform the operation herself—the silence will feel more voluntary and under her control. If possible, make lots of noise *before* going inside and adjust the volume at the last possible moment.

If you won't be next to your child to issue reminders, but she'll be able to see you, find a prop to use as a remote control. When she sees you point it at her and "click," she'll know it's time to turn the volume down again.

Lipper Zippers

A well-known gesture and friendlier than the Hushing Finger of Death. Show your child how to zip her lips closed, lock them with a key, and then toss the key away. The gesture from you can serve as a reminder when needed. Some children prefer other lip fastener metaphors—enlist your child's help in thinking up some to try, like laces, buttons, glue, Velcro, the ever-effective duct tape, chains and padlock, or maybe a little barbed wire. For the Houdini-tongued, you might want to trot out an assortment of methods—an elaborate lock-up routine may make the message more memorable.

Hushers

Nobody likes to be told "Be quiet!" or worse, "Shut up!" That's why it's a good idea to start using one of these hushing phrases or games that teachers find effective:

- **Inside Voices, Please!** My autopilot phrase from teaching days
- **Two-Inch Voices** Outside ones are foot high or even mile high.
- **Library Voices** (Or church voices, restaurant voices, etc.) These are good because they imply a certain tone and content as well as low volume; we also use phrases like party manners, grown-up manners, or restaurant manners.
- **Let's Play The Whisper Talk Game** Whoever forgets and talks in a regular voice loses.
- **Time For The Silence Game** This is an advanced version of the whisper talk game. First one to talk loses. (Fools them every time.)

TRY THIS!

Make sure you give kids a chance for appropriate loud voices as soon as possible after they've been quiet. They'll probably need it, and knowing that the silent time *does* end eventually helps them be more cooperative the next time.

Butt Glue Sticks
SIT STILL STRATEGIES

If you tried to use one of these techniques for too long, the kid would just explode. At least that's what mine tell me. But these will work with most preschoolers for at least five minutes. Maybe ten. After that, put up your umbrella, so you don't get showered with guts when your kid explodes.

Butt Glue Sticks

Take out a really large invisible tube of Super-Duper Sticky-Stucky Butt Glue (also available in a convenient giant glue stick). Slather it liberally over your child's chair and posterior. Press the two surfaces together and hold for ten seconds until it sets up. During this time, read the label out loud, so your child knows the glue will hold him firmly in place for whatever time period you need. Just make sure to have some invisible instant adhesive remover available for those emergency trips to the rest room.

Heavyweight Champions

A 20-pound weight will hold most preschoolers in place. *Just kidding!* But a full-size Beanie Baby, buckwheat hull pillow, or even just a bag of rice stuck in a small pillowcase will remind a restless child to stay seated. Almost anything he has on his lap will help, but it's best if it isn't something that will scatter and clatter when he forgets and stands up to yell, "french fries!" as the bride walks down the aisle (like one of my toddlers once did).

Periscopes and Elevator Knees

Seating your child so that he can *see* (and hear or participate) will make him much more likely to sit quietly. (But also select seats that allow for a quick and easy exit.) Try to get aisle seats, bring along a booster seat, or allow your child to perch on his knees. Standing next to his chair may also help a squirmy child to be less bothersome to others. Periscopes are too cumbersome to be a good idea for real, but opera glasses or binoculars can distract your kid while giving him a better view.

Not the Old Underwear Trick!

Know how public speaking experts are always advising you to picture the audience in their underwear (or less)? This technique is supposed to make the people seem less intimidating, but I've noticed it also makes them more interesting. The strategy also seems to make boring social events more intriguing to four year olds. But rather than picturing folks in their Fruit of the Looms, your child can imagine everyone with slugs coming out of their nostrils or with giant purple frog eyes or something else kind of gross or cool. Just beware of an unfortunate side effect of this approach: giggle attacks.

Sign Language
HOW YOUR CHILD CAN TELL YOU IMPORTANT THINGS LIKE "I'M ABOUT TO PEE MY PANTS!" WITHOUT MAKING A PUBLIC ANNOUNCEMENT

My kids have taken several American Sign Language (ASL) classes in school. I wish I'd known this method of communicating when they were younger. They used to mouth their needs at me (but I could never tell what they were saying), or simply shout out the information. Now a discreet hand gesture puts me in the know. I apologize in advance if my ASL is imperfect—I've learned much of it from books or secondhand from my kids. A final note: use facial expressions as well as gestures to help convey meaning.

- *Toilet* As in "I need it now!" Make the ASL *T* sign (fist, with thumb stuck between the pointer and tall man fingers). Shake it back and forth. Look desperate.
- *I need help* Place the right fist on top of the left palm. The left palm lifts the right fist up and toward the chest.
- *How much longer?* Tap wrist (where a watch would be) several times and raise eyebrows questioningly. A child-friendly response is to use hands held apart to indicate "just a little longer" (hands barely apart) to "a long time still" (hands far apart, sympathetic expression).

- ***I'm hungry*** Bunch fingers and tap lower lip. A pathetic look may get faster service.
- ***I'm thirsty*** Form fingers into the shape of a *C*, as if they were holding a cup. Raise hand to lips. A pathetic expression is good with this gesture too.

ON THE WEB

There is some evidence that learning sign language early in life may foster better language development later on. Certainly, kids who are taught some signs (which they generally learn easily, just as young children learn second spoken languages easily) are more likely to use gestures to communicate when they need to be quiet. There are many books, videos, and websites to help your child learn sign language. Try www.handspeak.com to look up individual signs or check out the videos *Sign-Me-a-Story* by Linda Bove and *Sign Songs: Fun Songs to Sign and Sing* for signing instruction aimed at young children.

- ***I feel sick*** Open hand, use middle finger to slide across forehead and repeat. Pained expression. He can also put middle finger on his forehead and use his other hand to show the area that hurts.
- ***I'm scared*** Move both open hands in front of the chest, as if grabbing someone to protect him from something scary. (This also looks kind of like a cool rapper gesture.) This is useful for kids who want your help in getting them out of a difficult situation, but feel embarrassed to admit it in front of others.
- ***I love you*** Hold up the hand, palm forward, with the thumb extended, index and pinky fingers raised, tall man and ring man folded down. An easy sign and a good way to offer reassurance from a distance.

It's useful to invent your own "family signs" to stand for different family members or favorite catch phrases. We also use traditional gestures, like "thumbs up" and the OK sign (circle with thumb and index finger).

Church Mice and Putty-in-Your-Hand
EMERGENCY PROPS

The right props can help keep your preschooler too busy for shrieking and sometimes distracted enough that he's downright quiet. Certain props can also serve as reminders of your kid's mission: to remain *silent*—at least until his attorney arrives.

Church Mice

One family I know always takes a set of tiny toy mice to holiday church services. Their girls, appropriately enough, call them "church mice," and recognize them as a signal for quiet play. The parents add miniature props appropriate to the occasion (e.g., a small crèche at Christmas or little baskets at Easter). The novelty of the props keeps the activity fresh and appealing. On the way to services, the dad tells his girls a story about the church mice to help prepare the kids for the upcoming experience.

Gather toys appropriate to whatever setting you'll be in. For example, a toy bride and groom might delight children attending a wedding, and doll dishes with scraps of food can busy children in a grown-up restaurant setting. Toys like these will be especially effective reminders if you *only* make them available during quiet-please situations.

Putty-in-Your-Hand

Silly Putty is a great take-along toy. It's small, silent, versatile—and engrossing. (One potential problem: it can get stuck in upholstery or carpeting, so be selective about where you use it.) Aside from simply stretching and rolling it, try these activities:

- Transfer images from the newspaper. (Comics are our favorite.)
- Stretch and distort the pictures you've transferred.

- "Dress" action figures or plastic dolls or animals or wrapping small objects like coins.
- Use strings or snakes of putty to shape pictures, shapes, letters, or numbers.
- Mix two different colors together. (Roll pieces of different colors into snakes, twist them together, and then roll and knead until marbled or combined as desired.)
- Pok or imprint the Silly Putty with small objects, like game pieces, toothpicks, and coins.

Pipe Cleaners

Also called chenille stems. Easy activities:

- Wrap them around a pencil to make springs, which can be sproinged gently at a target. Or just enjoy squishing and releasing them.
- Thread objects onto the pipe cleaner. Try using lengths of drinking straws, foam shapes (prepunch holes with a hole-puncher), cereal O's. and dried pasta. Or weave the stems through a sewing card or plastic berry basket.
- Make wacky (or pretty) hairdos by twisting stems around sections of hair. (Obviously save this activity for an appropriate place.)

Quiet Foods

A good distraction for *desperate* times. Dole out the goodies one or two at a time on a schedule. The following snacks are noiseless or nearly so:

- *Treats* Gumdrops, marshmallows, candy corn (eat one stripe at a time), LifeSavers (make a rule that they must be sucked not chewed), licorice (cut into small pieces in advance), mini-chocolate chips, caramels (precut in smaller pieces), fruit roll ups, gummy bears and other gummy creatures

- *Quiet Healthier Stuff* Cheese cubes or sticks, raisins and other dried fruits, peanut butter sandwich cut into bite-size squares, bite-size pieces of lunch meat

Serve food from zipper plastic bags or string treats into a "Goody Necklace," using thin elastic or dental floss (how ironic).

MORE TO KNOW

Other good quiet props include a small hand mirror for making faces; pom-poms, tassels, and fabric scraps (store them in a large sock or a cloth bag); a travel-size magnetic drawing board; a length of string (show your child how to make knots in it and you may keep him busy for hours); precut foam shapes for making designs; finger puppets; and a small calculator (for pushing buttons).

CHAPTER THREE

Surviving Doctors' Offices, Hairdressers, and Other Places Your Child Hates

If you have children, sooner or later you will find yourself dragging them to places they would rather not be. Like the emergency room. During one bad two-month period, I took children to the emergency room three times! None of the injuries was my fault, honest!—I wasn't even there when two of them happened!—but still I'm grateful that I didn't get investigated by the child abuse people. The one good thing about this stretch of bad luck is that I learned a lot about dispensing lousy-situation TLC. This kind of knowledge is pretty useful to have, so I've tried to share it with you here. The same general techniques also work at the doctor's office with kids facing unwanted checkups and shots or at the dentist's office when it's time for a filling. And I've included other ideas for cheering your child at the hairdresser or when he has to accompany you to the gynecologist's.

I figure I might as well take a couple minutes here and tell you about how the above injuries happened in hopes that you'll feel a little less like a bad parent if you find yourself heading to the emergency room—at least you probably won't be there three times in sixty days like I was! Or for such silly accidents!

Lessons from Accident One When your child says, "I'll go to bed in just one second. Let me just show you this good trick first," you should say, "No way, José. Upstairs and brush your teeth right now." Especially if the trick involves spinning around as fast as he can right next to a low wooden bookcase with sharp corners. And even more especially if the bookcase with the sharp edges is sitting on the newly installed carpet. Because then you're going to have to figure out how to get the bloodstains out of the new carpet as well as take your kid to the emergency room. The one good thing, from the kid's point of view, though, is that he'll have a cool new nickname to impress the guys at preschool: Mr. Staplehead.

Lessons from Accident Two Don't run in the house. At least not in your stocking feet. Or at least not on a hardwood floor. And especially not at a friend's house. Or if you do, and you crack your head open, remember that it's not polite to sit in the friend's dad's favorite light blue recliner. Because then you have the bloodstain problem again, and it's more awkward when it's not your own stuff you've stained. Incidentally, this was a different child, *and I was not even there at the time. Really.*

Lessons from Accident Three Make a rule that if your child doesn't know how to juggle and he doesn't know how to balance on a basketball, he should not try to juggle while balancing on a basketball. This should prevent the accident that happened to Mr. Staplehead when he tried this trick less than two months after having the staples from the first accident removed. You shouldn't need to bother with the longer version of the rule—"No juggling while balanced on a basketball in the cement driveway next to the stone wall." For one thing, it takes too long to say and for another, it's harder to remember. For the record, I was not home when this accident occurred; I just returned in time to take the bloody child to the emergency room and blush every time anyone asked me if my son had ever been a patient there before and why did I look so familiar? The good thing from the kid's point of view: a second set of staples in your head is nearly as cool as the first one.

Creative kids are always finding ways to hurt themselves, so bone up on these tips and pack your Emergency Comfort kit, just in case. And if you feel a bit faint when it's time to call the doctor, remember to lie on the floor and elevate your feet while you make the call. Finally, to remove bloodstains from carpet, use a white towel to blot the spot with cold water or club soda. Repeat until clean.

Dry Runs
DRESS REHEARSALS AND INSTANT REPLAYS

Preparing kids for unpleasant or new experiences is one of the best and easiest ways to help them cope—and to prevent major Public Displays of Fussing. Here are some ways to help kids rehearse or prepare for some of the difficult experiences that many young children face.

Read All About It!

There are picture books on almost any childhood experience you'll encounter—and that's a lucky thing. Books provide a visual context, as well as teaching words that will help your child discuss her experience. They may also contain details you hadn't anticipated. Books can be examined at a pace of your child's choosing, and can be revisited as often as he needs. The *First Experiences* series by Fred Rogers covers many situations, like visits to the doctor or hospital and attending school or daycare, and the Berenstain Bears books by Stan and Jan Berenstain address many of the same situations. For more ideas on managing specific experiences, search the website of the American Library Association (www.ala.org— go to the pages for parents and kids) or look on one of the online bookstores like www.amazon.com.

The Talk-Through

This is the method you'll probably use most often. Outline expected events and the order in which they'll take place. Reassure your child that you'll be there to support her. (If you won't be there, let her know who will be helping her.) Encourage her to ask questions and share her feelings. Do not lie about expected pain or other negatives, but don't dwell on them either. Discuss ways that your child has coped successfully in the past, and what she can do this time.

The Walk-Through

Visiting a site *in advance* of the actual event is often the ideal way to prepare your child. The real place will provide sensory information—like smells, that even the best books or videos can't supply—and may spark questions your child otherwise wouldn't have thought to ask. Visiting beforehand lets him rehearse without the stresses that may accompany the real experience. Casual, repeated visits are best—so let younger siblings tag along to their siblings' schools and doctor visits or come to the barber with you. Take advantage of tours before planned hospitalizations, visit classrooms before school starts, or plan an outing to the airport a week or two before a first flight.

Play It Out

If you can't visit a place in advance, use props or miniatures to act out the situation. Your child may particularly benefit from playing different roles. For example, to give him a feeling of control and mastery over the situation, let him be the doctor as well as the patient. (Seeing him in the adults' roles will also give you a window into his perceptions and provide an opportunity for you to correct any confusion about procedures or reasons for them.)

The Instant Replay

The military, emergency response teams, and other groups who routinely face difficult experiences know how important debriefing is.

Reliving the experience will help your child share her emotions, receive comfort or reassurance, and gain additional information she needs. Simply

MORE TO KNOW

Many experiences that adults perceive as ordinary are anxiety provoking for inexperienced children. The following events may be stressful for preschoolers: doctor or dentist appointments, hospital stays or emergency room trips, visits to someone ill or injured (in the hospital or elsewhere), the start of school or daycare, travel, outings to someplace new, nights away from home, visits to the barber or beauty shop, gift-giving or -getting situations, and adult-oriented occasions or places.

talking about the experience (especially emphasizing how well she coped) is often enough. Many children, though, will want to replay what happened with toys or reread the books that helped them prepare. Debriefing is especially important for events that have caught your child by surprise, either because they differed from her expectations, or because you simply didn't have a chance to prepare her.

Groomer-Soothers
GENTLE TOUCHES FOR ROUGH TIMES

Touch is comforting to people of all ages. These games will help distract your child by capturing her imagination, and ease her distress through your caring touch. They're especially useful in places like the doctor's office or for relaxing after a difficult experience.

Put on a Happy Face

Have your child sit (or lie if possible) with her head in your lap or leaning against your chest. In a soothing "spa attendant" voice, tell her to close her eyes and relax, while you give her a "facial" and apply her "makeup."

Massage her forehead, using medium pressure and small circles. Next, lightly apply "moisturizer." Have your strokes begin at the midline of her face and move toward her hairline. Gently smooth hands over her forehead, eyes, cheeks, and lips.

Finally, apply imaginary makeup, from foundation to powder, and touches of perfume. Talk quietly while you work, telling your child what you are doing and complimenting the smoothness of her skin. (This will help her relax her muscles.)

For a boy, do the facial and finish up with a shave and a little aftershave. And, who knows, maybe your child will want to reverse roles! Aaah!

Dress Up to Calm Down

Let your child choose an imaginary costume or fancy outfit to wear, and then "dress" him in it while he sits in your lap. A British valet voice is a nice accompaniment.

For example, for a pirate, comb his hair back with your fingers and put on a bandanna or captain's hat. Trim his beard and wipe the gunpowder from his fingers. Stroke his legs from his feet to his knees as you put on his stockings. Fasten his breeches at the waist, and slide a blunderbuss into its holster. Tie his puffy shirt at the neck and fold up his cuffs. Finish up with a parrot on one shoulder, an earring in one ear, and a cutlass between his teeth.

More suggested outfits:
- ball player uniform
- astronaut or scuba diving suit
- fancy gown for Cinderella or other fairy tale character
- work clothes for firefighter, police officer, surgeon, or cowpoke
- robes, crown, and jewels for king or queen
- favorite Halloween costume

Finger Creepers
TOUCHY-FEELY DISTRACTIONS

Some situations call for a lighter—and more light-hearted—touch. Try these nervy experiments that tickle kids' skin and their fancies.

Finger Creepers

This is a simple but cool activity. Be prepared to repeat it endlessly. Have your child close his eyes and straighten one of his bare arms, palm up. (This doesn't work as well if his arm is bent at the elbow.) Very slowly and softly, creep your fingers up his bare arm from the underside of his wrist to his inner elbow. Ask him to tell you when you reach the spot where his elbow bends.

Most people will "feel" the bend in their elbow an inch or so before the actual spot. Pretty neat, huh? Repeat and see if he can improve his ability to tell. Then let your child try it on you.

One Touch or Two?

Nerve endings are distributed unevenly over the body. Your fingers and your face have a large number of endings; your back has relatively few. This fact makes for an interesting experiment on sensitivity.

You need two opened paperclips, two pennies, or two dull pencil tips to *gently* poke your child's skin. Have your child stand with his back to you. Hold a "poker" in each hand. Touch your child's back with either one poker or two at the same time. See if he can tell how many pokers touched his skin. At first, keep the two pokers close together. Gradually move them farther apart when you do the two-poke touches.

Most people have a hard time distinguishing two pokers until they are significantly apart. Repeat the experiment on the palm side of your child's fingers or his cheek. Are the results the same?

Squeezy Fingers

Another "nervy" game my kids like is performed as a pseudo-magic trick. Have your child push his clenched fists together hard. Then using two fingers of each hand, tap rapidly back and forth on the sides of your child's fists and then the tops of his knuckles. Keep this up for about a minute, reminding him frequently to keep squeezing. Say some magic words. Then tell your child to try *slowly* to move his hands apart. It will feel very difficult.

The magic words and tapping are actually unnecessary. Simply pushing your fists together hard for a while causes the sensation of being stuck. But the other features make the trick more *fun.* Reverse and have your child do it to you. A variation is to clench your fist and have the other person gently stroke the skin on the inside of your wrist. Then slowly try to open your hand. Or push your arms tightly against your sides, while the other person strokes them shoulder to wrist. Then try to lift your arms.

Puppet Pals
FRIENDS-IN-NEED

Preschoolers often find it difficult to talk directly about fears or other upsetting feelings. Fortunately, play can give them an outlet to express their worries about the thing that the doctor pokes in their ear or to practice being brave in the face of an enveloping hairdresser's cape. Puppets and other figures are especially good props for emotionally supportive discussions and enactments.

Puppet Fingers

Put your hand in your pocket, wiggle your index finger, and say, "Oh! What's in my pocket?" Have your finger "jump" or "creep" out of your pocket and say hello. Your finger/puppet can begin a conversation with your child. Most preschoolers are completely "captured" by the finger's assumed identity and will speak freely with the puppet as if you weren't there.

Puppet fingers are useful for preparing your child for a new experience. For example, before a first trip to the dentist, your finger could ask, "What's going to happen? Will I like it? Show me how to open wide. Wow! You have lots of shiny teeth!"

You will probably find this kind of play easier if you have a couple of stock characters. Some useful characters:

- A child (or small animal) who puts your child in the "big" person role
- A character who is silly, and/or physically affectionate (especially useful when you want to distract your child from what you are waiting for, like a shot at the doctor's).

TALES FROM THE TRENCHES

My friend was having a conversation with her three-year-old son, using a hand puppet. The little boy was telling the puppet with great animation about a big dog he had seen. The mom, forgetting herself, said in her normal voice, "Boy, I bet that dog scared you!"

Exasperated, the boy put his hands on hips, gave his mom one of those looks, and said, "I wasn't talking to *you!*"

The favorite characters at my house were named Little Mouse, who needed to have *everything* explained to him (he was prone to asking "Why?" and "What does that mean?" endlessly, like certain three year olds we've known), and Tickle Bee who "spoke" in expressive buzzing and was given to tickling fits.

If you are not waiting to be presented to the Queen or for an audience with the Pope, add to your puppet's mystique by drawing on a face or dressing it in a bit of tissue.

Little Guys

Jumpstart imaginative play by grabbing a couple of objects and having them "talk" to each other in different voices. We've used rolled up newspapers, prescription pads, lollipops, shoes, belly buttons (Squeeze them to make them move their "mouths.") and almost anything else you can name to play a wide variety of roles.

Doctor, Doctor, I Declare!
YOU CAN SEE MY UNDERWEAR

Preschoolers go to the doctor for annual checkups and most will make occasional visits for illness or injuries as well. The following tips may help with common preschooler concerns at these visits.

The Shot Question

This is the Big Worry at the doctor's for most preschoolers. Currently, experts recommend three immunizations between the ages of four and six: DTaP (diphtheria, tetanus, and pertussis), IPV or OPV (polio), and MMR (measles, mumps, and rubella). Because pediatricians may schedule these shots for different well visits, you should ask about shots when you make the appointment. Double-check when you are shown into the examining room, so you can prepare your child for what to expect. (See "Sleepy Puppy" on page 67 and "Pricker Presents" on page 69 for tips on helping your child cope.)

The Naked Truth

Preschoolers are typically unworried about modesty, but being naked at the doctor's office may make them feel vulnerable or uncomfortable. Newer pediatricians have mostly been trained to examine children fully clothed or nearly so. If your child is asked to undress and it makes him uncomfortable, first talk with the doctor about whether an exception is possible. If not, request a blanket or sheet to keep him warm, leave as many items on as possible (even if it's just his socks and undies), and/or wait until the last minute to undress. Undressed children may feel more relaxed with a little nake-y humor, like telling the doctor a variation on the classic "Teacher, teacher" school rhyme: "Doctor, doctor, I declare! You can see my underwear!"

Always prepare your child for the doctor to check his "privates," especially if you have warned him not to let other people touch his genitals without his permission. Explain that doctors have to—and are allowed to—touch him during an examination with you present.

TRY THIS!

Be an assertive advocate for your preschooler. Don't let healthcare providers lie to him ("This won't hurt a bit."), rush him unreasonably, ignore his questions, or treat him roughly or unkindly. Insist on your right to comfort your child and remain with him, except when doing so would endanger him or you. After a horrendous trip to an allergy doctor (where the nurse literally called my five year old a baby and was less than gentle), I vowed I would never let a health professional treat my child that way again—and I haven't. You don't have to either.

Stranger Anxiety

Preschoolers who visit the doctor infrequently or who go to large practices may not know or remember the doctor who sees them. Make a point of introducing the two (and yourself) before getting down to business. If the doctor does not spontaneously get down on your child's level or address him directly, boost your child up to the doctor's level and encourage your child to interact with her by saying something like, "Show Dr. Patootie how big your muscles are these days."

Gag Me!

Throat exams and swabs for strep throat tests make many kids gag and even throw up. If your kid tends to gag, make sure she has an empty stomach before the visit. You can help her learn to hold her tongue down and out of the way, too, so that a tongue depressor is unnecessary for exams. Have her pant like a puppy for throat swabs—this tip really helps many kids.

Sleepy Puppy
AND OTHER PAIN MANAGEMENT STRATEGIES

Researchers know that three psychological processes can increase tolerance of pain: feeling in control, distraction, and deep relaxation. Try these techniques to help your child better manage the pain or discomfort of shots, fillings, and other procedures.

Control Tower

It hurts less to pull a splinter out yourself or to rip off your own bandage, doesn't it? You probably can't let your child give his own injections, but you can help him feel more in control—and less in pain—by doing things like

- having him close his eyes, relax, and raise a finger when he's ready for his shot;
- choosing which arm to have the shot in or which chair to sit in while he gets it;
- giving him information (e.g., "This will sting, but the pain will stop as soon as the needle comes out.") and providing some advance warning (but not so much that he has time to get completely worked up).

The Old Hit-Your-Thumb-With-A-Hammer-When-Your-Stubbed-Toe-Hurts Trick

A competing strong sensory experience can help block out the feared one. And it doesn't even have to involve hammers! Try these ideas for distracting your child:

- *Read*—something funny and fast-paced. Be sure to use a loud, expressive voice and get your kid to look at the pictures.
- *Suck*—on a lollipop, especially something strong tasting or sour. Scratchy sugar cubes are good too. Closing his eyes and hearing you talk about the taste will help a kid focus on the sensation rather than the pain.

- *Hug*—your child tightly and calmly, whispering loving messages in his ear. Squeeze or massage other body parts.
- *Listen*—to rousing or soothing music on headphones. Again, closing eyes or focusing on a neutral visual stimulus (like a picture on the wall) will distract more effectively. (I bet doctors' offices could reduce crying by showing cartoon videos during shots or other distressing situations.)

Sleepy Puppy

This deep relaxation technique worked great with my imaginative daughter. Relaxation can reduce actual pain, as well as the perception of it. Demonstrate this to your child by having her close her fist loosely. Poke your finger into her fist. Easy, right? Then have her squeeze her fist tightly. Your child will see that it is much harder for your finger to poke its way in between her fingers. Explain that the same thing happens when the muscles in her arm are loose or tight and the needle has to go in. Tell her you'll help her relax like a sleepy puppy (or other image you choose) so that the shot will go in easier and hurt less.

Hold your child comfortably in your lap and have her close her eyes. Reassure her that you'll let her know when she's about to get the shot, and that she can just "let go" and listen to your voice. In a calm, deep voice, say something like this:

Take a deep breath in, filling up your belly like a balloon. Hold it…and let it go. Now you feel heavy and tired, just like a sleepy little puppy that can't keep its eyes open. (Stroke your child's "fur," trace her eyelids, rub her ears.) *Your ears feel heavy, your head feels heavy, even your belly feels heavy. Your tail is sleepy and so are all your legs and paws. You're so tired you hardly notice when a fly bites you.* (Pinch—a little hard—your child's arm; if she doesn't mind, motion for the doctor to be ready with the needle.) *You're so tired, you won't even*

mind when the vet gives you your shot—it will just feel
like a little fly biting. There, now it's all done, and you
can go right on sleeping peacefully in my lap. And in a
minute, when you're ready to wake up, we can go home
and play fetch and puppy tumble. (**Pause**) *Ready? One,*
two, three, open your eyes.

The biggest drawback of this technique is that it takes a few minutes—and fewer healthcare workers today have the luxury of being able to give you extra moments.

Post-Relief

Ask your doctor whether it's okay to give your child acetaminophen or other pain relievers to prevent the discomforts like fever, swelling, or stiffness that often follow injections. (Often it's best to give the pain medication shortly *before* the procedure, so that it has had time to take effect—but check with your doctor to make sure this is okay too.) Exercise, massage, and application of heat or cold may also prevent swelling or secondary muscle stiffness. Consult with your pediatrician or dentist about best approaches.

Pricker Presents
LIGHTS AT THE END OF THE TUNNEL
AND OTHER COPING MECHANISMS

Some things just are yucky—shots do hurt, fillings can feel scary, and sometimes a body just has to do something she doesn't want to. Although you don't help your child by shielding her from normal discomforts and difficulties, there is nothing wrong with helping her learn how to cope. Having something to look forward to—a light at the end of the tunnel—helps people survive everything from small derailments to major disasters. Try these ideas to help your child learn to look beyond the darkness of the moment to the light ahead.

Pricker Presents

When my brother-in-law had to undergo a series of painful medical procedures, my sister and her young son wrapped up small gifts that they called "pricker presents" for him to open after each one. Fortunately, Doug is healthy now, but pricker presents have become a family tradition when the kids need to have shots or anyone has to face a trying situation. I recommend giving young children a wrapped present to hold or have in sight during the unpleasant experience. Keep it inexpensive—just a nice surprise or small treat. (A major gift is likely to frighten or overwhelm your child, and create a cycle of greed.) You can talk about the present during the experience to help distract your child while she's in the throes of discomfort. Afterward, let her know how well she coped by focusing on a good thing to come.

Speed Bump Mentality

It helps to think of difficult experiences as speed bumps—a small obstacle to get over on the way to something good. Emphasize that your child's pain or discomfort will be temporary (if it will be) and that she will be back feeling good or doing fun things very soon. Even better, plan a fun outing for immediately after an unpleasant experience or allow a normally off-limits treat like a weekday TV feast. When I was growing up, after appointments at the pediatrician's office we always went to the drug store next door to get ice cream at the fountain. (I still want to have ice cream after I go to the doctor.) Another friend always schedules doctor and dentist appointments to conflict with activities her kids dislike (school, mostly, but also music lessons—her kids are older), and doesn't make them return afterwards.

Cocoons

Bring comforts from home to make your child feel loved and secure. Swaddling an ailing child in a soft fleece or flannel blanket, like a caterpillar in a cocoon, may make him feel warm and safe. Bring a pillow for a child who needs to rest his head, a favorite stuffed animal for him to hold (especially if you won't be able to remain with him), a cool drink to sip (after his temperature has been checked), a damp washcloth (to cool his fevered brow), or other comforts you'd provide at home. And remember to think about the comfort of healthy children too, and let them have a few luxuries to enjoy during a difficult time. One friend used to let her daughter wear her engagement ring on a chain around her neck at the doctor's office so she could look at the sparklies to her heart's content.

Sara's a Sandwich
BUCK-UP GAMES

Facing an unpleasant experience can plunge your child into a nasty mood—and that mood can make a bad experience even worse (especially for the adults who have to deal with her). Getting her "bucked up" may make the moment easier for everyone involved. Humor and touch are the magic pills that can transform a rotten mood into one that's sweet—or at least just a *little* overripe.

Sara's a Sandwich

This game was inspired by the silly William Steig picture book *Pete's a Pizza*. Announce that you are going to make a sandwich. Grab your child and put her on the "table" (which can be the floor, your lap, an examining table, or whatever surface is available). Decide what kind of bread she is (a baguette is nice), and "slice" her in two lengthwise, which should be a rather tickly operation. Next build a hero-style sandwich. We slap on slices of cold cuts, sprinkle on grated cheese, stack up sour pickles, toss on some lettuce, and so on. Finish by putting your child back together and poking in a frilly toothpick. Then gobble her up, burp, and pronounce her delicious. It's very hard to be grumpy and serious after you've been made into a sandwich.

Crab Removal Service

Pull your child close and look in her ear. Say, "Ah ha! I see what the problem is! You have a crab stuck in here." Pretend to start working it out. Tug on her earlobe gently as you pretend to pull out one that's got a good grip on her. Then have her open her mouth wide. Find something like a wild grumpus snake in there and start pulling and pulling and pulling it out, reminding her to keep her mouth open wide the whole time. If she's still out of sorts, check her nostrils for bad mood bugs (remove by pinch-honking her nose repeatedly), and her eyelids for low-energy elephants (blow them off with her eyes closed). Sometimes you'll even find a flock of tiny bothers under her fingernails—squeeze gently from the base of her fingers to her nails to remove them. If all else fails, exterminate the whole joint with your secret formula kissing potion. That'll take care of the problem for sure.

Hopping Mad

Say to your child, "I see you are hopping mad." Then when she just stands there glowering, tell her, "Well, start hopping!" Have her hop and hop until she doesn't feel mad anymore. You can hop with her. If you'd like, and she doesn't hit you, sing a little hopping song for encouragement, like these verses from "There Came a Girl from France," which can be heard on Raffi's *The Singable Songs Collection*:

> *Hopping on one foot, hopping on one foot,*
> *Hopping, hopping, never stopping,*
> *Hopping on one foot!*

> *And, hopping on the other, hopping on the other,*
> (repeat)

> *And hopping on both feet, hopping on both feet,*
> (repeat)

And, hopping like a frog, hopping like a frog,
(repeat)

Eventually she'll probably be too tired to be whiny and miserable. Or maybe you'll just be too out of breath to care that she's in a bad mood.

Open Why?
DENTISTRY WITHOUT PAIN IN THE BUTTINSKI

Preschoolers should visit the dentist every six months. Pediatric and family dentists use child-friendly approaches to examining and cleaning teeth. Having grown up as a cavity-prone kid who was *terrified* of the dentist, I was pleasantly surprised to find that for my kids, as well as many others, visiting the dentist is a *fun adventure.* Some kids, though, are anxious or resistant. These approaches may help to calm, reassure, and elicit cooperation.

Find the Right Dentist

Look for kid-friendly features, like child-sized chairs, pictures on the ceiling for a reclining child to examine, and prizes (even just a new toothbrush) handed out after the checkup. The waiting areas should be stocked with books and toys, and the wait should not be excessively long—anxiety builds the longer your child must wait. Even more importantly, look for dentists and hygienists who

- speak directly to your child in friendly voices and communicate openly with you;
- explain what they are doing and why (including showing cavities at all steps of the repair, demonstrating equipment before putting it in your child's mouth, and sharing a look at the X rays);
- do not scold, punish, or shame imperfect patients;
- allow you to remain with your child and comfort him if necessary.

If you are dissatisfied, don't be shy about switching to a different provider. Childhood attitudes about the dentist may last a lifetime and affect your child's dental health.

Make the Visit Comfortable

- Let your child bring her own comforts from home, such as sunglasses (so the examining light doesn't hurt her eyes), a small pillow, worry beads, a stuffed animal, or a hand mirror to help her keep an eye on things.
- Stay with your child if she wants you to. Very anxious children may feel better if they can recline on top of you, or rest their heads in your lap for the exam.
- Agree on a way that your child can signal the dentist to stop (like raising her hand) if she needs to close her mouth and take a rest or if she has a question (very important for fillings).
- Use humor and imagination to secure cooperation. Try asking your child to open a little wider so the dentist can see what she ate for lunch and how pretty the food looks all mushed up, or calling a noisy drill by a funny name like "The Growler."
- If the noises bother your child, bring a portable tape player and headphones to help her block out the sounds of dental equipment. An eye mask may help children who prefer not to look, and a dab of perfume on her wrist may give her an alternative scent to sniff during breaks if the smells of the office bother her.
- Take an "After" photo of your child's dazzling smile and record how many teeth she has and any other interesting findings from the visit.

Play Dentist

Oral mirrors and "tooth counters" can be purchased inexpensively in most pharmacies. (Be careful with the sharp tooth counters and let your child use them only with supervision. Avoid using them to scrape plaque because of the risk of injuring your child's gums.) My kids liked to practice on stuffed animals that could open their mouths (especially those that had pretend teeth). Play-Doh makes a set called "Dr. Drill 'n Fill" that will let your child practice dentistry on a funky guy with a big mouth. Playmobil also makes a toy dentist office set, complete with a reclining chair, miniature tools, and appropriate figures.

Introducing the Hair Fairy
AND OTHER TRIM TACTICS

Haircuts upset a good many preschoolers. Some of the fear comes from ignorance and lack of

LITERATURE LINKS

See the hilarious book Open Wide: Tooth School Inside by Laurie Keller to help your child learn about the importance of dental care and receive giggly reassurance about emotional reactions to having a cavity. To help prepare your child for a checkup or filling, look for other books and videos like The Berenstain Bears Visit the Dentist by Stan and Jan Berenstain, and A Trip to the Dentist Through Pinatta's View, which presents a dental visit using a child-level camera angle and emotional perspective. It can be ordered through www.amazon.com.

experience. Preschoolers may not really understand that their hair doesn't get "hurt" when it's cut and that it will grow back. They may feel uncomfortably restrained by having to wear the capes or hold their heads still, and be frightened by chairs that move or sharp scissors that snip near their faces. These techniques may help children relax (and maybe even enjoy the experience) or at least cooperate more fully.

The Hair Fairy

This idea was suggested by a preschool friend who asked his mother, "You know how the Tooth Fairy comes when my brother loses a tooth?

How come the hair fairy doesn't come when I lose my hair?" I think he was angling to clean out his hairbrush for a little nightly income, but the hair fairy just *might* come to your house if your child puts a lock of trimmed hair under his pillow (in an envelope or bag). And she might bring a surprise like a new comb or, for a girl, some hairclips.

Get a Haircut, Harry Doll

One of my childhood friends had one of those dolls whose hair "grew" so you could give it a haircut and then restore its locks. I loved that doll, but my parents would never buy me one. And that's why I understood when my son gave his doll Scottie a rather *interesting* hairstyle one day. About the same time, we discovered that Kyle was much more cooperative with haircuts if we let him trim another hunk out of Scottie's punk 'do before his own turn at the barber. Just be sure to get a doll with nice *long* hair to start, and make it clear that, unlike your child's, the doll's hair won't ever grow back. And that kids are *never* allowed to cut their own hair without permission. (But consider letting him cut a few strands beforehand so he can remember how it feels.)

Attention Grabbers

Focusing your child's attention on something intriguing will help him hold his head still. A detailed picture in his lap (like a hidden picture puzzle from *Highlights for Children)* is useful for those times when he needs to keep his head bent down. Many kids' hairdressers now show videos to capture their clients' attention, but simply looking in the mirror works well, especially if you hold a hand mirror behind so he can keep track of the action on the back of his head.

Holdy-Locks

Getting to keep his hair may make your preschooler more cooperative; it really is hard for children of this age to give up something that they see as part of themselves. The problem that arises: what the heck do you do with the hair you take? Try these ideas:

- Take a before and after photograph of your child at each haircut and paste the pictures in the album with a lock of his hair.

- Let your child sprinkle hair around plants in the garden to discourage deer and other pests. (This is supposed to work, but apparently the deer in my yard don't mind a few hairs in their tulip snacks.) You can also tie some in a bundle and hang it in a tree for birds to collect for their nests.

- A good outdoor activity: let your child make a hairy picture. Draw a face and spread glue all around it. Sprinkle on some hair and let it dry thoroughly. Shake the picture well to remove loose strands before you bring it in the house. Or draw an animal shape and let your child glue "fur" on it.

- Use it as a secret potion ingredient (another good outdoors activity). This suggestion is so appealing to certain children (usually the sort with Y chromosomes and a fondness for jokes about farting) that they may beg for another haircut.

No-Toy Joy
FINDING AMUSEMENTS AT GREAT-AUNT ETHEL'S AND OTHER NO-FUN PLACES

I'm qualified to give this advice because once my sitter canceled on me at the last minute and I had to take a five year old, a three year old, and a toddler with me to my gynecologist's appointment. I was so rushed I forgot to pack up any toys or other distractions. We muddled through, with spirits intact and a modicum of my modesty preserved—and now I can give you ideas for keeping your kids amused at your doctor's office or in No-Fun-Great-Aunt-Ethel's parlor.

Make-It-Do

If you find yourself stuck in an adults-only environment without a toy supply, think about back-to-basics playthings that can be fashioned from materials on hand. You may have to be assertive in requesting what you need, but here are some small-mess toy or game substitutes you can find in many no-kid places:

- **Target Games** Drop coins in a shoe or boot, toss cards into a hat or pan, or shoot balled mittens into a basket. The more breakies about, the lighter the objects you'll want to use, and the more you'll want to stick to dropping or rolling rather than throwing.

- **No- or Low-Supply Art** Draw patterns and pictures in a plush rug using a finger or blunt stick (like a chopstick), arrange found objects in patterns or to form a picture (such as "drawing" with a piece of string or making a mosaic from coins or dry cereal). You can make a quickie puzzle by arranging a row of tongue depressors, drawing a picture across it, and scrambling the pieces.

- **Puppets and Guys** Dolls and puppets can be fashioned from a huge variety of objects. Try drawing faces on tongue depressors or rubber gloves to make finger puppets. (You can also make nice chicken head guys from inflated rubber gloves). Other objects can be drafted as furniture or props for the "guys." My son once played for hours with an empty salt and pepper shaker "couple," using plastic dishes, silk flowers, and a hanky or two to furnish their home.

- **Safe Treasures** My mother's parents had few real toys in their small apartment, but they had a collection of cast bronze dog figurines that we were allowed to remove carefully from the whatnot table and pretend with when we visited. Even the least child-friendly environments usually have a knickknack or two that is sturdy enough for play.

- **Un-Blocks** Preschoolers will be happy to construct cities in the kitchen using cereal boxes and cans from the pantry. Empty plastic containers can be stacked and nested. Try building a small log cabin from handful of straws, plastic spoons, or pens and pencils. Sponges are good block substitutes too.

- *Forts* Use items like throw pillows and blankets, sheets, or even your coats and jackets to construct cozy forts. (This was the solution I used in the gynecologist's office; I helped the kids make a fort from sheets, gowns, and visitors' chairs, which kept them happy—and not watching—during my exam.)

Make-It-Easier

Look for ways to adapt the environment to make it easier to hang out with a young child. Go outside to sit or stroll while you visit or even head for a nearby park. Set your child up to play safely on an enclosed porch, or at the sink in the kitchen or powder room. Ask permission to preschooler-proof a room filled with valuables or dangers, or simply shift into a more casual room. Most people won't mind—in fact, they'll probably be relieved not to have to worry about their possessions. And be sure to praise your child for her flexibility and respect when you're done, and give her a chance to run around and let off steam.

Warning: I'm Packing!
AN EMERGENCY COMFORT KIT

My sister-in-law read over an early draft of this book and laughed when she came across this suggestion for a kit for rough times, like trips to the emergency room. "Carol," she said, patting me, "some people *never* have to visit the emergency room with their kids." (It really hasn't been *that* many times, especially considering that my kids are "active.") Two weeks later, Karen called me to apologize for laughing at my idea—she'd spent the previous evening in the emergency waiting room with her son, wishing she had the kit. So I've put the idea back in. I hope you never need it for the emergency room, but it comes in handy for other minor disasters, such as being stuck on the subway because of an accident on the line, a last minute sitter cancellation that forces you to take the kids to your meeting, or a long wait at the doctor's with a sick kid.

The Basics

I'm assuming you have a first aid kit. This is more of an emotional first aid or comfort kit. Keep it small so you can always tote it with you. Suggested supplies:

- One or two small wrapped presents (Good gifts are activity supplies like drawing/writing supplies, pipe cleaners, Silly Putty, or stickers.)
- Candy and/or gum (We're talking emergencies here—time to bend rules.)
- A flashlight with working batteries and/or a lightstick or two (Power outages are very frightening to young children.)
- Something to cuddle (A soft receiving blanket or a satin ribbon, a small stuffed animal, or a soft hand puppet are comforting.)
- An unfamiliar book or kids' magazine (Jokes and riddles, search books, or novelty books like pop-ups are best bets.)
- A list of waiting games or other distracting activities (Have the list handy so you don't have to try to think some up when you're stressed out too.)

Additional Options

Extras should be tailored to your child's temperament and based on what has soothed him during past upsets. Ideas: a photograph of your family and pictures of happy times (especially helpful if you can't remain with your child), something that smells like you (a piece of clothing, a hanky scented with your usual perfume or soap), a pacifier if your child uses one or has just given it up (Regression is normal during crises.), a warm blanket and/or small pillow, chemical hand warmers/ice packs, a music box or other soothing sound maker, a "Loving Heart" pillow (Cut two heart shapes from soft fabric, stitch or glue them together, fill the pillow with a mixture of rice and sweet-smelling herbs, and seal.), eye mask, change (to buy junk from the vending machines), hand-held games.

A Comforting Presence

The biggest comfort for a distressed child is, of course, the presence of a loving parent or other familiar caregiver. The following behaviors will soothe better than any of the "things" in your Comfort Kit:

- ***Remain Calm and Act Competent*** Force yourself to breathe deeply and to reassure your child that you will take care of him and that he will be okay *even if you are worried sick or scared.*
- ***Touch More*** Firm hugs, distracting tickles, gentle strokes, holding—whatever helps. At a minimum, stay near and "touch" your child with your voice.
- ***Use Humor*** Laughter is healing and breaks tension.
- ***Express Love*** Physically and verbally.
- ***Talk—and Listen*** Let your child know what is happening. Help him to express his feelings and accept whatever he is feeling. Continue to offer reassurance.

CHAPTER FOUR

Going on Outings without Going out of Your Mind

The title of this chapter is excessively optimistic, because it's not really possible to take kids on an outing without either being or going a little bit insane. In fact, my kids are lucky that I ever took them on any outings, because before I had kids, I was a teacher. That meant I had been on field trips. Many of them.

So, not only did I know how totally exhausting even small, ordinary outings with children could be, I also knew all about the unexpected things that could go Wrong. Like how you could take everyone on a nice, educational visit to the farm. And how one minute you could be standing innocently on one side of a fence with your group of little guys clutching paper bags of bread crumbs for feeding the ducks. And how everyone could be looking at the "cute" piggy on its proper *other* side of the fence (who secretly amazed you by being way bigger and uglier and bristlier than you'd realized pigs were). And how suddenly the next minute, the ugly, bristly 600-pound pig could be trying to smash right through the fence to your side to gobble the little paper bags of bread crumbs, and you could be wedging your whole body up against the fence trying to protect your little darlings from the piggy and screaming would somebody please come and save you all and then fortunately someone else could have the Very Good Idea of throwing all the bags of bread crumbs right over the fence to the piggy and hightailing it to the safety of the big yellow bus but unfortunately some of the kids would not want to do that because they were saving their bread for the ducks and everyone would be crying and then you would need to go home and have a very stiff drink even though it was only 2:30 in the afternoon on a Tuesday. Or many other things that I would rather not think about, even though years have passed.

But, as I said, I took my kids places anyway. Partly it was a way of repaying a debt of gratitude to my parents, who took my siblings and me to interesting and educational places all the time. But mostly it was because we live in an area with long, cold winters and after a few days stuck inside with three small kids, my grip on reality loosened, and I started to think that a morning at the natural history museum would be delightful. Heck, I even took my kids to the *farm* on occasion, where fortunately, we never encountered any more rampaging pigs. And despite a few Exciting Experiences on these outings, mostly of the wandering child variety, I'm glad that I made the effort and I know the kids were too.

I say all of this by way of preparing you for reality. Because by far the biggest threat to your sanity from outings is expecting them to be charming excursions with your well-dressed and even better-behaved little sweeties. You'll stay much saner if you realize they'll probably be whining or dawdling or making fart jokes in front of old ladies as you shepherd them through the museum exhibits or sit with them at the kiddy ballet. (Hmm, maybe you should take them to the park instead.) My advice to you is simple and straightforward: prepare well, be patient, and plan to laugh later. This chapter has tips on getting yourself and your kids ready for successful outings to a variety of places, from museums to ball parks, as well as suggestions for where you might go in the first place. It also has ideas for avoiding those awful Missing Child Moments that can ruin an otherwise lovely day and for solving problems you're likely to encounter, like eating on the go, managing meltdowns, and navigating the shoals of the gift shop.

Oh, one more piece of advice before I let you go: *never* take bags of crumbs on your visits to the farm.

Stopping at the Expectation Station
PROGRAM PREVIEWS

Preschoolers can seem so sophisticated at times—mine could program the VCR before I could. It's easy to forget about the huge craters in their knowledge. On some occasions the resulting misunderstandings are cute, like the time a friend took her T. rex–loving four year old to "see the real dinosaurs" at the museum, only to have him bitterly disappointed because he'd thought the dinosaurs would be *alive,* not just fossils. At other times, the misunderstandings are anything but cute, like having your five year old rub her hands all over priceless works of art at the museum. It's impossible to put yourself in your child's brain or to prepare your child for everything that might happen on a given outing, but the closer you come to doing both, the more likely you are to have outings that are smooth and pleasant experiences.

Step One: Choose Appropriate Activities

And tweak them to suit your child. This step seems obvious, but as it's where many outings go wrong, it helps to think twice at the outset. (See the next activity for suggestions of places to consider.) Before you settle on a plan, take into account variables like these:

- *Stimulation Levels:* crowding, noise, lighting, scariness, sugar, overall excitement
- *Kid-Friendliness:* tolerance of touching and movement, emotional suitability for young children
- *Timing*: time of day, length of activity, number of other planned activities, possibility of delay

- ***Energy Levels:*** your child's—and *yours*
- ***Your Child's Idiosyncrasies:*** current passions and fears, temperamental characteristics, stage of development
- ***Cost-Benefit Analysis:*** Expensive outings can lead to major frustration if your child doesn't enjoy them as much as you'd hoped, or if he wants to leave too soon.

Sometimes you can make adjustments so an outing will suit your child better, such as coming late or leaving early. And sometimes you can't (e.g., you know your four year old will be terrified by the PG movie her brother wants to see, even with her eyes closed), so devise a Plan B, whether it's a baby-sitter, a postponement, a divide-and-conquer approach, or another compromise.

Step Two: Predict and Prepare

Most people enjoy new experiences more when they have some idea of what to expect—and that goes double for young children, for whom so many seemingly mundane activities are novel. (And it goes *triple* for children with spirited temperaments.) Try to do the following:

- Outline the agenda.
- Detail major rules and expected behavior, especially if they're different from those for other places you visit regularly.
- Inoculate your child against disappointment, frustration, etc., by warning her about possible blips and helping her plan how to cope if needed. (Say things like, "If you feel scared in the movie, you can close your eyes and cover your ears. Or we can go out in the lobby until the scary part is over.")
- Have supplies on hand to comfort and distract.

Step Three: Enlist Cooperation and Enthusiasm

In the process of making sure your child is prepared to handle difficulties, don't forget the main point of going on outings: having *fun.* Help your child to picture the pleasures that await him, and let him catch your own enthusiasm for the upcoming event. Use visual aids, like photos of the place you'll be visiting, or tell stories about it. Use the word "we" frequently, let your child help with preparations, and tell him in advance what he can do for you to make the outing a success (e.g., being a trouper, not begging for things, remembering to say thank you).

Step Four: Know When to Quit

"Always leave them wanting more" is a show business axiom, and a good mantra for parenting. Exit the scene *before* fatigue and whining set in. And if an outing turns out to be a mistake, give it up gracefully and head home or elsewhere.

Step Five: Remember—and Revise

Don't forget the debriefing—it's your chance to do a little spin-doctoring if necessary, or simply an opportunity to cement a happy memory. Make a mental note of things to do differently the next time, so that outings can become a delightful tradition.

Oh, the Places You'll Go!
BEST BETS WITH YOUNG KIDS

It's easy to get in a rut and just do the same stale outings over and over. Variety will enrich your child's learning—and maybe keep her from being a bored pain-in-the-butt. Besides the typical, but still fun, visits to the zoo or natural history museum, here, in no particular order, are some places to go:

- *Farms* Many cities have nearby working farms set up especially for visitors.
- *Fruit or veggie picking* You can often easily find places to pick strawberries, apples, pumpkins, blueberries, and peaches.
- *Concerts* There are lots of options, including symphony, folk/bluegrass, children's, outdoor, school, and marching band.

- *Parades* Search especially for ones where your child can participate.
- *Fairs and festivals* Depending on your area, you might be able to find those featuring arts and crafts, Renaissance and other historic re-enactments, county or state, apple or maple, holiday, and so on.
- *Amusement parks and carnivals* Be safety conscious, especially at traveling ones.
- *Parks* You can probably find state and national parks, as well as historic sites like battlefields or monuments.
- *Playgrounds* Gradually tour as many within driving distance as you can.
- *Hikes* Try a variety of locales, but stick to easy trails for beginners.
- *Theater* Your kids may enjoy children's performances, street performers, puppet shows, or high school musicals.
- *Special events* Consider ice shows, circuses, and other children's extravaganzas.
- *Sporting events* Sample different sports, age levels, and venues.
- *A construction site* Bring a camera and track the progress.
- *Your workplace* Try to arrange a visit for a time when you can show your child around.
- *Kid-friendly shopping places* Don't forget flea markets, swap meets, rummage sales, garage sales, and farmers' markets.
- *Pools, beaches, and other swimming spots* Supervise children carefully near water.
- *Sports facilities* Children often enjoy places like ice rinks, tracks, athletic fields, bowling alleys (look for bumper and cosmic bowling), and miniature golf courses.

- *"Explores" (like the ones Christopher Robin enjoyed)* Try strolling through different nearby neighborhoods. Take a tricycle or a wagon sometimes.
- *Dance performances* You can attend children's ballet performances, recitals by kids, high school shows—or take your child to participate in a square or folk dance.
- *Food places* Eat in or get takeout food from ethnic restaurants to sample new dishes, browse at ethnic food markets, stop by a nearby coffee place for a "cuppa" hot choc, schedule a dinner date with one parent or grandparents.
- *Transportation centers* There's a lot to see at places like airports and train stations when you're not in a rush. These visits will make these places feel familiar and comfortable when you are traveling.
- *Public transportation* One of my kids' favorite mini-outings was to meet Dad one stop before his usual and ride the rest of the way with him.
- *Boat ride* There are many options, like paddleboats, rowboats, and tour boats. Make sure all kids wear life vests, and that all adults have them handy.
- *Library and bookstores* Check calendars for special events or performances.
- *Cemetery trek* This is fun for preschoolers, and may spark lots of questions.
- *Museums* Depending on your kid's interests, consider science, children's, art, history, sculpture gardens, and specialty museums like railway or toy.
- *Nature places* Your child may like to explore arboretums, botanical gardens, or greenhouses.
- *Science places* Don't forget aquariums, aviaries, nature centers, and planetariums (for older preschoolers who aren't afraid of the dark).

TRY THIS!

Stuck for ideas on where to take your kids? Magazines like *Family Fun* feature monthly samplings of current events around the country; these publications may give you ideas, even if the featured places are too far away. Check newspaper listings (usually once a week, often on Fridays) for a local calendar of events. Finally, many areas have a free parenting magazine published monthly that includes listings and advertisements for local attractions and events. See www.parentingpublications.org to search for a magazine published in your area.

Red Shirting
AVOIDING THOSE EMBARRASSING "WILL THE PARENTS OF _____" ANNOUNCEMENTS

As preschoolers, my three kids ran the gamut in lose-ability. My youngest was a barnacle who preferred to be physically attached to my body whenever we were out in public. The oldest was middle-of-the-road. He didn't care to hold hands, but he could generally be counted on to stay nearby. My middle child, though, was an absent-minded professor sort, who was also completely oblivious to danger. His toddler and preschool years were harrowing for my husband and me—and that's why I'm an expert on how to avoid losing your child completely. (I know right where he is at this moment. I think…)

Red Shirting

How you dress and accessorize your child can make it harder to lose him—and easier to find him if you do. It can also affect his safety. Here are some dressing strategies to help avoid the lost-kid syndrome:

- Wear barfy matching outfits. Or wear the same color shirts, preferably in a bright color. At least put them on the kids. That way if you forget what one kid is wearing, you can glance at one of the others and remember.

TRY THIS!

Larger pet stores often have machines that will make real dog tags while you wait—and your kid will *love* having the real thing.

- Use accessories to make your child stand out. I normally hate any clothing that makes noise, but I used to put jingly things (always disguised as a cool action figure accessory) on my wanderer. A helium balloon can help a short child stand out above the masses; tie on a "tail" to make it easier to identify your kid's. Finally, if you have a child who gets lost regularly, make sure he carries a noisemaker, like a whistle, or something that flashes lights, like a telescoping "light saber," so he can summon you to his side.

- Avoid letting your child wear clothes with his name displayed. You don't want strangers to be able to win your child's confidence by using his name, thus making him think they know him.

- If you do lose your child in a crowd and can't remember his outfit, or can't see a small child easily among bigger people, check feet—chances are you'll recognize his shoes.

- Make dog tags for your kid, with his full name, address, cell phone number, parents' names, etc., to wear pinned in his pocket (which is safer than around his neck). Many lost preschoolers become completely tongue-tied under the stress, and can't remember identifying information.

Hand Holders and Boundary Markers

Preschoolers usually consider themselves too cool to do babyish things like hold hands. Try these strategies to keep your child at hand:

- *Must Hold Zones* Most preschoolers will hold hands more willingly if they only have to do it when necessary. Designate parking lots, streets, escalators, and other places that pose safety risks as "Must Hold" areas.

- *A Knotted Rope* Daycares and preschools use this technique because it's useful when you have a number of children to keep track of. Knot a large soft rope at intervals. (The distance will depend partly on how far apart you need to keep warring siblings.) You hold one end and each kid holds onto one of the knots. This lets them wander a little, seems less obnoxious than actually putting them on a leash, and can be made more appealing by pretending you're mountain climbers lashed together.

- *Boundary Markers* When you enter an unfamiliar place, let your child know how far away she can go. Try guidelines like, "Where you can see me *and* I can see you," or "Do not leave this room without me" (best for older preschoolers in please-touch museums, indoor playgrounds, and other roam-a-bit places). Finally, teach your child to *stay put* if she does get lost (as long as it's safe to do so), until you find her or a helper (police officer, guard, uniformed employee) comes by.

SAFETY ZONE

Literal-minded preschoolers may take instructions like "Stay where you are if you get lost" so much to heart that they'll freeze in the middle of a busy intersection or other dangerous places. Remind them to step out of "Danger Zones" like streets, driveways, parking lots, places where machinery is being operated, anywhere they would be hidden from the sight of searchers, or any body of water. Occasionally, when you're out, ask your child to point out places where it would be safe or unsafe to wait for you to find her.

The Buddy System
FRIENDS MAKE IT FUN

Taking a friend on a fun outing is like whipped cream on a hot fudge sundae. Not essential, certainly, but it does make something good even better. Try these tips for including buddies of various sorts on outings.

The Buddy System

Most schools assign kids a partner for field trips. The idea is that the kids can keep track of each other. The buddy system works in families too, especially if you have several children or are bringing friends. Kids can pair up with a sibling, a friend, or an adult, but they should know where their buddy is at all times. This system helps in case your family gets separated because of crowds or different interests or needs. Or in case you thought your husband was watching the toddler, and he thought you were. Older siblings *sometimes* like the responsibility of helping younger ones, especially with tricky things like buttons that need pushing, and that may lead them to be a bit kinder and more helpful. And younger ones *sometimes* enjoy the help of a big sib and that may make them less whiny and tired. Otherwise, try to match everyone with an adult, even if you have to put several buddies together.

Peer Pressure Points

I thought I was out of my mind the first time I let my four year old invite a friend to join me and my two other kids (ages four months and two) on a jaunt to the science center. Four small kids and only one adult seemed like a recipe for disaster. Instead, it was the easiest outing we'd had in months. Kyle didn't pick on his little brother nonstop, the friend was downright *nice* to the two year old, and the boys occupied each other when we had to stop so I could feed or diaper the baby.

Since then, I've found that the right friend can make almost any outing *less* work for me and *more* fun for my kids. (Note that I said the *right* friend.) "Active" (euphemism for wild) kids are usually toned down by a quieter, more in-control buddy. (A slightly older playmate is likely to have the most influence.) And timid kids may follow the lead of a braver friend, leading to less clinging and more fun. But leave the "active" (still a euphemism for wild) friend behind with *his* folks—you can invite him over another day when you have loads of energy. Or maybe the kids can just see each other at school…

Zoo Bears

Friends don't *have* to be human, or even alive. My daughter has always liked to take an appropriate toy with her on each outing, like a plastic stegosaurus to see the dinosaur hall, a teddy bear to visit the polar guys at the zoo, or her Madeline doll to listen to story hour at the library. I like it too, because some of her chatter is aimed at the toy instead of me. I can also direct comments and corrections to the toy instead of to her directly and this usually leads to their being heard and followed more willingly. For example, I can tell Teddy, "We have to hold hands here and move out of the way of the tram," or "Hush, Madeline. Sit quietly please while the librarian is talking."

The Stunt Double

Intense preschoolers can get very frustrated when they are not big enough to do things they'd like to try. I found with one of my kids that we could often ease his disappointment by sending his teddy bear to take his place on the ride or to try out the climbing wall. (And, according to my son, Ted-Ted usually found the experience no fun or got hurt or something.) A toy can also act as a test driver for a timid child—let it try out the activity and demonstrate how safe and fun it is to a reluctant child.

We're Going Bear Hunting!
ANSWERS TO "WHY DID WE COME HERE?"

More and more museums and other visitor spots are beginning to offer activities with kid-appeal to help you keep kids from being b-o-o-o-r-ed when you're out and about. But if you find yourself heading someplace that doesn't provide preschooler-level entertainment, you can probably *create* a purpose for the visit that will suit your child. These ideas were tested and approved by my kids when I dragged them to less-than-kid-friendly places like "don't touch" art museums.

Bear Hunts

A scavenger hunt of some sort appeals to nearly every young child. Pick a theme for the visit, such as looking for bears (which we have done at both the art museum and a children's antique toy exhibit, as well as the zoo), or give your child a list (preferably visual) of items to search for. Can't draw a list? Stop first at the gift store or information desk to collect postcards or exhibit materials to structure your hunting. My kids particularly enjoyed pretending to be spies, detectives, or paleontologists searching for evidence of an as-yet-undiscovered dinosaur while they conducted their hunts. Naturally, hunting for things that are gross or ferocious will appeal most to certain segments of the preschool population, while others like to hunt for things that are glamorous or cute.

Artistic Jaunts

My kids were—and are—more enthusiastic about almost any outing if it includes a sketchbook and pencil. Naturally, you will want to be careful about the materials you give your child, and the situations in which you let them have any art supplies at all. (I once chaperoned a field trip art class—run by the museum, mind you—where the kids were handed *permanent Sharpie markers* to use in the art galleries. I was a nervous wreck the whole time.) Generally the finished products don't look like much, but sketching helps the kids to look at everything more carefully, and they usually garner attention from other visitors, including other kids.

Handing your kid a camera (a cheapo kids' one, a disposable one, or an old broken one without film if he's somewhat gullible) will usually have the same effect. (Just make sure that picture-taking is permitted.) Even looking at things through binoculars, kaleidoscopes, or magnifying glasses will spice up the view. Once we took a tape recorder to the aviary and let the kids make *interesting* artsy tapes of bird sounds and overheard conversations. Another family I know makes rubbings of architectural features or headstones in cemeteries. (Ask permission first.)

Monkey Shines

In art museums, young kids enjoy posing like the paintings or sculptures. (These make good photo ops, too, if allowed.) At the zoo or aquarium, they can imitate the animals' movements, facial expressions, or sounds. Enjoy your walk through the natural history museum, holding the hand of your allosaurus, until he morphs into a rare albino buffalo at the next exhibit.

First Watch
AUDIENCE DRESS REHEARSALS
AND OTHER VIEWING READINESS TIPS

Introduce your preschooler to film, theater, concerts, burping contests, and other live performances. Naturally, you'll want to start with shows aimed at young children, but don't forget outdoor concerts, street performances, bookstore entertainment, or other settings where restless or less-than-silent audiences are tolerated. When possible, reserve seats where your child will be able to see and move easily—aisle seats are often best. And don't forget to bring books to read while you wait for the show to start. The following ideas will help prepare your child for enjoying a variety of performances.

Preview the Performance

Young children enjoy a performance more when it is somewhat familiar. If you'll be attending a children's music or dance performance, listen to some or all of the score you'll be hearing a week or so in advance. Talk through the plots of plays, or even better, read a storybook version of the show. Check out how different puppets work before attending a marionette show, practice a few dance steps before a trip to the ballet, or learn about set design, lighting, and makeup prior to the theater. Emphasize that drama will be make-believe; the actors are pretending, just like your child likes to do.

TRY THIS!

If your child has a cough, take along lollipops (safer than hard candies) or gum (if she can chew it without swallowing) to ease the tickle during the performance. And don't forget goodies to nibble during intermission.

Audience Dress Rehearsal

Darkness, the volume of the music or actors' voices, the arrangement of the stage and seating, the presence of other audience members, and the structure of the show and intermissions are often unexpected elements that derail young children who have previously only seen shows on TV in the family room. Read a book about attending a performance, or even better, act out the experience in advance with your child or using toy figures. Finally, offer guidance on audience etiquette like this:

- "Sit quietly in or near your chair. If you move around a lot, it may bother other people watching the show or make it hard for them to see."
- "Whisper in my ear if you need to talk right now. Try to save your talking for the break or intermission and after the show."
- "When it's over, let the performers know that you liked their show. Clap with the rest of the audience. If you really liked the show, *stand up* and clap. That's called a standing ovation. After a musical performance you loved, you can shout 'Bravo!' or 'Encore!' Sometimes the performers will play another piece then."

Everyone's a Critic

Being asked to review a show tends to make even young children watch more carefully. With your child, read reviews of shows you've seen or are considering seeing. My kids liked to give performances "Thumbs Up" or "Thumbs Down," as well as "Sideways Thumbs" (for "not sure" or "so-so") à la Siskel and Ebert and other professional reviewers. I also liked teaching the kids to make up silly movie poster blurbs, like "Made me laugh, made me cry, made me pee my pants!" or "Super-glued my eyes to the stage; had to have paramedics remove them so I could go home!" Help young children evaluate specific aspects of a show, such as a particular actor's performance, special effects, costumes, or the set.

Fan-Tastic!
SHORT SPECTATOR STRATEGIES

The thrill of victory! The agony of defeat! Your child can learn these and other important lessons, like math skills, loyalty, and how to scream really loudly, by following a sport or rooting for a favorite team.

LITERATURE LINKS

Children's books can help introduce your child to the world of theater and other performing arts. A new series subtitled *Little Puppet Theater* features classic fairy tales that your child can perform using the cardboard stage and finger puppets packaged with the books. *Amazing Grace* by Mary Hoffman introduces young children to the magic of dance and theater in the context of a sensitive story about determination. Older preschoolers may also enjoy Wendy Wasserstein's *Pamela's First Musical* about a nine year old's first trip to a Broadway show. Good books to prepare your child for attending the symphony include the acclaimed titles: *Zin! Zin! Zin! A Violin* by Lloyd Moss and *The Philharmonic Gets Dressed* by Karla Kuskin. And the PBS show, *Mr. Rogers' Neighborhood*, frequently features kid-friendly operas and other performances.

Here are some ways to make spectator sports accessible to your preschooler.

MORE TO KNOW

Practical matters are important considerations when hooking young fans. Make sure your child will be comfortable (dressed appropriately for the weather, well-fed, near a toilet, able to get up and stretch) and safe (especially important in youth venues, which may not have nets, Plexiglas, or other protections for fans). Also be sure she can see—plan ahead and reserve aisle seats or bring seat cushions and field glasses if necessary. Also, plan to leave early. Expect that your child may be ready to go after the halftime show or the seventh inning stretch. (Listen to the rest of the game on the radio on the way home, if possible.)

Pick A Team, Any Team

And go root for it! Professional sporting events are often exhorbitantly expensive, but preschoolers are just as thrilled to attend college, high school, or even youth sporting events. Or games you're playing in yourself! Don't feel you have to stick to mainstream sports, either— the local ice rink may showcase youth figure skating competitions, the high school crew may row on a nearby river, or a local college may host fencing meets. Just make sure it's a sport (and a team or individual) that you too will enjoy watching and learning about. And one you won't mind your child trying when she's ready.

Suit Up for the Big Game

Preschoolers like wearing junior uniforms, sports-themed outfits, and team T-shirts, jewelry, or colors. (They also get a kick out of the crazy fans who paint their bodies or dress up in outrageous getups.) Props like kid-sized equipment or toy mascots may help your child feel like a well-accessorized fan. Have her dress up on important game days, even if your child will just catch a few minutes of the game on the TV or radio.

Give Me a C!

And an *H-E-E-R*! And what have you got? "Cheer!" Model how to cheer for your team with good humor, and only humorous antagonism toward the other team. Many cheers teach basic concepts almost effortlessly, like simple spelling (unless you're my brother-in-law who got to high school thinking "Victory" was spelled with a *B)*. Here are a few corny cheers (from my high school days) that my preschoolers liked:

V-I-C-T-O-R-Y!
That's the (team's name) *battle cry!*

My team is red hot!
Your team ain't doodly squat!

Lean to the left!
Lean to the right!
Stand up, sit down!
Fight, fight, fight!

We are the (team's name)*!*
The mighty, mighty (team's name)*!*
Everywhere we go-o
People want to know-o
Whooo we ah-are!
So we tell them!
We are the (team's name)
(Repeat)

Remember to enjoy the other sideline delights too. Kids often get a bigger kick out of rituals like the seventh inning stretch, the bands, the mascot's antics, and the other entertainment—and that's fine.

Be a Stat Master

Many math whizzes first become interested in numbers from following sports. Wins and losses are easy to count and compare. Make guesses about the final score. (Also explain the many ways different sports are scored—like football and basketball, where different ways of scoring earn differing numbers of points; golf, where you want *the lowest possible score*; and track, where time is important.)

Hello, Uncle Beasley!
RITUALS AND TRADITIONS FOR REGULAR STOPS

Small rituals and traditions can make regular outings easier and more comfortable by providing structure and predictability. As a bonus, the rituals tend to become favorite delights of young children. (Just be sure to start things you're willing to continue indefinitely, because you will *never* be allowed to stop.)

Hello, Uncle Beasley!

When I was a child, my family lived for a while in the Washington, D.C., area. We started every visit to the Smithsonian by greeting the large fiberglass triceratops, Mr. Beasley (named for the dinosaur in the book *The Enormous Egg* by Oliver Butterworth). You may not have a Mr. Beasley to visit, but you can probably find a favorite site or artifact to say hello to as you start your visit. This tradition builds a sense of belonging and respect for the place you are visiting. It also gives you a moment to take a deep breath and plan what you'll do during this visit.

"Something Old, Something New"

"Something for me, and something for you!" Use this saying to guide how your family chooses activities during your visit. Most young kids will want to repeat favorite activities from past visits, but you'll also want to encourage them to check out whatever is new and exciting or simply not yet explored. Finally, your child will feel more satisfied if he's had a chance to pick the thing that he most wants to do.

Rites of Passage

I think of these most in terms of our annual visits to Kennywood, the local amusement park. The excitement of finally being "big enough!" to go on certain rides is a central part of the thrill. Other types of outings also provide opportunities for rites of passage—big enough to wander around the "Please Touch" room without an adult right *there*, big enough to order and pay for your own snack in the cafeteria, and so on. And a child who attains certain milestones (a birthday, learning to tie his own shoes, for example) may also be rewarded with a special outing, just for him and a parent.

Seasonal Delights

Outings linked with times of year often become favorite family traditions. Strawberry picking in June, going to the model railway exhibit every December, and strolling through a different cemetery each Memorial Day are examples of annual outings that can be family traditions. Other ritual outings may occur more frequently. I know a family that celebrates Hump Day (Wednesday) with a trip for ice cream, and another who marks the full moon with a nighttime stroll through a park.

A Taste for Good-bye

Hold out a treat to entice your child to leave gracefully. Food, whether it's a goody to eat in the car, or a promise to stop for a picnic, meal, or snack on the way home, is an especially effective lure. (I kept a bag of lollipops in the car in case I forgot to pack something special.) Other treats may include things like throwing a penny in a fountain, fifteen minutes on the playground, or a chance to feed the ducks or pigeons. Or a climb on Uncle Beasley before you say good-bye.

Buy Me Some Peanuts and Cracker Snacks!
EATING, EATING EVERYWHERE

With preschoolers, eating is an unavoidable part of most outings. Young children have small bellies and get hungry (and therefore crabby) frequently. Experience has taught me that the whole eating thing can be one of the worst aspects of outings. If the kids aren't whining for candy from the vending machine, they're begging for hot dogs and fries priced so exorbitantly that you'll need to take out a second mortgage to buy lunch for the family. Here are some tips for balancing nutrition and treats, munching affordably, and making eating part of the *pleasure* of going out.

Portable Picnics

Bringing your own food is clearly the cheapest way to go. Here are some tips to make from-home-food almost as appealing as the bought stuff:

- Make sure at least some of the food you bring is special— comparable in appeal to what you would have purchased at the snack bar or restaurant. (It will still be cheaper, and most of the meal can be healthier.)
- Pack up picnics in a ritualized way, using the same cloth, hamper, or cooler and providing special touches like after- dinner mints or maybe a candelabra for an evening picnic.
- Put snacks in little individual containers so you can dole them out gradually. Plastic Easter eggs, recycled tiny raisin boxes, snack-size zipper bags, and small plastic bottles all make exciting containers to open to look for the "surprise."

- Include a small toy like the fast food restaurants do. (We just used recycled junk or fresh drawing stuff. The novelty will keep your child satisfied—and busy while you finish your meal.)
- Find a fun locale for your picnic. Tailgates are popular (as are spots next to a playground).
- Buy *one* inexpensive treat—maybe something like ice cream that you can't tote.

Ball Park Franks

Some foods are linked with certain outings, like hot dogs with the ball park. The special food tends to taste even better because of its association with the experience and the experience is even more fun because of the special food. Here's a secret—*you can choose whatever foods you want to link with an outing and fool your kid into thinking it's a tradition!* For example, instead of buying cotton candy at the zoo, always bring a box of cheaper and less sugary animal crackers. Carrot sticks, apple slices, and one sugar cube each are tasty treats for horses and kids when you visit a farm, as is whatever produce is in season. Take homemade trail mix (with a preponderance of healthy ingredients) on hikes, a package of Pop Rocks and a couple of Starbursts (after pinwheel PB&J sandwiches—see below) to the Fourth of July fireworks display, or Teddy Grahams treading a cracker "stage" to nibble (and play with) during intermission at the theater.

TRY THIS!

Fancy presentation can jazz up the usual preschool favorites enough to turn them into treat foods. My kids always oohed and aahed over peanut butter and jelly sandwiches when I made them into pinwheels. To make these very "fancy" treats, simply take a slice of bread and use a rolling pin or bottle to squash the bread into an absolutely flat square (trim it up with a knife if necessary). Spread it thinly with peanut butter and jelly. Then make four cuts from each corner *almost* to the center. Starting from one corner, fold half the corner into the center. Repeat at each corner. The resulting sandwich, which *will* be messy to eat, should resemble a toy pinwheel. Stack the finished sandwiches between layers of waxed paper if you're transporting them. Or make the less messy variation: PB&J "swirls" or "fireworks." After you've squashed the bread and spread the toppings on, roll the whole thing into a tight cylinder and cut into thin slices, which will look like red, white and—oh well—brown spirals. This technique also works with lunch meat and cream cheese.

Don't Forget Drinks

A child who complains of being hungry may feel magically better after a stop at the drinking fountain.

Pop-top sports bottles are my favorite drink container to go. (You can get ones with straps, so the kid can carry his own.) Get away with water as long as you can. Dress up water with a little lemon, lime, or orange juice to make it more appealing.

Freeze drink boxes or pouches to use as ice packs in picnic coolers. After several hours, they'll be thawed, but still cold.

Slide Rules
AND MORE GUIDELINES TO GO

It's annoying to encounter kids who push and refuse to take turns at the playground, who scream and throw things in restaurants, or who run around out of control in museums. Don't you *really* hate it, though, when it turns out that the uncivilized maniac is *your* kid? Much of the time, the kid's problem isn't brattiness or poor parenting—just ignorance of the etiquette for a new situation. Knowing the rules will not only make your kid nicer to be with, it will keep him safer *and* make him feel more secure and contented in new places.

SAFETY ZONE

Younger children are at increased risk of injury when they're copying older kids, so remind your child of safety rules, like "Don't jump from anything bigger than you, unless a grown-up says it's okay."

The Multipurpose Golden Rule

"Treat other people the way you like to be treated." You will repeat this rule endlessly, in one variation or another, right through the teen years. It covers most situations, but you'll still have to deal with the arguments like, "But *I* like it when other people are screaming!" Teach the corollary too (which many preschoolers don't really "get"): "Treat adults with the courtesy and respect you'll want when *you're* grown up."

Slide Rules

Guidelines for playgrounds and pools need to include both courtesy and safety. Teach your child rules like "A turn for you, a turn for me, that's the way it's supposed to be" to help her remember to let others use the equipment and to help her stand up to pushier kids. Read posted safety rules—preschoolers are big respecters of signs—and help her and other kids follow their specific guidelines.

Indoor Public Places

Remind your child to use her inside voice, to stroll like a peacock instead of jumping like a monkey, and to "Ask first, touch second." Signs describing banned behaviors come to your rescue again. Translate them into child-friendly language. When children need to sit quietly, get them settled with a traditional rhyme/song like:

> *Open, shut them,* (Open and close hands.)
> *Open, shut them,*
> *Give a little CLAP!* (Clap hands.)
> *Open, shut them,*
> *Open, shut them,*
> *Lay them in your LAP!* (Fold hands in lap.)

In the Great Outdoors

Encourage your child to keep to designated trails with phrases like "Eyes in the trees, but toes on the trail." When examining objects, teach your child to "Respect and replace." Explain that the rock she has lifted might be the roof for a creature's home—she wouldn't like it if a giant lifted off her roof and didn't put it back. State and national wildlife areas usually ban littering and prohibit taking any objects. In those places, tell your child, "Here we take only pictures and leave only footprints."

Uncrowding
AND OTHER RE-COMFORTS

All of a sudden, your previously well-behaved child is acting like a Wild Thing or a Whiny Cling-on! Time for a comfort check. (Is she hungry/thirsty, hot/cold, tired, bored, or overstimulated?) Sometimes comfort problems signal that it's time to go home. But other times, the right sort of break or emergency comfort measures will be enough to keep her going until everyone else is ready to leave.

Uncrowding

Masses of people tend to overwhelm young kids faster than they do older ones for a couple of reasons. One is that preschoolers have fewer "filters" to block out lots of stimulation. The other is that they're short—there may be no escaping the bodies that press in, around, *and* above. Techniques that can help your child cope with crowds and other excess stimulation:

- *Get her above the crowd* Carry her or let her stand on a bench.
- *Escape* Let her sit in a bathroom stall all by herself, or find another quiet spot.
- *Create a sensory deprivation tank* Have your child lean into your body and relax. (You can tell her to imagine she's a Beanie Baby or floppy doll.) Tell her to close her eyes while you cup your hands over her ears. Breathe slowly and deeply together.
- *Substitute soothing touch* Have her close her eyes while you blow gently on her face or arms. Stroke her arms from fingertips to shoulders and back, or draw spirals up and down her back. Hum quietly.
- *Use the power of imagination* Press some buttons to put up an imaginary force field or shield around her body. Use your body to "block" for her and give her some space. Have her close her eyes and imagine being transported to some-

place peaceful while you narrate her journey and describe the destination.

Tired Tootsies

This problem short-circuits many outings with children (and some adults). These ideas may give you an extra half hour or so. Beyond that...

- *Be shoe savvy* You can't beat well-fitting sneakers when you'll be doing lots of walking. Be wary of cute sandals, flip-flops, stiff or hot boots, party shoes that rub, and other impractical fashion choices.

- *Give those toes some air* And maybe a massage too. Have your child sit while you remove her shoes and socks for a few minutes. Blow on her feet to cool them down and tickle them. Check for red areas and blisters—and give them first aid as needed. (Offer a bandage for invisible hurties too.) Rub her foot or simply sandwich it between your hands and squeeze.

- *Change the pace* If you've been doing lots of strolling, try some jumping and running. This simple technique often works wonders.

- *"Gimme a break, gimme a break!"* Sit on a bench or offer a piggyback ride. (Specify a destination or time limit to save your back.) Or better yet, find transport. Many popular family

TRY THIS!

When I can't give my kids what they need, imagination works better than anything else. I've stretched endurance by feeding hungry children imaginary Kids Meals and Mega-Ice Cream Sundaes, kept sleepy kids relatively bushy-tailed by taking them on wacky, wild dinosaur safaris, and cooled over-heated children by having them imagine scooting down an ice slide with a pack of penguins. The other all-purpose technique I've found effective is touch—rubbing hungry bellies, blowing softly on hot faces and necks, squeezing out the crabbies with bear hugs, and tickle-stimulating the under-whelmed.

destinations rent wagons, which are more appealing to preschoolers than strollers. Or get a stand/sit-behind stroller add-on, like Seat 2 Go Safari from Litaf Industries, so your preschooler can hitch a ride behind a younger sibling.

● *Shine a light on the end of the tunnel* Preschoolers lack perspective. Give them a sense of how much time is left (measure it in kid-units, like number of TV shows), list the remaining activities, or point out the exit in the distance.

Gestapo Tactics for Gift Shops
KEEPING YOUR SANITY OR
AT LEAST YOUR CREDIT CARDS IN YOUR WALLET

Before I had kids, I loved gift shops—browsing, choosing a memento or two, collecting ideas for projects of my own. Now when I see one, I get a pounding headache. Too many experiences with greedy and indecisive kids. Which tells you something about how successful *I've* been in taming the gift store monster. But these techniques usually make visits a little less painful—or simply cheaper.

The Quick Nix

Staying out of them altogether is probably the most effective approach in the long run—but in the short run, it takes a tough parent. Explain *before* you reach your destination that you will not be stopping at the gift shop. If the kids whine and beg, you won't go the next time either. Make sure you stick to your guns. Or, for the less resolute, announce at the last minute that you must dash home *immediately*, so unfortunately you don't have time for the gift shop.

Visit the Gift Shop *First*

Before you've run out of energy and the will to resist your child's begging and when your child has enough reserves to accept frustration or disappointment. The only problem with this strategy is that it wastes valuable energy resources on shopping instead of the real point of your visit. Another option is to take a break mid-outing to check out the shop.

Limit Choices

Divide the store into buying and looking zones. Most gift shops have displays of cheapies—postcards, pencils, stickers, and the like. Let your child choose one item from this area, though you may still need to specify a price limit. Really indecisive kids (like my daughter) may find even the handful of choices there overwhelming—offer these kids just two or three items to choose between. If your kids haven't completely exhausted their energy reserves, let them browse through the rest of the store after they've made their purchases. Whip out your birthday wish book to record the items they're yearning to own.

The Souvenir Allowance

We've used this strategy very successfully with our kids as they've gotten older, but it can work for preschoolers with a few adaptations. You can give an allowance for a number of visits or budget an amount (either per visit or over a longer period of time). For example, let your child buy something inexpensive on two of every four "gift store outings" you go on. For a money allowance, preschoolers need a concrete representation of how much they have. One way is to give your child a chain made from paperclips, safety pins, or something similar. Each link represents a dollar (or quarter, or whatever unit you choose). When your child buys something, you help her subtract the appropriate number of links. When she's out of links, her shopping is done. You can give just enough links for one visit, or enough to last for a longer period of time.

Why Do You Think They Call It a *Gift* Shop?

I knew a mom who convinced her kids that it was called a "gift shop" because you were only allowed to buy gifts for other people there. Funny, her kids never wanted to spend much time in them...

CHAPTER FIVE

Don't You Hate It When the Kids in the Car Go Whine, Whine, Whine?

I know I do! Before I had kids, I thought driving annoyances were things like tailgaters, traffic jams, construction zones, and bad weather conditions. Now I know those things were *nothing!* What's a little delay compared to having a little delay while three kids are whining or fighting in the back seat? And the worst thing about kiddy road rage is that it is totally contagious—if you let it get established, before you know it, evil feelings are ping-ponging all around the vehicle and everyone has to have a time-out plus no dessert plus lose TV for an entire week when you back get home.

Major drug companies would have you believe that the best cure for Driving With Kids Irritability Syndrome is to load the driver up with Prozac or some other antidepressant. I doubt, however, that there is any drug that could make a parent indifferent to backseat bickering. And if there was such a drug, I don't think it would be safe for someone to drive a car after they'd taken enough to combat DWKIS.

That's why I've included this chapter. Your kids will still probably prefer to stay home and play with Danny across the street while you go driving around, and it certainly won't help with the traffic problems in your town. However, most of the chapter is devoted to games and activities that I hope will help you keep the kids distracted from their spitting, pinching, and fussing routines. The ideas I've included are ones that were favorites with my kids and that I could bear without gritting my teeth (well, mostly). There are more car games that are especially appropriate for longer drives in chapter 6.

The first part of the chapter features ideas for helping your child learn and cooperate with safety rules, like the one absolute commandment of going anywhere in any car with kids: ***EVERYONE BUCKLES UP!*** I know I state this rule in bold, all caps, italics and other pay-attention typesetting devices about a gazillion times in this book, but that is because I totally, absolutely, under every circumstance mean it and want to make sure that you mean it too whenever you're driving kids around. I worked in various hospitals and rehab centers while I was in college and graduate school, and saw some of the most heartbreaking cases—kids who suffered serious, irreversible brain injuries because they weren't buckled up properly. Please, don't take chances.

The chapter also offers ideas for keeping kids safe and reasonably contented on public transportation. There are ideas for solving some of the problems you might face during your shared commute, such as overcrowded subway cars or a kid who feels barfy on the day you're wearing your best suit and have a big presentation.

So, buckle everyone up! Watch out for the orange cones and brake lights! And everybody quit your whining! At least stop spitting!

No Cows in the Front Seat
AND OTHER IMPORTANT RULES OF THE ROAD

When I was a kid, I loved the movie *Please Don't Eat the Daisies*. I couldn't believe that there were boys who were so naughty that their mother actually had to spell out rules like "No gobbling up the centerpiece." Then I grew up and had boys of my own, and understood the necessity of being explicit—preferably well in advance of trouble. Here then, are some detailed rules for safer, happier car rides, including some the average safety expert probably hasn't realized are necessary. You might want to photocopy these, add any extras your family needs, laminate the list, and attach it to the visor as an Official Reminder.

1. No cows in the front seat. And nobody under thirteen either.

2. A seat for everyone and everyone in his seat! ***Buckled***. The car does not move until *everyone* is properly seated and buckled. This includes Daddies and Mommies, even if they think that no one could possibly get hurt in the driveway.

3. ***Stay buckled!*** If something falls on the floor, you'll just have to wait until the car is stopped to get it. Even if it's your favorite lollipop and dog hair is sticking to it. Ditto for anything you can't reach.

4. The driver should be drivering, not yelling at passengers or freaking out because she's been scared out of her wits. So, please:

   - Use *quiet* voices. No screaming, shrieking, screeching, loud squeaks, squawks, banshee yells, monster burps, T-rex imitations, Howlers, air horns, police whistles, cap guns, or any other loud or unexpected noise.
   - Save roughhousing for the backyard, teasing for when a grown-up can't hear you, and whining for later when I'm not busy.
   - Please wait until you are outside on the grass to spill your chocolate milkshake all over.

5. Please don't eat the steering wheel. And while you're at it, don't play with the doors, locks, or window controls. Or eat them. You are in Major Big Trouble if you touch or eat any car controls without permission, even if the car is turned off.

6. Warn the driver to pull over before you throw up. Try to throw up on/in, in order of preference: the ground outside

the car, an empty bag or container in the car, a towel or blanket, yourself, the upholstery, your little brother.

7. Be *careful* getting out of the car. Hold hands in the parking lot. I don't look so pretty with tire tread marks on my face, and neither do you.

Safety Seat Savvy
BOOSTS FOR BOOSTER USE

These ideas aren't perfect. I've had some Bad Mother Moments when I've had to resort to my knee and a Fierce Bad Rabbit voice—but most of the time, these approaches will get the kid buckled up peacefully.

Habit Helpers

- Have your kid buckle up *every single time* he gets in the car—even if you're just sitting in the driveway—and he'll soon feel naked without his seatbelt. (My kids all freaked the first time they rode in school buses for just that reason.)
- Make sure *you* always buckle up too!
- A buckle-up rhyme can help teach the skill, as well as promote the automatic behavior of a tradition. Here's a *very* simple one we made up:

> *Sit, sit!*
> *Strap, strap!*
> *Click, click!*
> *Let's clap!*

Madison Avenue Approaches

Advertisers are good at getting people to do things they might not have realized they wanted to. You can use their techniques too.

- ***Repetition, Repetition*** If your child refuses, simply repeat the command calmly and cheerfully. Eventually your child may tire of the broken record and obey just to shut you up. I think that's why people bought Wisk—to make the advertisers stop with the "Ring around the collar" commercials already.

- *"I Wanna Be Like Mike!"* Point out instances of high-status playmates or actors buckling up. Speak in the style of an old-fashioned commercial (good and hammy) featuring your child who is rich, famous, and beautiful all because he uses X brand of car seat—and always buckles up!

- *Add Some Razzle-Dazzle* Hot glue fake jewels on your child's "throne" (not on the straps—you don't want to weaken them) or add some push-button controls (an old TV remote works well) where your child can reach them so he can operate his space ship. A fish-eye mirror attached to the back of the front seat can improve his view and provide entertainment. Put toys and other distractions within reach in an over-the-back-of-the-seat organizer or shoe caddy.

Necessary Force

"Simply refuse to start the car until everyone is properly buckled." This is the usual expert advice about how to get your child to comply with the safety seat rule. That rule may work fine when you're going for ice cream—but how about when you're dragging an unwilling child to the doctor's office? "You won't start the car?" he says. "Great!" That's when you need to force the issue—with a carrot or a stick.

During a calm, away-from-the-car-moment, ask your child which approach works better with him: a reward for cooperating when he doesn't feel like it (like a sticker chart) or a punishment for failing to cooperate after a warning (like losing use of a favorite toy). You may be surprised that many kids do *not* choose rewards—both my boys admitted readily that threat of punishment was more effective for them. In general, I've found that the threatened punishment needs to be much "bigger" than the offered reward. Decide together what specific punishment or reward will follow; it saves you from overreacting when you're frustrated, and it helps the kid to know exactly what is at stake. With most kids, a reminder of the consequences is enough to gain compliance, but it may help to count to three (or ten) to give a child who needs to save face time to comply. At that point, if the child still is not cooperating, you *must* follow through with the promised punishment. No second or third chances.

SAFETY ZONE

I'm not sure about expert statistics, but in my experience, the preschool years are a period when many kids are not properly buckled in. Kids often resist booster seats as "babyish" and want to use a regular belt. *Insist on a booster every time your child rides in a car.* Standard seatbelts may cause *fatal* injuries in children under 80 pounds or eight years of age. See www.carseat.org for information on safely seating children of all ages and sizes and for lists of options and recalls.

Wiggles for Squirm Worms
IDEAS FOR WHEN YOU'RE DRIVING MISS ENERGIZER BUNNY

Not moving may actually tax your child's energy more than vigorous activity—it really does require effort for children to inhibit their natural fidgetiness. That's one of the reasons they object strenuously to car rides: safety restraints that fit well restrict movement. Car calisthenics can help drain off some of the squiggles while keeping the kid safely in place.

Wiggle Worms

Tell your child to perform a series of actions, isolating different parts of the body. Start each direction with the words "Wiggle worm, wiggle worm," then add a movement and a part of the body. "Wiggle worm, wiggle worm, shake your fingers" or "Wiggle worm, wiggle worm, blink your eyes."

Spice up this activity with imaginative movements like these: scrunch your nose like a rabbit, push a button with your tongue, shake a pigeon off your noggin, bob your head like a chicken, brush your teeth till they sparkle, smile on one side of your face and frown on the other, chew up a rubbery whale, sing a silent opera, wiggle-waggle your shoulders, rock 'n' roll, flap "wings" like a dragon, play honky-tonk piano, squeeze a balloon till it pops, stretch high and pluck stars from the sky, push a monkey on a swing, get ants in your pants, point directions with your feet, swim like a frog, climb a ladder to the moon, catch butterflies, pick up leaves, and sweep up a pile of walrus boogers.

Pat Your Head and…

This game works well in the car, but the classic "pat your head and rub your belly" is too challenging for most preschoolers. Actions that use both sides of the body (and brain) tend to be easier, as do similar movements. For example, try having your child pat her stomach with both hands while blinking her eyes, or tap her feet while she pats her crossed arms. Another good challenge for preschoolers is to try to remember and perform a series of actions. For example, tell your child to *first* flap her arms, *second* kick her feet, and *last* roll her eyes.

Car Yoga

This isn't *official* yoga—but I've found that breathing and stretching exercises not only feel good for confined kids, but they're also calming for stressed drivers. We do these when we're stuck in traffic jams or running late for an appointment:

- *Belly Breathing* Tell your child to pretend there is a balloon (or bubble gum) in her belly. Talk about what kind it is (color, decorations, flavor). Then have her rest her hands on her tummy and pretend to inflate her balloon/bubble as she breathes in. Hold it for a couple of seconds. Then let the balloon/bubble deflate again as she breathes out. Repeat a few times. (You do this, too—provided you keep your hands on the steering wheel and your eyes on the road.)

- **Stretchers** Direct your child to do some stretches. For example, she can take a deep breath in while she places her palms together. On the exhale, have her stretch her hands toward the ceiling (or sky), as if they were a baby mountain growing up and up toward the sky. Hold the stretch, belly-breathing for several breaths. She can then link her fingers, and stretch her hands palm up toward the ceiling too. Another good stretch is the "half body hug." Have her stretch her left arm across her body and hug her right side of her head, then her right shoulder, arm, waist, thigh, and so on until she's hugged half of herself. (Use terms like "window arm" and "inside arm" if your child doesn't know right and left.) Repeat with the other side. Have her imagine that she's being hugged by a soft friendly bear or some other animal she likes.

Tales R Us
STORIES TO GO

At three, my oldest started demanding that I "read" to him while I chauffeured him to school and around town. After I refused repeatedly, explaining that it wouldn't be safe, blah, blah, blah, I finally figured out that he meant, "*Tell* me a story." No problem—except thinking up one. Here are some story starters for tales that satisfy the preschool set and leave most of the driver's brain free for the road.

Fairy Tales—with a Twist

The traditional favorites are easy telling, but my kids especially liked it when we spiced them up with new characters.

- *The Three Little Ants and the Big Bad Anteater* who sucks and sucks till he sucks the hill down—but just wait until he gets a snoot full of that concrete anthill!

- *The Silly Trolls Gruff* and the mean old nanny goat that lived under the bridge that stood between them and the delicious cow pies in the pasture on the other side of the river.

- *Cindersmelly*—A stinky pig is mistreated by her perfumed step-piglets until her fairy groundhog helps her go to the Compost Ball. When Cindersmelly departs at midnight, leaving one pee-yoo sneaker behind, Prince Swine is heartbroken. He combs the kingdom searching for his beloved, sniffing the feet of every sow until he finds the one whose hooves smell just like the sneaker.

I always tried to get the kids to fill in lots of the details, which they were happy to do and which made my job even easier.

Snow Fairy Stories

Adventure stories starring your child as the hero are always popular. My oldest liked us to recount his daring rescues of the snow fairy who lived in our backyard during the winter (and in Antarctica or on mountain peaks during summers). These stories are a little trickier to tell—you might have to think a bit—but the plot is simple and follows a standard structure. Danger threatens (wild animal attacks, natural disaster, or the favorite—bad guys) and all looks black, but then your child saves the day. (Magical powers are perfectly acceptable if you can't think of any other way to make things work out.) Your child will especially enjoy the story if you weave in his friends and family members and add a healthy dose of wish fulfillment. (He's rewarded with lots of candy or toys, gets to stay up late, can fly or turn invisible—that kind of stuff.)

Tell Me About When I Was a Baby

My boys were mostly uninterested in old photos or videos, but they loved to hear stories about when they were babies or little kids. They particularly liked stories about anything silly or gross that they did, like peeing all over the wall when I changed their diapers, or spitting up on big brothers who squeezed them. Your kid will too. Can't think of anything? Make it up. And go ahead and make it *outrageous* while you're at it—tell them about the time they barfed on a burglar and scared him away or when they were just learning to talk and their first words were, "Get this ugly lace hat off my head, lady." Get the kid to add parts too (and of course, make sure he knows it's all just fun, not for real).

Red Light Magic Spells and Love Bug Hugs
DRIVING TRADITIONS

Keep road rage at bay with little driving traditions like these.

Red Light Magic Spells

We are constantly testing incantations, looking for one to make red lights turn green. We haven't found a perfect one yet, but we'll keep trying. Meanwhile, your child can practice with these spells that sometimes work:

- "Abracadabra and one magic bean. Presto and change-o, red light, turn *green!*"
- Count backward from ten, and then shout "Presto change-o!"
- "Things that need changing: a pumpkin to a carriage, a poopy diaper for one that's clean. A caterpillar to a butterfly, and this traffic light to green!"

Traffic Jam Sandwich

A friend told me that her family used to yell "Traffic jam sandwich" whenever they hit a slow-down—and then her siblings would squish her, since she usually got stuck with the middle seat. She taught the tradition to her kids, but with a less squashy, better-in-safety-seats gesture: her kids make sandwiches with their hands. Hold out your hands and put them around your sibling's hands, like you were going to clap their hands between yours—and then *squeeze* (but not too hard).

Love Bug Hugs

I wish. Around here, Volkswagen Beetles are called "Punch Buggies" and the first kid to spot one gets to punch his sibling until the sibling correctly names the color of the spotted bug. I *hate* that tradition. (It seems to be a regional thing—my neighbors all grew up doing it, but I'd never heard of it before I moved to Pittsburgh.) So, I'm proposing a kinder variation. When I was a kid, we called VW's "Love Bugs" (like Herbie of movie fame), so I suggest exchanging hugs or blowing smooches when you spot one. Of course, siblings will undoubtedly find a way to make hugs and smooches aggressive, so maybe you should just give up right now and stick with punching. Sigh.

Hold Your Breath and Pick Up Your Feet

That's what you'd have to do if you were driving on a bridge over a cemetery. My husband taught our kids to hold their breath when we pass a cemetery because, as my three-year-old daughter earnestly explained to me, "It'th not polite to breathe when otherth can't." We also hold our breath in tunnels, trying to make it from one end to the other (and in Pittsburgh you get lots of chances to practice this skill). Here are some more driving traditions:

- Lift up your feet when going over a bridge or railroad tracks.
- Salute every flag and statue.
- Try to say, "Spot stop, stop spot!" three times between the moment you see a stop sign and the moment the car comes to a stop.
- Pull an imaginary air horn (and make a *quiet* blast) when you spot an eighteen-wheeler.
- Click an imaginary bell and say "ding-a-ling, ding-a-ling" when you see a bicycle.
- Hold your nose and say "Pee-yoo-mobile" when you spot a garbage truck and cover your ears and say "wee-oh, wee-oh" when you see anything with a siren.

"This Is the Song That Never Ends"
AND MORE DRIVE-BY SINGING

I love to sing—loudly and with gusto. Unfortunately, I inherited my father's complete absence of musical ability. (I was the *only* girl in my class not to make sixth grade chorus—even after I pleaded with the music teacher, promising just to mouth the words during performances.) Fortunately, my kids were six or seven before they realized how awful my singing is. Any album of kids' music can provide a nice selection, but these songs have features that make them especially nice driving music.

"This Is the Song That Never Ends"

I grew up watching Shari Lewis and Lambchop, and I was delighted to find them back on PBS during the 1990s—until they introduced this major league annoying song to my kids. But I turned it to my advantage by telling the kids that when I was little, the point of the song was to sing each round a little more *quietly* than the last. And it was a kind of *competition* to see who could sing it the longest and quietest. And that worked! Here are the lyrics, in case you've been lucky enough to miss it.

> *This is the song that never ends.*
> *Yes, it goes on and on my friend.*
> *Some people started singing it,*
> *Not knowing what it was,*
> *And they'll continue singing it forever just because...*
> (repeat)

"Riding in My Car"

This is an old Woody Guthrie song. We sing it over and over with a variation: for each stanza, the kids take turns picking another vehicle to go ridin' in. Then you can pretend it's educational—building vocabulary, creating a font of knowledge, and so on. Plus, it drags it out so you don't have to think up quite so many songs to sing before you get to Shop 'N' Save. We also vary the activity. "Let's go pet shoppin' and buy a _____" gives the kids a chance to name every animal they can think up. Here are the very simple lyrics to the refrain:

> *Take you riding in the car, car,*
> *Take you riding in the car, car,*
> *Take you riding in the car, car,*
> *I'll take you riding in the car.*

And some vehicle suggestions to get your brain limbered up: car, truck, submarine, sailboat, yacht, armored tank, Humvee, stretch limousine, camel, horse and buggy, elephant, go-cart, race car, hot air balloon, helicopter, Concorde jet, rocket, and bike.

Aikendrum

This is a bizarre song I first learned when I taught daycare. The kids there loved it, and so did mine, especially since we used it as a "fill-in-the-blanks" song.

> *There was a man lived in the moon, in the moon,*
> *in the moon.*
> *There was a man lived in the moon and his name*
> *was Aikendrum.*
> *And he played upon a ladle, a ladle, a ladle,*
> *He played upon a ladle, and his name was Aikendrum.*
> *And his hair was made out of* _____
> (Let kid fill in the blank, and continue body part by
> body part)

The traditional construction materials for Aikendrum are different kinds of food, but we sometimes branched out and used lovely things like slug slime or toad warts to construct our moon alien friend.

SOUND BITES

"This is the Song that Never Ends" was the closing theme song on the Shari Lewis PBS show and can be heard on *Lambchop's Sing-along*, Play-along CD if you can manage to track down a copy of it. (Try the Amazon auction links or z-shops). Raffi sings "Aikendrum" on his *The Singable Songs Collection*, and Woody Guthrie does a great rendition of "Ridin' in My Car (Car Song)" on his *Nursery Days* album. You can hear samples of the last two songs on www.amazon.com.

Car Talk
IT'S MORE THAN CHITCHAT WITH CLICK AND CLACK

Nothing against Click and Clack—I love their show, even though I think cars are about the most boring topic in the world, right after golf. Plus, a conversation about carburetors isn't going anywhere with the average four and a half year old, so you're going to need a different subject or a verbal game to keep the chatter going. Try these talk starters:

Conversation Starters

Besides the usual topics (preschool, buddies, why snot runs but boogers stay put), the following prompts will usually lead to a lively and interesting discussion:

- Design the best birthday party ever (games, cake, favors, presents, guests, decorations).
- You just won the castle of your dreams. Tell me what it looks like. What cool features does it have? You know, like a slide from the highest turret into the swimming moat? Who lives there with you?

- Let's make up a new superhero. Is it a boy or a girl? What special powers does she have? What does her costume look like? Who are her enemies?
- Which would you rather be able to do: turn invisible or fly? Why?

A Number of Things

I don't know what it is about car rides, but they always prompted my kids to ask math questions (or to have me ask them math questions). My oldest figured out the concepts of addition and subtraction (and learned most of his basic facts) before he even reached kindergarten by asking over and over, "How old will I be when ____?" (My little brother is six? I have two more birthdays? You're 100? And so on.) Questions that will grab the attention of young kids also include the following:

- Anything that involves candy, cookies, or sharing toys (like dividing ten candy bars between your kid and his best friend). Bonus: some interesting discussions involving morality and nutrition.
- Anything phrased in a silly way, like "The three bears invite the three little pigs to dinner. How many chairs will they need? What if baby bear barfs before dinner because he ate all the onion dip?"

Encourage kids to use their fingers for figuring and help them talk through the solutions.

Rhyme Time

The simplest is to say a word, and get the kids to think up others that rhyme with it. Oodles of research show that rhyming play prepares kids for reading, but preschoolers also just think it's fun. For a more advanced rhyme game, give the kids a word, and have them try to make up a sentence using the target word *and* one or two words that rhyme with it. The rhymes should be kind-of-real words, and the sentence ought to more-or-less make sort-of sense. You're probably guessing that some of these rhymes are *creative*, shall we say? Like for the word "ship," my kids might say, "The *ship* got a *drip* and then it went *thwip.*" Close enough for government work, I'd agree, once the teller explained that "thwip" means "sank." But most people don't know that. Some good rhyme words for beginner poet laureates: car, cat, truck, dog, dad, fox, lick, no, cow, ball, hit (but watch out for that one potential rhyme), door, bee, shoe, hippopotamus. (*Just* kidding!)

Truth or Goof?
AND WHO SAID THAT?

Mini-games like these are useful when someone is starving and the snacks are gone or someone else has to pee badly but he just has to wait until you get home in ten minutes because there's no place even to pull over.

Truth or Goof?

Occasionally, I like to tell my kids outrageous fibs like, "I used to be able to fly, but my wings fell off when I turned sixteen." Playing this game has taught them to be suspicious when I tell them something ridiculous, which has made it much harder for me to pull their legs. Oh well.

The game is very simple. Players take turns making a statement that might or might not be true. We often play with categories like:

TALES FROM THE TRENCHES

When my middle son was about four, he discovered that certain people in the family did not always tell him the truth, so he took to demanding, "Are you *for-realing* me?"

- **General Knowledge** ("Honey is bee barf."—Truth.)
- **All About Me** ("My favorite color is rainbow."—Truth for my daughter at age five; she didn't like to hurt any of the colors' feelings.)

- **Books We Know** ("Madeline says 'Poop-poop' to the tiger in the zoo."—Goof; she says "Pooh-pooh.")
- **Family Facts** ("Kee Dad is Daddy's father and Poppy is Mommy's father."—Goof; it's the other way around.)

Everyone guesses "Truth" or "Goof." The person who made the original statement then acknowledges whether he was stating a fact or pulling everyone's leg. The nice thing about this game is that it often leads to interesting discussions.

Who Said That?

This simple game will prepare your child to be an English major in an Ivy League university—he'll be a whiz at literary allusions, at least those from kiddy lit and film. Some preschoolers may not be able to think up quotes, in which case you can provide all the phrases, but I was always impressed with how many lines my kids could recall from their favorite books and videos (and depressed by how few my husband and I remembered). Some lines to get you started:

- "Oh, stuff 'n' fluff." (Pooh in the video *Winnie the Pooh and the Blustery Day*)
- "Would you, could you in a box?" (Sam-I-Am in Dr. Seuss's *Green Eggs and Ham*)
- "We'll eat you up, we love you so!" (The Wild Things in Maurice Sendak's *Where the Wild Things Are*)
- "I smell...I smell...Ducky!" (Petrie in the video *The Land Before Time*)

We also play variations like "Who Did That?," "What's the Book?," and "Who Is It?" (In the last version, we describe a character without naming him and see if anyone can figure out who it is.)

Finger Fun
STAYING OUT OF THE DEVIL'S WORKSHOP

Keeping the kiddies' fingers busy will often keep them out of their sibling's hair, at least in the literal sense. These were some of our favorite finger games for car rides.

Five Little Monkeys

A bit gruesome—but maybe that's why it's so popular.

Five little monkeys swinging in a tree,	Wave five fingers side to side.
Teasing Mr. Alligator, 'Can't catch ME!'	Waggle index finger, make snotty face.
But along came Mr. Alligator,	Open and close hand like a gator's mouth.
Quiet as can be…	Hold finger to lips.
SNAP! (pause)	Clap hands suddenly.
Four little monkeys swinging in a tree,	Wave four fingers side to side.
(repeat)	

Five Green and Speckled Frogs
Mmmm. Delicious bugs!

Five green and speckled frogs	Hold up five fingers and "hop" them.
Sat on a speckled log,	Use other arm as a log and seat frogs on it.
Eating some most delicious bugs, yum! yum!	Delicately pluck "bugs" out of air, eat.
One jumped into the pool	Hold up finger and jump it down.
Where it was nice and cool,	Make frog swimming motions.
Now there are FOUR green, speckled frogs.	Hold up four fingers and hop them.
Glug, glug!	
(repeat)	

Double, Double

This is really a clapping game, the kind that grade school girls love. We found that preschoolers could manage it alone, though, especially if you started *slowly*. Build speed as your child gets good at it.

Double, double	Tap closed fists together twice.
This, this.	Clap palms together twice.
Double, double,	Tap closed fists together twice.
That, that.	Clap *backs* of hands together twice.
Double this,	Tap fists, then clap hands.
Double that.	Tap fists, clap backs of hands.
Double, double,	Tap fists twice.
This, that.	Clap palms, then backs of hands.

The Old Floating-Sausage-Between-the-Fingers Trick

This is a very simple illusion, but it fascinates my kids every time. Have your child hold his index fingers together a few inches in front of his eyes and stare past them as if he were looking right through them. Then he can slowly pull his fingers apart, until he sees a little "sausage" that appears to be floating in between his fingers. Have him move his fingers nearer and farther from his face and vary the distance apart from each other. If he closes one eye or pulls his fingers too far apart, the sausage disappears. Pretty cool.

Stirring and Stirring My Brew
QUICKIE CAR SILLIES

I'm not sure why driving around town brings out the sillies in me and my kids, unless it's that being silly is often one step away from hysteria. And hysteria is a constant threat when one is trapped in a small, enclosed space with preschoolers. Here then, are some *controlled* ways for everyone to be a bit silly without losing it altogether.

Stirring My Brew

We got started playing this pretending game at Halloween one year. I taught the kids a song they liked very much—mainly because it involved shouting "BOO!" at the top of their lungs. I quickly realized it was better to save the song for when I wasn't driving, but the pretending part is fine in the car.

Help your child imagine a very large black cauldron. You can pretend to be witches, wizards, or any other spooky guys. Take turns adding gross or silly things to your brew. Be sure to talk in scary voices. If you want to make the activity more challenging, you can add a counting, alphabet, or memory element. For example, add "one eye of newt, two bat toes, three used tissues;" or only use ingredients that begin with the letter *B*, like bug bandages, baboon boots, etc.; or recall all the earlier items as each new one is added. You can also use recipe terms, like "one cup of mashed lizards, two teaspoons of engines, a dollop of ear wax, mix well."

Variations on this game include Treasure Chest (take turns adding or removing items from a pirate's chest) and Love Potion (good for around Valentine's Day—let everyone pick things like puppy kisses and baby belly buttons and other things that make them feel happy and lovey).

"I One It"

I learned this game and the next one from my grandmother, and I've yet to meet a four year old who doesn't think they're hysterical.

Start by describing something very gross, like a run-over skunk lying in the road with flies all over it. Then say "I one it." The next person says, "I two it," and the third person (or first person again) says, "I three it." Continue until someone says, "I eight it." Then everyone says "Eeeyoooooo! That is so disgusting. You ate _____!" That person gets to start the next round, including thinking up the gross thing. Play until you feel like vomiting. Then you can play the next game.

"Just Like Me!"

This game has one person telling a progressive story, with the other person echoing, "Just like me" after each line. The teller might say something like, "I went into a dark and scary house." And the other person says, "Just like me." The teller says, "I walked up a tall, creaky staircase." Other: "Just like me." And so on, until the teller says something like, "And there I saw a horrid monster with green teeth and slime all over his face!" and the other person says, "Just like me." Very funny, right?

Pete and Re-Pete

Say to your child, "Pete and Re-Pete went for a walk in the woods. A big tiger ate up Pete. Who was left?" When your child says, "Re-Pete," say, "Okay, Pete and Re-Pete went for a walk in the woods…" (and so on). Then let your child do it to you. We liked to vary the disasters that befell poor old Pete. A similar story is, "Adam and Eve and Pinch Me went down to the sea to bathe. Adam and Eve were drowned, and who do you think was saved?" This story leads to too much pinching to be safe while you're driving, so you can substitute something like "Blow-Me-A-Kiss" for Pinch-Me. But of course, as one of my pinch-loving kids pointed out, that doesn't rhyme. Plus, it doesn't give you a good excuse to hurt your pesky little brother.

Pre-Boarding
WAITING SAFELY AND CONTENTEDLY

Taking public transportation with small children is *not* my idea of heaven. Probably it's not yours either, but sometimes it's a cool adventure to share with your child—and often it's a necessity. Either way, these ideas can make the wait for the bus or subway a little safer and slightly less boring.

Giant Steps for Safety

Teach your preschooler to wait *at least* three giant steps back from the safety zone on the subway or train platform or away from the street. This will give her an extra cushion of safety. Mark an invisible line with your child and help her notice landmarks that will tell her whether she is in the safe area. If there is a bus shelter, have your child wait with you inside. If you take public transportation regularly, you might want to get in the habit of carrying a piece of sidewalk chalk or string with you to mark the "kid safety zone." Even a pebble or a stick can serve as a line marker. Have your child remain near you at all times, so that you will be able to board together quickly once your transportation arrives.

It's All in the Timing

My kids like to bet on the arrival of the subway or bus. Usually everyone picks whether the bus will arrive before or after something like finishing the picture books we're reading or singing a certain number of verses of "The Wheels on the Bus." Winners either get to choose where we sit or push the button for our stop. Other times, we assign minutes to each person, rotating turns. If the vehicle arrives during your minute, you win! (A watch with a stopwatch feature helps for this game.) This game is very effective in reducing the "When is it *coming*?" whines. Plus, you can play other waiting or car games while you wait.

The Chicken or the Egg

Similar to the game above, but there can be multiple rounds. Tell your child the old riddle, "Which do you think came first: the first chicken or the first egg?" After a nice discussion of this issue, ask, "Now which do you think will come first: a person pushing a stroller or someone walking a dog?" Make guesses and see who is right. If neither happens, it's a "cat's game"—kid-speak for a tie. Take turns making up sights to choose between. You can also pick a category, like people with briefcases, and count how many go by before your transport arrives.

Exercise in Place

Let your kid work off waiting wiggles safely by exercising in one spot. Try jogging or marching in place (This is difficult for younger preschoolers.), doing windmill toe touches (Spread legs and arms, bend over, and touch one hand to opposite foot, alternating sides.), pretending to climb a ladder (Try different speeds—quickly, slowly, like you're being chased by a gorilla.), jumping jacks (They're also tricky for many preschoolers.), squatting then popping up like a jack-in-the-box, pretending to throw with one hand and then with the other (Tell your child something silly to pretend-throw, like smelly socks or a jelly sandwich.), spinning jumps (Quarter turns are good for young kids.), and in-place dancing, using steps like the twist, the swim, and other goofy sixties dance fads. Exercises are especially good for chilly outdoor waits.

LITERATURE LINKS

Picture books can help prepare children for public transportation experiences and they're especially appropriate to read while you wait. Some to try: *Jason's Bus Ride*, an easy-reader by Harriet Ziefert (Even pre-readers can hunt for the word "bus."), *The Bus for Us* by Suzanne Bloom (This story deals with the waiting experience, and has a fun refrain to repeat.), *The Wheels on the Bus* illustrated by Paul O. Zelinsky (This one makes a bus ride enticing to anyone, and has incredibly cool paper engineering.), *Subway Sparrow* by Leyla Torres, and *Subway Sonata* by Patricia Lakin. (These last two books will give new riders visually interesting previews of the subway experience.)

Step Right Up!
ALL ABOARD AND END OF THE LINE STRATEGIES

Kids are more likely to be injured when entering or exiting a bus than in a bus accident. These are also the times when you may have to deal with a balky preschooler who is suddenly fearful of getting on a big vehicle or reluctant to end an exciting ride. Add the crowds and confusion that often accompany these junctures, and you have some Fussable Moments. Try these tips to increase both safety and cooperation.

Ready, Steady

New—and even experienced—riders need to know what to expect. Tell your child what will happen when the bus or train arrives, including where he'll stand (with you, well back from the curb or platform edge, holding your hand). Discuss things that often frighten young children, like the squeaky sounds of brakes, the whoosh of air, the automatic doors, and how other riders might push forward. Remind him to wait with you for all of the passengers to get off, before you enter quickly together. (Let your child know if you need to enter at the front and if you'll need to pause to pay the fare—and what he should do then, like hold onto the pole.) Make sure he knows not to bend down to pick anything up or to let go of your hand (or shirt, or whatever he's holding onto); you'll take care of any problems. The same thing goes for your exit strategy—the fewer surprises, the better for everyone.

Grab-Ons

Your child will need to have some way to hold onto you as he enters. *Do not trust a preschooler to handle this step alone.* Holding hands is ideal, but not always possible. If you're pushing a younger child in a stroller, tape an area of the handle to show your preschooler where to hold on. I once saw a woman in the New York subway with a novel solution to the full-hands problem. She had several short leashes attached to her belt loops—with a small child holding tightly to each handle. (She was even being very nice, pretending to be a dog that the kids were walking.) It was slow going, but she made it onto the train with all the kids and packages.

Jodies

The American military chants marching rhymes, called "jodies," to help keep time. Use your best drill sergeant singy-voice (and manner) to move your troops on or off safely. Try a call-and-response chant, with the kid repeating each line after you. This will cement the lesson in your child's memory. A simple "Hup, two, three, four. Up the steps and in the door" will work nicely, but you can also make up your own rhymes (or don't-quite rhymes) to suit your child and circumstances. Here's an all-aboard jodie and an end-of-the-line jodie to get you started.

Train is coming down the track.
That's why we are standing back.
Wait for riders coming out.
Grab a hand, don't push or shout.
Quickly move your marching feet.
Step on in and grab a seat!

Even though we're having fun,
Now our ride is almost done.
Hup, two, three, four,
Grab your things, march to the door.

SAFETY ZONE

Many of the safety rules that apply to school buses also work with other forms of public transportation. For example, teach your child to take three to five giant steps out of the "Danger Zone" (the area in which the driver can't see her, and not to bend down or return to pick up something dropped or forgotten. Make sure your child is wearing clothes unlikely to get caught in the door. See www.nhtsa.dot.gov for kids' and parents' pages on school bus safety.

That's My Stop!

Enlist your child to help watch for your stop. Look at a map and count the number of stops until yours. Hand your child some tokens (pennies, scraps of paper, whatever's handy) to equal the number of stops. At each stop, she can give you one. When there's only one token left, move near the door and be ready to exit.

The Kids on the Bus Go...
WITH LUCK, NOT OUT OF THEIR MINDS FROM BOREDOM

Here are some easy diversions for bus rides.

Ad Lib

List three things (including letters or numbers) that you can see on the ads inside the vehicle. When your child finds three matches, trade off and let him give you items to find.

Window Shopping

Have your child look out the window and try to find five things he'd like to buy. More things to spot: the car of his dreams, an interesting place to live, someplace he'd like to visit some day, a perfect pet, a fun place to play, someone you'd like to make friends with, someone who looks like a kind grandma.

Fortune Telling

You can make up your own "rules," but here are some omens you might find on buses and other transit cars:

- If the third person to come through the door is wearing shoes that tie, you'll soon visit someone you love.
- If you can remain absolutely silent between one stop and the next, your words will make you rich and famous some day.
- If someone drops a coin during the ride, you'll be rich when you're grown up.

- If the subway car comes to a halt between stations, expect an extra long playtime before the day is out.
- If you wave at someone outside the car or bus, and she waves back, you'll marry someone kind and wonderful.
- If another passenger starts snoring, you'll have a happy dream that night.

This Bus Ride is Brought to You by the Letter *B*

Pick a letter of the day, and have your child hunt for things on or outside the bus that start with that letter. You can also play this game with numbers (watching for numerals on signs, or groups of objects that equal the number). Or try hunting for colors or shapes (either two dimensional like rectangles and circles, or three dimensional like boxes, spheres, and cylinders).

Spoonerisms

A spoonerism is a slip of the tongue where you reverse the starting sounds of two words, for example, saying "led right" when you meant to say "red light." Look for things out the window, and see if your child can make a spoonerism from the phrase you tell her. Or, give the spoonerism as the clue, and see if she can figure out the correct phrase (like telling her "dig bog" for "big dog"). Just don't try this game with the phrase "fire truck."

Houston, We Have Some Problems!
AND MAYBE SOME SOLUTIONS!

Crowds and kids' small bladders may pose problems during your journeys. Here are some tips for keeping your child relatively safe and perhaps dry during your commute.

Un-Pushing and De-Squashing

Small children are in danger of being mown down or simply over-crowded and frightened by other commuters in a hurry. If at all possible, avoid traveling with your child during rush hour. But if you must, try these measures:

- Have your child sing a song, recite the alphabet, or count steps loudly as you move toward the platform or vehicle to make sure that other people are aware of her. (You sing or count along with her too.) Or, if you regularly ride during peak hours, make your child a flag from a wrapping paper tube and some bright fabric so that people will see her.

- If people are crowding your child too much, help her assert her right to some space. Sticking her arms out like chicken wings will help keep people at elbow's length, and if she sings a nice duck song like "Five Little Ducks Went Out One Day," she may even get some smiles and friendly attention.

- Younger preschoolers may be best off in an umbrella stroller or riding along with a younger sibling. (See www.rightstart.com for stroller attachments that let older kids perch behind younger siblings.)

Standing Room Only

Personally, I think passengers should be courteous and give up their seats to people traveling with small children. But too often, no one does. Try these ideas for easier wibble-wobbling with a young child:

- Teach your child the "Subway Surfing" stance—legs wide, knees slightly bent, one hand holding on and the other slightly extended for balance.

- Protect your child from toppling-over injuries. Use your body to cushion her and make sure she has enough space. Once I saw an experienced subway mom pull a short length of foam tubing (the kind that's slit to wrap around pipes) from her diaper bag. She slid it around the pole, just above her daughter's hand, so that when the child rocked forward, at least she didn't smash her teeth or nose on the metal pole. (A foam tube could also be carried as a "see me" flag and used as an extended "hand holder.")

- Help your child see standing as a fun challenge. Sing the old commercial, "Weebles wobble, but they don't fall down!" or pretend you're on an exciting amusement park ride.

Bodily Function Emergencies

Young children invariably need to use the bathroom during inconvenient times or get motion sickness when you least expect it. Try these tips for rough moments:

- Be prepared. Always tote a spare set of clothes, diaper wipes, Purell-style cleanser, and a couple of zipper-close bags (for catching barf and holding soiled clothing). Carry lemon lollipops for kids prone to motion sickness.

- Have your nauseous child close her eyes and lean against you while you gently squeeze her wrists. (There's a pressure point in the wrist that often relieves nausea.) Face forward and move toward the front of the vehicle. If necessary, use her shirt to catch the barf—your goal is to soil as few surfaces as possible.

- Encourage a child who has to pee to hold herself, even though that's not normally polite in public. Have her take five deep breaths and see if the urge has passed for the time being.

- If possible, get off at the next stop, and find a bathroom or rest. Your schedule will be messed up if your kid throws up on you too.

- Notify train personnel if your child does pee her pants or throw up.

- Reassure your child that it was an accident and it's okay. You'll take care of her.

CHAPTER SIX

Getting There Can Be at Least 10 Percent of the Fun

Notice that I am not pretending that getting there could be anything like *half* the fun, the way travel writers are always insisting. They must not be traveling with preschool children. Or with my husband. His personal opinion is that getting there is 0 percent of the fun, so you might as well hold your pee, close your eyes to the intriguing antique stores or interesting caves, and stop for gas only when you're traveling on fumes.

At the risk of sounding sexist—okay, *being* sexist—I'm going to say that this attitude toward travel is one of those gender-linked traits. My father was that way, as were my father-in-law, my grandfathers, my brother, my sons, and virtually every guy I've ever known. Females, on the other hand, like my mother, my mother-in-law, my grandmothers, my sisters, my daughter, and my girlfriends, will stop at the antique stores, get gas before they need it *just for a chance to stretch their legs*, and definitely take a break to relieve their bladders. And they'll stop at real rest areas with actual toilets instead of simply pulling over to the side of the road.

And now, at the risk of compounding my sexist sins, I'm going to suggest that the *female* approach to traveling is the better one with young children. It's not that I think that only females are suited to caring for young children; it's more that preschoolers have the same bladder issues as pregnant women and those who have had several children, so *they need to stop frequently if it is remotely possible.* And, like women, they like to stretch their legs and examine the interesting sights to be found en route.

I'm not going to get carried away and ask the guys to stop at the antique stores—I know that would be a mistake with the preschoolers—and I'm not going to insist that the journey be half the fun. (I do think 25 percent of the fun is possible, but I'll settle for 10 percent.) But the reason I insist on some fun and frequent stops is that the reality is this: *for young kids, the mood of the travel portion of the trip infects the mood of the being there portion of the trip.* So, if you made the whole getting there part a miserable ordeal, chances are you'll spend the rest of the trip trying to recover from it, or at least trying to get the smell of pee out of the upholstery. It just isn't worth it.

Even 10 percent fun does not come cheap or easy. It takes weeks of preparation and making lists. I do not know how people travel successfully without lists, but apparently some do. I've tried to make that step a little easier here for you by making some lists for you to use, but you'll still have to make a few of your own about things like taking the dog to the kennel or buying gifts for all those belated birthdays of the people you're going to visit. I've also included ideas for games in the car or on the plane, and for handling discomforts like sore tushes, empty bellies, and motion sickness. All these things can up the "fun" proportion of the trip into the perceptible range.

You'll notice that I have not included many ideas for cruises. This is because I have never been on a cruise. Not even once. I'd be more than happy to include original, right-on-target tips for happier cruising in future editions of this book, if you'll just send me a ticket. I'll even save you money and go all by myself or just with my husband. January is usually a good month for me.

Anticipation/Preparation
PLANNING FOR PEACE AND PROSPERITY

Without a doubt, getting ready to travel is trickier (and probably crabbier, no matter how hard you try) when you're doing it with small kids in mind and underfoot. But there are things you can do to make it somewhat easier and to set the stage for a good trip.

Countdown Strategy

Do this for your child—and for yourself, so you aren't a frantic, screaming maniac trying to cram everything you might need into suitcases fifteen minutes before you absolutely, positively must leave for the airport and your overwhelmed four year old is in contagious panic mode and running around in tight little circles weeping inconsolably in the background. I've tried that, and this way is better.

Get a bunch of small containers, like plastic Easter eggs, jewelry gift boxes, or film canisters, and number them. On slips of paper, write jobs you must do to get ready for your trip, such as: "Do laundry," "Gather tickets, maps, and travel documents and store them in a Velcro-close portfolio," or "Cancel newspaper and confirm that Naomi can pet-sit." Write corresponding tasks for your child, like "Make play dough men while Mommy folds the laundry." Put the tasks in chronological order and place each in its appropriate container, along with—*and this is the crucial part*—a treat, like small chocolates for everyone or a promise of something nice (like "Play War even though Mommy hates it"). Starting at the appropriate point before departure, open the container for that day and do the tasks. Try to save the treats for a reward when you're done.

Pep Rallies

In the flurry of getting ready, I think I sometimes left my kids with the impression that we were bound for some terrible ordeal. Make sure you talk up the trip between sessions of grumbling about the preparations—though take care not to over-promise. In fact, part of what you want to do is plant the seeds that you can have a good time, *even if yucky things happen,* like it rains every day, you can't get near Mickey Mouse to give him a hug, or you miss your connecting flight. Sometimes these pep talks will even inoculate *you* against disappointment. The best time for the pep talks, by the way, is not at bedtime or even dinner—end of the day excitement too often interferes with sleep—but at the breakfast table or in the car.

Dress Rehearse

Theater people stage dress rehearsals to catch possible glitches that they might otherwise miss. They'll help your child too, to preview the trip—and they may open your eyes to issues or feelings you hadn't anticipated. Mini-real experiences, such as visiting the airport or sleeping in the tent in the backyard will be most effective, but even just pretending will help get your child ready. Some things to practice with your child:

- Carrying whatever packs or luggage he'll be expected to manage
- Trying out the kind of transportation you'll take (at least for pretend)
- Greeting friends or relatives (especially if they're unfamiliar)
- Walking distances longer than normal
- Sleeping in a different bed, room, arrangement, etc.
- Using unfamiliar potties, eating unusual foods, dining in restaurants or by a campfire
- Sightseeing (Look at pictures of attractions you'll be visiting and describe what to expect.)
- Hearing foreign languages or different accents

If the dry runs go poorly, keep in mind the theater superstition that a bad dress rehearsal foretells a stellar opening night.

TALES FROM THE TRENCHES

Before one kid's first flight, we set up rows of chairs in the family room and played "Going on an airplane ride." We discovered that he was mostly looking forward to the experience, except for one thing: he was worried about getting shrunk so he'd fit in the tiny planes he saw in the sky.

Packing for Pleasure
WHAT TO REMEMBER BESIDES UNDERWEAR AND TOOTHBRUSHES

The packing phase of our trips is always a flurry of laundry and folding and cramming, since we never seem to have enough clothes to do it well in advance of departure. If you can afford it and travel frequently, get duplicates of many frequently needed travel items and store them ready to be stuffed in a suitcase as needed. Mark your suitcases with artistic designs in colored electrical tape to make them easy to spot on the carousel. One more tip: if you're taking a car trip, consider packing in something other than a suitcase. For our yearly beach trip, I now use rectangular laundry baskets; they're easy to see in to find what I need, and it's a breeze to toss in one more thing that I almost forgot.

Must Haves

See travel or camping websites like www.family.go.com for lists of the usual stuff you ought to pack. This list is for other stuff you really need for traveling with kids:

- *Bathing suits* All I know is that every time I skip them because I think there is zero chance we'll go swimming, the motel *does* have an indoor pool or someone invites us to go swimming, and then everyone is mad at me.

- ***Clothes your child will actually wear, not the cute outfits you* wish *she'd wear*** Even if there's nothing else to wear, she's not going to put on the cute outfits without a fuss. And then you're going to have to let her wear the same ratty Powerpuff Girls T-shirt day after day or go shopping.

- ***Shoes*** This may seem obvious, but once we put the kids in the car in their jammies and arrived to discover that one of them didn't have any shoes. It is very embarrassing to take a barefoot child to the shoe store in the winter. Plus expensive. Plus a waste of vacation time. And remember socks while you're at it.

- ***Something warm and something cool, even if you're going to Florida in August or Colorado in January*** Freak weather or, more likely, excessive heating or cooling, will leave you wishing you had some off-weather clothes. Also, pack compact rain ponchos instead of umbrellas; you can't hold a kid's hand, two suitcases, and an umbrella at the same time.

- ***Sleep aids*** No, I'm not recommending you give your kid sleeping pills. But if she can't fall asleep without her Puppy Pee-Pee, a nightlight, or her own pillow, you'd better make sure you pack it.

- ***Peanut butter and crackers or some other healthy nonperishable food your child will actually eat*** Better to bring your own than risk the possibility of not being able to find the right brand or needing it desperately when you don't have any.

- ***Duct tape, zipper-seal plastic bags, bungee cords, twist-ties, and/or Velcro closure strips*** These things all have multiple uses and can take care of many emergencies, kid-related and otherwise. And no, you may *not* use the duct tape to solve either the "Are we there yet?" or the "But he started it!" problems.

• *Lots of underwear and a new toothbrush or two* Some-one—maybe even you—is bound to forget them. Or pee them (the underwear, not the toothbrush, I hope). And while you're at it, get some extras to leave at home, because somehow they never all make it back.

Genuinely Useful Tips from the Pros That Will Make Everyone Less Fussed

• Put comfort and practicality ahead of style in clothing selections.

• Pack *light.* The general rule of thumb is to take *half* of what you think you'll need. You can wash or re-wear clothes. You can live without stuff. You can also *mail* things to and from your destination. The extra expense may be worth it, especially if you're taking public transportation.

• Pack complete outfits in separate plastic bags. That way you don't have to hunt through the whole suitcase for the socks that match that cute blue jumpsuit, *and* you'll have extra containers for wet bathing suits and souvenir pop can tabs. Plus, you'll be able to tell quickly what's clean and what's dirty.

• Make your child pull his weight. Preschoolers are old enough to lug a lot of their own things. Older preschoolers may be able to manage pull-behind wheeled suitcases everywhere except steps or escalators. And nearly all preschoolers can carry their own backpacks of "stuff."

• If you're flying, pack at least one outfit for everyone in each suitcase, instead of packing separate cases for each person. That way if some luggage goes astray, everyone will still have something to wear. Also, *never* pack essential items like medications or Puppy Pee-Pee in checked baggage.

• In this day and age, don't even *think* about letting your four year old pack the most innocuous toy weapons. Ask him repeatedly under threat of never watching TV again if he snuck one into his suitcase.

Totes of Note
WHAT TO CARRY ON OR CARRY IN

For a good chunk of my childhood, my family lived in Virginia—and nearly all our relatives lived in California. Most summers we made the 6,000-mile roundtrip between the two coasts—and we did it *s-l-o-w-l-y,* traveling by train or station wagon rather than zippy airplanes, which were out of our budget. And here's the amazing thing! *All* of us kids survived! And we didn't have a tape player, much less a VCR! I credit our survival (and my parents' apparent continued sanity) to the cute matching travel bags my mom sewed for my sisters and me. She filled each one with goodies like lemon drops, joke books, and those magic-erase boards that seemed cool but didn't really work. If you're going to do any significant traveling with young kids, I strongly suggest packing some similar treat totes. And stick in lots of practical stuff while you're at it. I won't, however, insist that you actually *sew* cute matching bags to contain everything.

What to Pack

These are the things you'll want to have accessible in transit. But don't forget that lots of it can go in your kid's pack or in a stay-in-the-car container.

- *Plastic container with lid* Small enough to fit easily in the tote, large enough to: protect crushable or squashable snacks like crackers or gorp en route, corral small toys, act as a tray when your child eats, or hold a monster vomit if he gets sick.
- *Plastic bags* Two kinds. You'll need grocery store bags for each person's garbage; tuck them over the back of the front seat in the car and into the seat pocket on planes. (Flight attendants really appreciate it if you hand them a bag of garbage instead of a stream of sticky wrappers, and they might be extra nice to you.) Also, take zipper-seal plastic bags for holding found treasures, new toys opened en route, soiled clothing, or wet washcloths.

- **Purell and a washcloth** Purell will take care of most wash-up problems, but if a child vomits or spills his entire meal down his front, you'll be glad to have a washcloth. Baby wipes are nice too, but they don't make much of a dent in a pile of puke.

- **Tissues** Snot can be a surprisingly major problem. One friend prefers a half-used roll of best quality toilet paper, since it's also good for those "Yikes!" moments in a rest room.

- **Medium-size towel** Does duty as an emergency blanket or, rolled-up, as a pillow. Can protect clothes, mop spills, or even dim lights. (Throw it over the kid's head.)

- **Rectangle of flannel-backed oilcloth** I forget who told me this idea—sorry, especially since it's a great one. Take a flannel-backed vinyl tablecloth and cut it into rectangles big enough to cover laps generously. The lap cloth can be a giant napkin/bib, makeshift rain gear, drool protector for *your* clothes or pee cloth. (Slip under a sleepy or gotta-go child to protect the seat or, if it's too late, put it between the seat and the changed kid to protect his fresh clothes.)

- **Snacks, bottle of water, and toys**

- **Medications and mini-first aid kit** Prescriptions; medications for motion sickness, pain, diarrhea, and congestion; lots of Band-Aids

- **Lightweight sweater or jacket and a change of clothes**

- **Travel toothbrush and paste and a comb and brush** (if you have room)

- **Extras** A perfume-size atomizer filled with water (for combating dry-air effects, cooling, easing motion sickness), a light stick or mini flashlight.

Recommended Amusements

- Travel Magna Doodle (especially great because there are no loose pieces)
- Sticker books (the ones with reusable stickers, like those produced by Usborne)
- String (tie knots or braid)
- Pipe cleaners
- Paper, clipboard, colored pencils, and hand pencil sharpener
- Vinyl stickers that adhere to windows or plane trays
- Magnetic play sets (like the Madeline one made by Eden toys and available from upscale toy stores)
- Guys (small action figures, dolls, plastic animals, or dinosaurs—but nothing that's a favorite in case it gets lost)
- Books and other reading material (still number one for my family)

For *long* trips or medium ones on public transportation, go electronic without guilt. Books and music on audiotape are great, but also consider DVDs on a laptop, videos on a portable car TV/VCR, or handheld games like Game Boy. Just make sure you have earphones and an adequate power supply. (You can often buy adapters that plug into car cigarette lighters or long-lasting rechargeable power packs for many electronic toys; otherwise, be sure to pack extra batteries.)

Journey-Wear
OUTSTANDING OUTFITS AND PUPPY TAGS

What your child does or does not wear for traveling can have a big impact on mood. His clothing can affect everything from general irritability to how quickly you get through security checkpoints to how likely he is to have an accident. Keep these clothing pointers in mind as you suit up for the big trip.

Features of Outstanding Outfits

The best travel suits are:

- *Soft* Avoid lace or other annoying trims, scratchy fabrics, stiff jeans, pilled and bothery sweatpants, and clothes that make noise (electronic or jingly). Again, *put comfort ahead of style.*

- *Loose and layered* If you layer clothes, it will be easier to adjust for comfort and you may be able to get away with just removing one layer in case of accidents. Clothes with elastic waists, wide necklines, and generous sleeves will be easier to slip on and off and are much easier to manage when your child is desperate for the potty. *Avoid waists with zippers, buttons, or snaps!*

- *Practical* Patterns are less likely to show stains. When flying, dress for quick trips through security by avoiding clothes with metal trims (metal zippers, studs, belts with large buckles, some shoe trims). Put anything your child is carrying in his pockets into a zipper sandwich bag in case he has to empty his pockets. (Also, plastic-zippered pockets will keep your child's treasures from escaping.)

- *Memorable* You'll want to be able to spot your child quickly in a crowd, and she'll want to able to see you. This might be a good time to let her use the accessories she's been dying to wear in public, like that hot pink boa or the funky dragon hat. Cool decorations on shoes may be especially easy for your child to spot in a crowd of standing adults. At any rate, have everyone make a conscious note of each other's outfits. (See also "Red Shirting" on page 89 for tips on stand-out clothing strategies.)

- *Good for Feet* Businesswomen often wear sneakers and tote their heels when commuting. Keep this in mind for kids too; shoes should be *comfortable* and securely attached to their feet, so they don't fall off if you have to run or ride escalators. Velcro or zipper-fastened shoes are easier to get on and off quickly and are especially useful if your kid is "randomly" selected to get his shoes checked every time you pass through airport security. In transit, kids may be more comfortable wearing socks or slipper socks. Have them store shoes in the seat pocket, or bring an extra tote to contain everyone's shoes en route.

Puppy Tags

Try these keeping-track tips:

- Put tags on everything—luggage, carry-ons, Puppy Pee-Pee or other special toys, security blankets, anything you couldn't bear to lose permanently, *including your child!* Lost kids often panic and cannot remember any crucial information.
- While in transit, label your child and other essentials with information that will help them be reunited with you promptly, including names (theirs and yours), flight number, destination, cell phone number, business phone number, etc. Home address and phone number may seem like the obvious labeling info, *but you won't be there, will you?* It would be inconvenient not to have your luggage catch up with you until you got home, but it would be a disaster not to be reunited with your kid promptly.
- Dig out the old Polaroid camera or your new digital one before you head off on a long trip and take photographs of all the precious cargo. Having Puppy Pee-Pee's picture to show the baggage guys may greatly speed reunion. And an out-the-door photo will ensure that you know what your child was wearing.
- Ideas for making labels: blank address stickers (inside your child's clothing), airline baggage tags (loop these, folded, around the kids' wrists or buttons), and actual dog tags. (Get them made before you leave, and pin inside their clothes.)

SAFETY ZONE

Make sure any labels with your child's name or other personal information are tucked out of sight. Put your child's labels inside her clothing, and fold over or otherwise cover tags on luggage and objects. Kidnappers have been known to use this information to trick children into thinking they know them and can be trusted. Before every trip, review basic stranger safety rules with your child too:

- Don't talk to strangers unless we say it's okay.
- Don't take candy, toys, or other treats from a stranger.
- Never go anywhere with a stranger. Don't leave our sight without permission.
- If someone tries to make you leave with him or her, make a fuss. Yell, kick, and scream.

For more tips, see www.childconnection.org.

Ready to Roll
GOOD-BYES, GOOD PEES—AND GOOD LUCK!

Getting out the door and on the road always makes my husband very crabby. He thinks it shouldn't be such a production, but it always is. So take a deep, cleansing breath…

Good-Byes

Most preschoolers do not have the intense separation anxiety that toddlers do, but it's still an issue that can loom large on occasion. And it's not always people whom they fear leaving—they may have almost as much difficulty saying "Ta-ta for now!" to their homes and toys. Try these ideas to ease the separation:

- Reassure your child that you *will* be returning. (It's obvious to you, but not always to a young child. A friend's three year old sobbed after they returned from their beach vacation, "Oh! I thought we'd left forever!")

- If some family members are staying behind, talk with your child about how you'll stay in touch and when you'll be together again.

- Be sure your child is aware of arrangements to take care of your pet, home, and other obligations in your absence. Your child may enjoy getting a special treat for a pet to have in your absence, or arranging a nice place for a favorite stuffed animal to "sleep."

- If you tend to be a bit "grumpy," shall we say, during the good-bye stage, warn your child in advance. While you're at it, let your child know that she may feel out of sorts too. Short tempers are normal during times of stress and are heightened by separations. Everyone will soon be back to normal.

- Develop a "good-bye" ritual for all departures. A phrase that you always say ("To infinity and beyond! And the beach!"), a blowing kisses game, a teddy bear in the window to "wave" to you—whatever you choose—will make the good-bye seem familiar and predictable, and help your child feel more secure.

- Prepare a "Welcome Home!" treat. (Coming home is also a grumpy occasion for me, what with laundry, finding places for all the junk, and returning phone calls.) I recommend an untouched carton of chocolate chip cookie dough ice cream in the freezer, but you might have an even better idea. One more good thing to have waiting: a new bath toy to lure your grubby traveling companion into the tub.

Good Pees and Other Out-the-Door Tasks

Last thing before you get in the car: make *everyone, including yourself,* go potty. Even if you just did or don't feel like you need to. Same thing just before boarding a plane or bus. More out-the-door tasks:

- Check to make sure everyone has shoes. Prepare a checklist of essentials (all the suitcases, carry-ons, tickets, money, cell phone, going potty, etc.—and really check it (which is the part I usually skip, to my later regret).
- Give your child a job, like Door Checker or Seat Belt Monitor.
- Talk in a sickly sweet voice or with your teeth tightly clenched to avoid screaming at everyone.

Frustration Station Master
SURVIVING AIRPORTS AND OTHER DEPARTURE POINTS

The first issue you have to confront at the airport or other departure point is how you'll balance the stress of cutting it close with the stress of hanging out for a long time in a not-so-child-friendly place. Once you've decided that, turn your attention to these issues.

General Tips

Plan ahead and be prepared.

- Don't have brain freeze and forget that *everything* takes longer when you have kids with you.
- Information like terminal maps, security procedures, luggage requirements, and available airport services can be found at the website www.quickaid.com, which links you to individual domestic and some international airport sites. This information can help you manage a myriad of details, from estimating how much time you'll need to get from the long-term parking lot to the terminal to finding out if there is a kid's playground (and how to find it).

- Take a deep breath and stay calm. Kids will absorb and magnify your stress, and everything will get much, much worse. Talk about what to expect.

The Must-Dos

- *Getting there* Consider taking a cab, which will save parking time and fees—maybe enough to pay for the cab—and will allow you to disembark curbside. We drive, but usually have one parent drop kids and most bags (You did pack light, right?) at curbside. The other parent parks the car, while the rest of us get in line at the check-in.

- *Lines* Usually only one adult has to wait in line, while the other hangs out *nearby* with the kids. (But if you do this, make sure you alert those behind you that there will be more in your party at the last minute—remember all those lessons about not cutting in line that you're teaching your kids.) All passengers will need to be present at check-in time, so don't go far. Make sure you're ready, with all necessary tickets, IDs, baggage tags, etc., to speed your own trip through the line. I talk aloud with the kids about the things I'm doing to be ready when it's our turn; sometimes, that spurs the clueless people ahead of us into getting ready too. If you can afford it, business class lines are usually shorter. Final advice: be super, super nice to airline employees and act just a bit confused and overwhelmed. Sometimes they'll take pity on you.

- *Security Measures* Tell your child in advance about security procedures, such as having to walk through the metal detector alone. Armed guards, beeping machines, conveyor belts that swallow Puppy Pee-Pee, and other security measures often terrify inexperienced young travelers. Knowing about them in advance really helps.

Waiting

- *Go potty* Again.
- *Move around* If there's a kid's playground and you have time, take advantage of it. Just be sure to forewarn your child that she must leave without fussing when you say it's time to go. (I used to hold out a treat to have as soon as we were boarded, so I could say, "Time to go have our fruit snacks!" instead of "Time to leave this fun play area.") Invisible Ball is a good game to play at the gate. Hand your child an invisible ball and then direct her to do different things with it, tailoring your request to space and crowds. Try bouncing, dribbling between her legs or in a circle, throwing, shooting a basket, rolling it from fingertips across her back and down her other arm, kicking it into a soccer goal, balancing it on her nose like a trained seal, and so on. See chapter 2 for more wait and move activities.

Boarding

- Pre-board if you have lots of stuff to cram in overhead bins, if your seats aren't reserved (like on some commuter flights), or if your child is fearful in crowds. Otherwise, you might be better off waiting until the last minute. (It took me a long time to figure that out; I always felt compelled to pre-board, following directions like a sheep, but most of the time I think it made the trip feel longer and harder.)
- Don't buckle up until you must. Have a wet cloth or mister to cool your child in overheated cabins, or an extra sweater to keep her warm in cold ones. (Often the temperature control stuff isn't working while the plane is at the gate.)

Food to Go
KEEPING TUMMIES HAPPY
WITH FEWER STAINS, CAVITIES, OR ANTS

Food en route is a really big deal with kids (When isn't it?), so you'll want to be prepared with foods that: 1) keep the kids happy, 2) don't leave you covered with red dye #2, and 3) don't get the kids so sugared up that the other passengers vote you off the plane.

Multipurpose Foods

Food with entertainment value gives you more bang for the buck. Edibles shaped like little guys (fish crackers, bear cookies, fruit gummy creatures) can be used for pretending play before they're consumed, especially if you get your child started. Most preschoolers will naturally sort snack mixes into categories, which keeps them occupied a while; just make sure they have a flat container to hold everything. Stick pretzels can be shaped into alphabet letters, numbers, or games like tic-tac-toe, and other small-piece snacks can be used to make faces or other pictures. (Try having your child make a face, eat one piece, and then rearrange the remaining pieces to make a new face. Repeat until he can no longer make a face.)

If you're eating out, make the eating experience pleasurable, not an additional ordeal. Picnics at a rest stop where kids can run around are ideal; second choice is a fast food restaurant with a playground.

Less-Mess Meals

"Why are there ants in my seat?" One of my kids actually asked that about his car seat once—how embarrassing! Bite-sized foods (like cereal, raisins, sandwiches cut in small bits) minimize, but never seem to eliminate, the ant food problem, as do naturally not-so-crumby/sticky foods (cheese sticks, licorice twists, celery sticks). A plastic container as plate/tray confines the mess better than plastic bags or small containers. And don't forget the towel or lap cloth ideas mentioned in "Totes of Note" (page 146). A tongue depressor is a good crumb scraper; catch the crumbs in your plastic container.

Teeth Cleaners

Hard cheese like cheddar has enzymes that inhibit decay (but needs to be kept cold if won't be eaten for more than a couple hours). Apples, carrots, celery, and sugarless gum have all been shown to help clean teeth too. Follow treats with drinks of water. (Show your child how to swirl it around his mouth before he swallows it.) And don't forget the obvious—your child *can* brush his teeth en route (with toothpaste if there's a rest room available; without if there's not).

Plane Fare

On longer meal flights, you can usually preorder kids' meals. Not only will they probably be more appealing to your child, they're usually served before the regular meals. Your child won't get so hungry and crabby waiting, and he may be done eating before you're served. Remind your child that he probably can't go to the bathroom during meal service since the cart blocks the aisle. When you board, ask the attendant at what point in the flight they'll be serving, and try to time a trip to the bathroom before then.

SAFETY ZONE

After reading an account of how a mom vaulted over the front seat in heavy traffic to do the Heimlich maneuver on her choking preschooler, I've been more cautious about what I serve my kids while driving. Save potentially dangerous foods like gum, carrots, and popcorn for occasions when you're next to your child and available to help in an emergency.

Beverages

Once you give into pop, there's no going back. Try really, really hard to stick to water, preferably in a pop-top bottle. Water is cheapest and best for preventing dehydration, and it doesn't stain. Plus, it can be used to cool a hot face or blot a stain. If your child begs for other drinks, make a rule that limits them, such as one per leg of the trip. Juice boxes invariably squirt all over, so if you give them to your child, put the straw in and drink some before handing it to your child. Have him hold pouches by the top.

Adequate fluid intake during flights is especially important, since the cabin air is very dry. (Dehydration can worsen jet lag and other travel ailments.)

Chocolate

Yes, I know it's potentially a melty mess. But there's no better way to boost blood sugar and spirits quickly. So at least bring some for yourself, even if you have to sneak-eat it in the rest room.

Sit-Able
TIPS FOR TUSHES AND TEMPERS

Having to sit still in a confined space and "be good" is often the match that lights the tantrum fuse for young children already worn down by excitement, new experiences, and stressed parents. So keep calm, feel sympathetic—and then help your child cope.

Alternate Seating Arrangements

If you're lucky enough to be traveling with another adult (and not more than two or three children), you can experiment with flexible seating arrangements. For example, though I'm always reluctant to give up my relatively roomy front seat, I must admit that the kids are happier and better behaved if I sit in the back with them, at least for some of the trip. (Naturally, I make my husband take a few turns too. We remember when we used to fight over who *had* to drive on long trips; now we fight over who *gets* to.) On a plane, bus, or train, try getting separate pairs of seats so that the kids can trade one or more times. This arrangement gives each child time with each adult, reduces boredom, provides an excuse to move around other than going to the bathroom yet again, and gives tired parents a break from the most challenging child. I also know some families that rent bigger vehicles for their vacations, both to accommodate their luggage and to make it possible for squabbling sibs to spread out.

If you're traveling alone or with a whole herd of kids, you'll have fewer options, but some creative seating strategies may still help. Let kids rotate seats in the car at each stop. (Remember, though, that kids under thirteen must ride in the back.) If you're traveling by public transportation, ask for an aisle and a window seat, with luck leaving the middle one open. (Believe me—that empty one next to a small child will be the last one filled.) Or try seating a younger child with a responsible older sibling for at least part of the trip. (Place yourself in an adjacent row.) This tactic sometimes works amazingly well. Accept offers of help from flight attendants or friendly fellow travelers. (Take care not to overburden anyone, though.) Finally, consider shelling out the extra bucks to bring a helper, like a grandparent or a sitter, if you can possibly afford it.

Sit 'n' Stretch

Also see "Wiggles for Squiggle Worms" on page 115. We've found these exercises and adjustments can also increase comfort on long stretches of travel:

- *Tushercise* Direct your child to bump on her bottom several times (as much as allowed by the safety seat or belt). Then have her squeeze, hold, and release her bum muscles. Tell her to squeeze one cheek, and then the other. Have her imagine that she's sitting on a flying carpet that's gently lifting her, tush and all, into the air. She can butt-bounce off the carpet onto a soft fleecy cloud and notice how comfy it is under her booty. And so on. This generally gets everyone giggling, and it really does help sore buns if she can stop laughing long enough to do it.

- *Pad It* Before your trip, consider ordering a fresh seat pad for safety seats or replacing a worn booster with one that's a bit cushier. If that's not an option, buy a small piece of "egg crate" foam to fit the seat bottom. A rolled towel under your child's legs or behind her lower back may also provide relief for sore spots.

- *More Stretches* Every half hour or forty-five minutes, have everyone but the driver take a stretching break. Stretch along one side by reaching that arm toward the ceiling and stretching the leg on the same side as far down and out as permitted by the seat. Then do the other side. Raise both shoulders and drop them. Then rotate them in circles forward and backward, and twist side to side. Look up at pretend stars on the ceiling, and down at an imaginary river flowing on the floor. Look to each side like for crossing the street, moving slowly to feel the stretch. Lift legs toward chest and return to sitting position. Repeat several times. Point and flex toes, then rotate ankles in circles.

Stop

Yes, Steve and all you other male types, the trip will *take* longer if you stop every couple of hours to stretch legs and jump around a bit. But it will *seem* at least ten times as long if you're cooped up with major whining that you could have prevented. Make the most of every have-to stop, and have the kids get out when you stop for gas. Let them help you check the oil and the tire pressure, even if it isn't necessary. If you find a rest area well off the road, an inflatable beach ball or large punch ball balloons can provide lots of fun and exercise, without taking up much of your packing room. Try bringing a string too, so you can suspend the ball just above everyone's heads and let them jump to bat at it.

Barf Baggage
RIDING OUT MOTION SICKNESS

When your lap is soaked with vomit, it's probably small comfort to know that motion sickness is extremely common, especially in young children. Fortunately, there are steps you can take to reduce your child's chances of developing it, as well as things you can do to comfort her if she does.

Prevention/Intervention

- *Diet* Feed your child a small high-carbohydrate meal (like cereal) before traveling; an empty stomach, a too-full stomach, and greasy foods may all prompt queasiness. Foods that seem to combat nausea include: mint (Candy usually has little real mint, but sweetened peppermint tea works.), sour fruits (We find that lemon lollipops and sour gummy bears are best.), ginger (Try gingersnaps and ginger ale.), and dry, salty snacks (like pretzels or soda crackers).

- *Position* Have your child ride where the motion is smoothest: as close to the front of the car as possible (but for safety, not *in* the front seat), on the deck in the middle of a ship, as close to over the wings as possible in a plane. Reclining seems to help, especially once symptoms have started.

- *Behavior and Emotions* Keep an eye out for symptoms and monitor your kids' activities. Watching videos, staring at scenery out the side windows, and looking down at books or games can all bring on the "boofs," as one of my kids calls it. Watching the horizon or a fixed-point helps (but that tends to be hard for kids in the backseat or on a plane). Closing eyes and taking deep breaths is most effective for many young kids. Stay away from strong odors, like fuel, smoke, or perfume. Research has also shown that stress and anxiety make motion sickness more likely, so take extra care to have your child well prepared and comfortable for traveling.

- **Temperature** Stay cool. Fresh air—an open car window—helps. I know people who swear by spraying their faces with misters or wiping them with cool washcloths (especially good on a plane because of the dry air). Also, avoid over-dressing your child, and be sure she isn't wearing anything that squeezes her tummy (though some people find that holding a small pillow against their bellies helps).

- **Acupressure Products** Several products claim to prevent motion sickness by stimulating a point on the inside of the wrist. To find that point, have your child lay three fingers across his wrist, ring finger aligned with the crease closest to the hand. The point will be under his index finger.) Some independent research backs up the claims. You can buy fairly inexpensive bands (www.travelband.com) or bandages (Naustrips at www.cirrushealthcare.com) to stimulate this spot, but I also know people who just use ordinary rubber bands. There is also an expensive ($100 plus) electronic product called Relief Band that has shown promise for severely affected riders. For best results, put the bands on at least a half hour before travel. A suggestible kid might even benefit from the placebo effect alone; in a pinch, offer him any bracelet and tell him it's a special "no-sick" one.

- **Medications** Consult your doctor before using any of these. Dramamine, available over the counter, is used most fre-quently for kids. *Have your child take it at least one hour before traveling;* it's useless for stopping symptoms once they've started and takes a long time to take effect. The chewables also taste *terrible;* be prepared with a lollipop chaser. Most other medications, including scopolamine and herbal supplements, have not been tested for safety in chil-dren. All these medications can have significant side effects, from drowsiness to dry mouth. Use them as a last resort if motion sickness is an on-going problem for your child and the symptoms haven't responded to other measures.

Go Prepared

If your child is prone to motion sickness, make sure he has something ready—and I mean in hand—to catch vomit. (Even if your child isn't, be watchful after a meal, on winding or hilly roads, and during turbulence.) Zipper-seal bags, large margarine tubs with lids, and other waterproof, large-opening, disposable containers are the best choices. Take any complaints that your child doesn't feel well seriously, and take preventive measures *immediately*. You'll also want to bring a change of clothes and extra sealable bags to hold soiled clothes; the scent of vomit can trigger a fresh attack—or a new one in someone else. Pack water to rinse his mouth out and to slowly replenish fluids. Carry mint-flavored gum and/or a toothbrush to erase the taste and protect tooth enamel. One mom I know brings lavender sachets for her girls to sniff after an attack; they help to erase the puke odor that lingers in their nostrils.

MORE TO KNOW

Motion sickness isn't just barfing. Recognize the *early* symptoms and take steps to combat it before it progresses to the vomiting stage. These include: unusual fatigue or sleepiness, pallor, sweating, headache, dizziness, and mild nausea. Symptoms—and puking—can continue long after the motion has stopped.

When the Worst Happens

You're glad you were prepared and brought clean clothes for your child and you. Right? Comfort your child and reassure him that it wasn't his fault. Make a joke and get him laughing as soon as he feels a bit better. Clean up quickly, both to help your child feel better and to reduce the chance of further vomiting. On public transportation, notify attendants (though often they have surprisingly few resources to help with this problem and you may be stuck cleaning up the seat and everything) and expect them to toss coffee grounds all over the upholstery to mask the smell and absorb any remaining fluid. Make sure your child reclines and closes his eyes. Hold off on food for at least an hour, and go easy on beverages (try ice chips first) until it's clear everything is staying down. And if your child has thrown up on other passengers, it's good etiquette to offer to pay for their dry cleaning and to be extremely apologetic. And to get the heck out of there as soon as you arrive.

How to Say "No, We're Not There Yet!" Without Clenching Your Teeth
SMILE-POSTS AND ADVENT CLOCKS

It's totally clichéd—and totally true—that if you have young passengers, it's tough to get to the end of the block, let alone three-thousand miles from home, without hearing the are-we-there-yet question enough times to drive you insane. Here are some ways of dealing with it.

Smile-Posts and Advent Clocks

Preschoolers have poor senses of time and distance, and partly they ask the question just because they really don't know. Anticipate this need by breaking the trip into a series of segments based on mileage, time, or landmarks. (Danger, Will Robinson! Pad the total if you're using time, or delays will seem even worse than they already are.) Help your child see the Big Picture of your journey by giving him:

- a paper chain with links he can remove as each travel segment is completed
- a piece of paper with marks for each segment that he can cover with stickers
- a map and a marker to highlight each segment as it's completed

- a toy (like a small Lego kit) or puzzle to assemble gradually, making sure the pieces will match up reasonably well with the total segments of the trip.

When your kid asks you the inevitable question, simply refer him to his graphic aid, so he can answer the question for himself.

Sweeten the pot by handing out treats or starting new games or activities as you pass each marker. Or promise a rest stop within a reasonable period after each one (or after designated ones).

Okay, Fine!

I've seen this method mentioned so many places that I think it must work for some people. I'm including it here for that reason, but I must say it was a flop when my kids were small, mostly because they just didn't care much about money. (It works better now that they're older.) The idea is to give your child a handful of quarters at the start of the journey. Each time he asks, "Are we there yet?" (or whines excessively, beats on his brother, or whatever other bothersome behaviors you specify), he has to forfeit one quarter. Some people advise handing tokens out as rewards when the kids are being quiet instead of using them as fines, or letting the kid earn back quarters for better behavior.

I tried using the method with candy instead (which my kids did like), but ran into two problems with that. One kid snuck and ate all his candy instantly (and then had a whopping stomachache to boot), and the other argued every loophole when I fined him. I gave up on this technique after that, but maybe your kids aren't so blasé, sneaky, or argumentative.

My Silly Aunt Sally
AND OTHER THINKING GAMES

Even if you're equipped with a VCR and tapes (which, *mea culpa*, we resorted to a few times on several exceptionally long drives), you'll need some games as breaks between tapes; otherwise you'll arrive at your destination with a car full of glassy-eyed zombies.

My Silly Aunt Sally

This classic game is more appropriate for older kids. My silly Aunt Sally likes books, but she hates reading. She likes swimming, but she hates water. Can you guess the rule? She likes words with double letters. Since preschoolers can't spell, you'll have to play with little kid rules. We've played successfully using words that rhyme (she likes hogs, dogs, and logs, but not pigs, cats, or bricks), words that start with the same letter (trucks, toys, and turnips, but not cars, games, or spinach), and things that are the same color (the sun, lemons, bananas, but not the sky, limes, or oranges). Guessers respond by saying, "I know—, she also likes_____," and the hinter can agree or disagree. This way the game can continue even when some people have figured it out. Each round can take a long time. After a while, especially with younger kids, you might want to start giving hints. Preschoolers tend to stick with the same idea over and over, so you might play the second round with a different rhyme, a different starting letter, etc.

Serial Brain Killers

The traditional version of this game is "I packed my suitcase and put in _____," with each person adding something new and repeating everything put in before. Preschoolers may be more successful if you play the game with categories, like brands of cereal, cartoon characters, Pokemon guys, toys, or community helpers. In case you haven't guessed, silliness will boost their memory power too. We also play other serial memory games, like "This Is the Castle That Mommy Built" using the old rhyme about Jack and the house he built to create goofy stories featuring our own family. We take turns adding the next line: "This is Knight Kyle who jousted with Prince Eric who teased Queen Sara who lived in the castle that Mommy built." It helps most preschoolers if you start the "theme" for the story by choosing an interesting abode to construct or find. Try: cave, tree house, igloo, mansion, cottage, houseboat, cabin in the woods, tent, stilt house, nest, space station, and hot air balloon. And let younger kids go first, so they'll have the least to remember in each round.

Say What?

My oldest brought this game home from first grade, and it has been a favorite in our family ever since. One kid is "It" and he tries to get someone else to say "what" simply by engaging everyone in "normal" conversation and providing opportunities for people to ask questions like, "What the heck are you talking about?" As soon as someone goofs up, "It" says, "You're stuck with it!" and the stuck guy becomes "It." It's surprisingly hard not to say "what," especially if you're a befuddled adult. Sometimes we play with different words, like "no" or "like."

TALES FROM THE TRENCHES

The other game my son brought home from first grade is one I recommend *not* introducing to your kids. It's called "Doorknob" because that's what you say when someone passes gas. Then the doorknob guy punches the gas passer until he touches an actual doorknob. Someone who farts can quickly call "Safety" and then no one can punch him. But then you become acutely aware of how much toxic gas is accumulating in your small vehicle. If some kind reader has an idea of how to exterminate this game once started, I'd appreciate hearing it.

And May the Blue Cars Win!
LOOKING GAMES

Looking games are also classics, but some need some adaptations to be successful with preschoolers.

May the Blue Cars Win

This game is very simple, but entertaining nonetheless. Have everyone in the car pick a vehicle category, like blue, red, or green cars, or buses versus cars pulled over on the side of the road. Specify a watching/counting period. Kids who don't know how to count well can keep a tally if you show them how to make the classic four lines and a slash mark across them. At the end of the observation period, see which category has the most. With kids who are sore losers (i.e., most fours and fives), tell players that they're just observers finding the answer to a research question like "Are there more blue cars than red cars on this stretch of road?"

One Hundred Big Trucks

A noncompetitive version of the above game. Pick a category, like big trucks or, if your child is a more precise sort, eighteen-wheelers, and see how long it takes you to count 100 examples, or some other number you specify. This game is very satisfying to kids who are just learning to count to high numbers. We have also played counting to ten over and over, either until we've gotten ten sets of ten (100 again!) or counting in different languages.

Find Your Name

A junior version of the alphabet game. Write your child's name for him, if he doesn't know the letters well. Kids can work individually or together to find the letters for their names on signs or license plates. A similar game is "Find Your Age." Kids have to find the numeral for their age on signs—as many times as their age (so a four year old would have to find four fours, and an eight year old eight eights, which is good for handicapping among different-aged siblings).

Shape Hunt

Name a shape, like rectangle or circle. Have everyone look for examples of the shape. For example, the dashed lines between lanes are rectangles, many signs are rectangles, and the sides of trucks are rectangles. (We always played this noncompetitively, and switched shapes frequently.) Sesame Street fans have generally had some experience with this game and can be mighty good at it.

The Cow Game

If you're familiar with the commercial game "Pig Mania" you'll recognize the inspiration for this game. We play noncompetitively, with everyone adding to the score (usually "kept" by an adult or older sibling). We award points for seeing:

Cows in a field	1 point
A cow lying down	2 points (per cow—good way to rack up some big points)
A cow and a horse together	5 points
Cows going into a barn	10 points (standing near the barn's good enough)
Cow tipped over or cow loose on the road	1000 points (never yet seen either of those; still hoping)

Points are awarded only once per sighting, leading to some keen peering at fields as viewers try to get "credit." Make up your own version of this game to match sights you pass.

Glow Worms and Raindrop Races
ACTIVITIES FOR SPECIAL SITUATIONS

I frequently see recommendations that parents with young kids travel at night to avoid the challenge of entertaining the kids en route. We've done both, and initially, I planned to point out the pros and cons of the two approaches. On reflection, I'm just going to come out against night travel. Here's why:

- What parent of preschoolers isn't chronically exhausted? Do you really want to risk falling asleep at the wheel? Caffeine can only help so much.

- Do you want to be on the road with other sleepy and/or drunk drivers? And bad weather, construction, and other problems that are made much worse by the dark?

- Most of the time, it backfires and just screws everyone's schedule up. The kids don't actually fall asleep, or they wake up when you arrive and can't fall back to sleep. You start Day One exhausted and therefore less able to cope calmly when your child most needs your support.

The same evaluation should be applied to bad weather driving. Is it worth pressing on, or should you just spend a little extra time and money to be safe?

Okay, now that I've scared you half to death or made you feel guilty about your best travel strategy, I'll be nice and offer you some ideas for diversions when you are stuck driving under lousy conditions like heavy rain, snow and ice, or dark of night.

The Quiet Game

I've mentioned this strategy elsewhere, but it really is an exceptionally good one for when you have a headache or white knuckles. Challenge the kids to see if everyone can remain absolutely silent (for ten minutes, until you cross the big bridge, etc.). I continue to be amazed at how well this game works, but apparently kids like it. "That wath tho *hard!*" said my three year old after five minutes of determined shut-mouth. After someone successfully meets the challenge, you will naturally want to see if anyone can beat that record. But don't get carried away and do it for too many rounds, or the kids will catch onto you.

Raindrop Races

This tends to be another quiet, peaceful game, unless you let siblings play against each other. Read the Christopher Robin poem, "Waiting at the Window" in *Now We Are Six* by A. A. Milne, to give your child the general idea. Have him pick two raindrops and a finish point. Like Christopher R., most kids will pick a favorite they hope will win. Sometimes it's hard to tell who won, especially if you're zooming along the freeway and the raindrops are just going sideways. But then the fact that the rain is moving sideways instead of up and down is fascinating, and may keep the kid amused anyway.

Wiper Chants

Not so quiet or soothing, but we specify that kids must imitate the *volume* of the wipers as well as the rhythm. Have your child sing or recite a rhyme, using the wipers as a metronome to set the pace. Variable speed wipers can make this game more interesting.

Glow Worms and Padiddle

This is such a simple idea that probably everyone out there already does it, but I didn't think of it for years (although once I was stupid enough to hand out mini-flashlights—don't do that). Get a cookie tray and a whole assortment of glow-in-the-dark stuff, like stars and little toy animals. (Check dollar stores and science/museum shops.) Make sure you "charge" everything well before dark falls, and then hand it out to play with. Enjoy all the oohs and gasps of delight.

The other night game my husband taught me, and that we played for years even before we had kids, is Padiddle. Everyone watches for vehicles with one headlight and calls "Padiddle" when one is spotted. You get one point per Padiddle. (You can play competitively or for a group score.) But if you call Padiddle and it turns out to be a motorcycle, you start over at zero.

Plane Speaking
EARS, FEARS, SNEERS, AND PEE-ERS

Being stuck in a car is tough with young children, but being stuck in a plane can be even worse. For one thing, you really can't use the "Don't make me pull over!" threat effectively. What's more, there are problems, such as the ear pressure thing, that are unique (or nearly so) to planes.

Ears

Once I flew when I had a bad sinus infection, and I suddenly understood why all those babies scream at takeoffs and landings. It really hurts! Treats such as lollipops (safer than hard candies) and gum or fruit gummy candies encourage swallowing and "popping," but are often not enough. Heat sometimes helps. In a pinch, try rubbing your hands vigorously until they're quite warm and cupping them over your child's ears. Pressing over sinuses may work, as may making goofy open-wide, wiggle-your-jaw faces. Over-the-counter decongestants, taken an hour before flying, seemed to lessen the pain if our kids had colds or stuffy noses. (It's not a bad idea to schedule a quick ear check at the pediatrician's for the day before your flight, though ear infections can develop in a manner of hours.) Avoid antihistamines, though. They tend to dry out sinuses already irritated by the cabin air and make some kids hyper and irritable.

There is also an earplug product called "Ear Planes" (available from Wal-Mart) that is supposed to prevent pain. The plugs must be removed during the flight and replaced after just a few trips. I don't know anyone who has tried them (and I've asked around and checked websites), so I'm not sure if they really work. Still, if ear pain is a frequent problem for your child, they may be worth a try.

Fears

Matter-of-fact explanations can ease many anxieties for first-time flyers. When you board the plane, point out features like safety belts, tray tables, and the bathrooms. Explain that there are times when seatbelts must be worn, or when the trays and bathrooms may not be used. Explain the safety lecture as something similar to fire drills at school and help your child examine the card and locate exits. Warn him about normal noises that may be surprising, such as the loud whine as the jets rev up, the clunks when the wheels retract, and the changes as the ventilating system starts working. Similarly, prepare him for the bumpiness and sounds of landing.

And listen for his concerns—young children can have many strange ideas, like my kid's worry about shrinking, that you'll be able to allay.

Sneers

I've traveled alone and with kids, and in truth I have sympathy for business people who cringe when they discover they're seated next to a small child. (Naturally, I have even more sympathy for the parent and kid—and there's no excuse for the hostile glares that some people direct at adequately behaved kids.) Your child will benefit in the long run, though, if you balance attention to his needs with courtesy toward fellow passengers. Try to sit between him and other passengers, and certainly stop your child if he insists on kicking the seat in front of him. Encourage him to use inside voices, and do your best to keep him occupied. Finally, be calm and reassuring to your child if someone is unfairly rude to him—unfortunately, it probably won't be the only time he encounters a jerk—and remind yourself that you'll probably never see the nasty passenger again.

Pee-ers

Plane toilets are an ordeal, in part because they're so small. And you'll have to go in with your kid, if for no other reason than the light usually doesn't come on until the door is latched and most small kids can't manage that. Plane bathrooms also have some distressing features. Reassure your child that he can't go down the hole and fall out of the plane—that the toilets work like Port-a-Johns and everything goes into a tank that gets emptied *after* the plane lands. Plane toilets tend to have unusually loud flushes, so I often let the kid leave before flushing. Watch out, too, for very hot water from the faucets—I've nearly been scalded myself.

CHAPTER SEVEN

When You're Sentenced to Life on the Road

I remember enticing my daughter to look forward to a vacation when she was in one of those everything's-got-to-be-familiar-and-unchanging stages that most preschoolers go through. I told her that this was no ordinary vacation. Her grandparents had arranged for us to go stay at a "cabin-in-the-woods," just like in the song. You know, the one with the little old man who "saw a rabbit hopping by, knocking at his door?" At the time, Sara was singing that song twenty or thirty times a day, elaborately pantomiming all the gestures, and I was pretty sure I'd come up with a lodging description that would appeal to her more than square footage or Jacuzzis. Sure enough, she forgot her demands that we take her bed with us, and adored our rustic guesthouse and the trees around it. She was thrilled that we even saw a couple rabbits hopping by, though none came knocking at the door. So, my advice to you is to look for aspects of your vacation lodgings that might appeal to your child's interests, however eccentric they might seem. Here's a hot tip for you if you can't think of anything else: point out how the motel's toilet looks *just like the ones* in Dav Pilkey's *Captain Underpants and the Attack of the Talking Toilets.*

In this chapter, I have outlined tips for getting your child acclimated to his new surroundings. A formal orientation is important, especially so your child will know where the potty is when he needs it. Even then, the where-the-heck-is-the-potty? problem invariably crops up on vacations, and your child may pee his pants because he can't find the toilet in time. Or, if he's like one of my nephews, he'll wake up in the middle of the night and pee on his brother's face. Better for future sibling harmony to try to prevent that problem. There are also suggestions for the other kinds of potty issues—namely constipation and diarrhea—that are frequently vacation problems for young children.

I've proposed solutions for the sleeping, eating, and bathing issues that occur when your child is away from her familiar teddy bear, peanut butter, and rubber ducky. I even have ideas for addressing problems that may arise if you decide to give in and let Teddy come on your vacation with you but you're terrified of losing him. (Useful tip: You don't need to get Teddy his own ticket. He flies free on your daughter's lap. He also sleeps free in the same room.)

I can only think of one issue I forgot to cover, so I'll bring it up here: unpacking. Many experts feel that unpacking is essential with young kids since it helps them feel more settled and secure. But I say those people have never tried to cram all the stuff back in suitcases when their plane is leaving in seventy-five minutes and their kid has scattered everything all over the motel room. Usually, I unpack if we're staying someplace like a beach house, where we'll be doing laundry and stuff anyway (and then I make sure I wash everything before I put it back in, which makes coming home and unpacking much more pleasant). Otherwise, I leave as much stuff as possible in the suitcase. That will be easier if you follow my advice to pack clean outfits in separate bags on page 145.

And, if all else fails, remember your sentence to life on the road really isn't for life—just for a week or so. So, welcome to your new (temporary) home.

Home-Instead-ing
CREATING HOME-FOR-NOW COMFORT WHEREVER YOU GO

When I travel, I like to stay in places that are quaint, exotic, or at least a bit unusual. Not so my children. I think they'd prefer to be turtles and take their own house along. That attitude is typical of young children, who crave familiarity in a world that is, after all, bursting with things that are new and surprising to them. Try these ideas to create a sense of home-to-go that will, with luck, help your child feel secure enough to enjoy other new experiences.

Home-in-a-Bag

Business travelers often carry framed photographs of their families, artwork by their children, or other artifacts to remind them of home. Young children appreciate tokens of home too, even on short trips. Pack photographs of your house and pets and a few small familiar items, such as something from your child's bedside table at home (so he has something familiar to look at as he falls asleep), a small cuddle blanket (even if he isn't attached to a specific one), a music box, and some mundane objects like his usual bathroom cup. Tote everything in a pillowcase and you'll have a familiar cover for his pillow, in case the one provided at your destination doesn't feel or smell quite right to your child.

The Just-Like-Home Game

I remember how surprised and pleased one of my preschoolers was to discover that the hotel room had toilets, "just like we have at our house!" A friend, who travels frequently for business and sometimes brings her kids, plays a game where she gets the kids to find five things that are "just like home." They also look for two or three things that are "even better than home" (room service usually wins), and maybe *one* thing the kids wish was "as good as home." It also helps young kids to feel like the new temporary quarters are "theirs." Use terms like "our hotel" or even "home" to describe your place and help your child feel settled.

The Life of McDonald's

I'm not really a fan of the mall-ization of the world, but I do think that chain hotels, and yes, even McDonald's, offer a lot of benefits when you're traveling with young children. You can expect every Holiday Inn you visit anywhere in the world to be reasonably clean, safe, and equipped with nice bathrooms. And while the predictable appearance of chains may seem bland to most adults, it's reassuring to overstimulated kids. Plus, most chains have child-friendly features, such as a free stay for kids in the same room as their parents, swimming pools or play areas, and kid-tolerant staff and guests.

Let's say you're one of those adventurous sorts who thinks it's a great idea to spend a week camping with several children under the age of six. Good luck! Seriously, I do know many families who have camped—happily, they claim—with more than one young child. Nonetheless, unless you are an extremely experienced camper—and an exceptionally patient parent—higher end campgrounds or relatively manicured state and national park campsites are better bets for camping with toddlers and preschoolers than backwoods or wilderness adventure sites, especially for first trips. It's hard to lug along all the kid stuff you really do need, and the sharp contrasts with everyday life can easily overwhelm sensitive preschoolers. Definitely try an overnight or weekend of camping before you sign up for a full week.

Flex Time
SCHEDULE ADJUSTMENTS AND THE TRAVELING BLUES

Traveling nearly always results in a shift of the family's daily routines—and those changes are the source of much of the unpleasant kid behavior that can drive you crazy and ruin even a well-planned vacation. These ideas can minimize (but still probably won't entirely eliminate) the kiddy traveling blues.

Introducing a New Improved Schedule!

Aim for a rhythm to your day, even if it's quite different from the routine you follow at home. A consistent wake-up time, meal schedule, and bedtime will help your child adjust. Weave in rituals, like a nightly moonlight walk on the beach before the bedtime story. Help your child anticipate and accept the changes by nudging her routine toward the different one before you go, discussing changes that are likely to occur, and praising her for her adaptability.

The Afternoon Freeze

Even if your child doesn't nap at home, she will need an afternoon rest when you're traveling. An hour or more of chill-out time will give her a chance to process the morning's stimulation and supercharge her immune system to help her fight off unfamiliar germs. The best freezes have the following ingredients:

- Brief water play (in the pool, the tub, or the bathroom sink) and/or rhythmic movement (rocking, swinging, or jumping)
- Cuddle time (reading a book or touch-me games, like knee bouncers)
- Stretched-out-doing-nothing time (nap, alone play, or watching cartoons).

Time for a Little Something

Pooh Bear and small children need to eat frequently wherever they are. Aim for getting a high protein food in your child just *before* major activities, and pause every two hours for a high-quality snack. Having the big meal of the day at lunchtime instead of suppertime will be easier on your wallet *and* make it easier for kids to fall asleep, since their tummies won't be overstuffed then.

Activity Timers

Wear a watch with a timer or alarm feature when you travel. (Timex makes fairly inexpensive durable watches that hold up well under family travel conditions; look for the water-resistant "Expedition" ones.) Set the alarm to go off after an hour of challenging activities (such as a visit to an art museum or other not-so-kid-friendly place) or two hours of other ones. At that point, take a break or change to a different activity, like running around outside. Remember the axiom: "Always leave them wanting more."

Hit the Snooze Button

Make sure everyone gets enough sleep, preferably on some sort of a consistent schedule. Follow as much of your at-home bedtime routine as possible.

Jet Lag Strategies

Jet lag is as miserable for little kids as it is for adults. Try these strategies to minimize its effects:

- Make an effort to adjust your child's schedule toward the new time over the week before you leave.
- On overnight flights, put Post-It Notes on everyone to let the flight attendants know that you do not want to be awakened for meals, the movie, etc. (My kids like to hang "Do Not Disturb" signs around their necks, like Eloise does in *Eloise in Paris* by Kay Thompson.) Use eye masks and earplugs or headphones (playing soft instrumental music or nature sounds) to create a peaceful island en route.
- Take a *short* nap (no more than two hours) on arrival. Going by the time in your new location, try to put your child to bed as close as possible to her usual bedtime.
- Get outside! Sunlight helps reset circadian rhythms.
- Take it slow and easy the first couple of days.
- Don't rely on antihistamines or other sleep-inducing medications—they often backfire and create more sleep problems in the long run.

Mark That Room!
NEW WAY FINDERS

Preschoolers are easily confused in new environments and many have a hard time making mental maps of new places. The resulting insecurity may make them feel irritable and out-of-sorts. Try these ideas to get and keep your child grounded in her new surroundings.

Freshman Orientation

Take care to walk your child around her new surroundings, talking through how you're finding your way and pointing out landmarks that will help her later. More than one preschooler has peed her pants because she didn't remember where Grandpa's bathroom was. Important sites to know: the location of all bathrooms, acceptable areas for play and spots where she must be extra careful or quiet, and places where adults will be. State boundary rules, such as never leaving the hotel room without an adult or going only as far as the trees you've marked with orange ribbons. Also point out the people, like hotel clerks, relatives, or camp rangers, whom she can ask for help if she gets separated from you.

Cement your child's mental maps and understanding of the rules by playing "What if?" with questions like these: "What if you went out in the hall and the door shut and locked behind you?" or "What if you were in Grandma's kitchen and you had to go pee very badly?" We also play "Follow the leader," having the child leader take us to the lobby or the playground or wherever, to help her feel confident moving around her new surroundings.

Mark That Room!

Do something to make your room or campsite easy to identify, even if your child is required to be with an adult whenever she is outside that area. Kids who recognize and feel possessive of "their places" feel more secure. (Neighbors who prefer not to have kids banging on their doors and shouting, "Is this our room?" will also appreciate the effort.) Try tying ribbons to the door handle, decorating an old "Do not disturb" door hanger to take along, or taping a picture to the door. A photocopy of an old family picture can mark the rooms of your group at a family reunion or other occasion, and the adults will appreciate the visual aids as well. If you're camping, try hanging balloons or an inflated beach ball at your campsite to help your child recognize it. Putting your new address to music can help children memorize their hotel names and room numbers.

It's also important to make it easy for your child to find the bathroom—and you—at night. In a hotel room, hang a light stick or position a nightlight next to the bathroom or leave the light on and the door ajar. You can use glow-in-the-dark objects to create a trail that will last several hours, or mark a campsite trail with stick arrows. (Make sure your child has a flashlight.) Plan to accompany your young child to the potty, especially at night. Make a rule that your child must wake you and sleep between her and the door or tent flap, so she'll at least step on your face on the way out. If you're staying in a home or someplace with multiple rooms, walk your child from her bed to your room and the bathroom before tucking her in for the night. Several practice runs are better than one. Mark her own door as well, since sometimes kids can't remember how to get back after going to the bathroom.

Happy-Tizers
MEALS OUT CAN BE IN—SORT OF

Meals out can be not only expensive when you're traveling with young kids, but—how shall I put this?—mind-boggling, horrific experiences. We've had our share (and then some) of those meals, and as a consequence, I've got a good idea of the usual pitfalls—and some thoughts on avoiding them. And, because I'm in a generous mood right now, I'm going to share them with you and spare you the pain of discovering them the hard way.

Strategy Number One for Eating Out Happily: Don't Eat Out

I mean that. I used to think *not cooking* would be a relaxing treat on vacations, but I've completely reversed my position on that. Now a good vacation is one where we eat out only once or twice. I strongly recommend that you choose accommodations with a kitchenette whenever possible, and prepare at least a couple of your own meals each day. Keep them simple, buy prepared foods that only need reheating, and use paper plates, so you're not spending your vacation slaving over stove or dishes. Or, try these ideas to eliminate or at least reduce the number of sit-down restaurant meals:

- *Order Room Service* Not every meal, since it's too expensive, but consider treating yourself after a long day or before a travel one. If you order right, the kids may be able to munch off your meal—or you may be able to order less costly kids' meals.

- *Get Takeout* Cheaper than room service by far, but with the same "We really get to eat in our room?" magic that will delight your kids. Pizza and Chinese need not be your only options, either. Many upscale and interesting places will prepare takeout orders. My husband and I sometimes feed the kids pizza early, and order something better for ourselves after they're asleep.

- *Go on Picnics* We picnic everywhere we go. Sometimes, we buy food at markets and prepare it (Bread, cheese, and fresh fruit always satisfy.), but more often, we buy vendor fare. Then we take it to a nearby park. This is usually the happiest option of all, especially on a warm, sunny afternoon, but we've had car picnics during rainstorms, as well.

- *Make Breakfast* Even in a standard hotel room, you can probably fix breakfast. Try packaged instant oatmeal made with hot water from the coffee maker, cold cereal (small cartons of milk and juice keep overnight packed in ice from the machine in the hall), bagels and peanut butter (Skippy brought from home and bagels bought fresh), and fresh fruit like bananas or apples.

Strategy Number Two: Make Restaurant Meals Less Painful

- ***Order Ahead*** See if you can place your order over the phone, and waltz in when it's ready. If you can't, have everyone decide what to eat, then send the kids and one adult out to play until the food comes. And always make reservations when allowed, so at least you won't have to wait before you even get seated.

- ***Choose Family Style Restaurants*** Not only will it be hard for you to enjoy a nicer restaurant with small fry in tow, but also everyone else in the place will hate your guts, and the wait staff may even retaliate and give you lousy service. In addition, family restaurants are more likely to have things like crayons to amuse the kids while you wait, faster service, and lower prices (and then you won't be so resentful of how the kids are spoiling the meal with their whining).

- ***Nibble While You Wait*** Bring your own munchies so that kids can snack before the food comes. If you're out of goodies, order a kid-friendly appetizer like chicken strips or let them chow down on bread.

- ***Make Use of the Waiting Time*** Make plans for the next day, and review favorite experiences from the current day. Have the kids dictate postcards to Grandma or tape things in their scrapbooks. And don't forget to bring amusements and play some of the waiting games from chapter two—the above will take only 7.2 minutes.

- ***Eat During Off-Hours*** Early dinners are easier on kids and kinder to other diners. If you want to try a nicer restaurant, consider visiting it at lunchtime, when it will be cheaper and usually less formal—and you won't have end-of-day fatigue adding to the difficulty of keeping everyone content. Also, request *plain* food for your kids if there's no kids' menu— chicken sautéed without sauce, pasta with butter (and Parmesan on the side), or bread and cheese. Many restaurants will accommodate these requests, and you'll only have to endure the raised eyebrows of the waiter instead of the shrieks of your disgusted child.

Traveling Hygiene
GETTING CLEAN WITH NO MORE TEARS (THAN USUAL)

Lazy parents like me rely mostly on swimming to get kids clean on the road, with just a quick rinse to remove chlorine or salt afterwards. An evening bath routine, though, can be a big help in settling excited young bodies, especially if that's what you do at home. Also, you'll definitely want to keep everyone's hands clean to reduce the chances of vacation-ruining diseases. Try these tips for on-the-road wash-ups.

The Bare Minimum

Doesn't actually involve getting bare—*just make sure you wash hands frequently!* Maybe faces too. I'm far from germ-obsessed, but I *hate* those sick bay vacations. Make the kids wash their hands before every meal and following any "hands-on" play at

MORE TO KNOW

I really don't own stock in Purell! Other brands of alcohol-based washing stuff work just as well, so buy whatever's cheapest. The important point is that Purell and similar products have been shown to be more effective *in actual use* by kids than soap and water or wipes. Why? Mostly because kids rarely wash as long or thoroughly as they must to kill germs, and they don't rinse or dry adequately either. If dry skin is a problem (alcohol has that effect), choose a variety with added moisturizers.

TRY THIS!

For young kids, bring their own shampoo, as even family-friendly places rarely have no-tears stuff in those little bottles, and your usual soap, especially if your child has sensitive skin. For years, my kids would only brush with bubblegum-flavored toothpaste, and I soon learned the little extra bit of luggage space the full-sized tube required (couldn't find that flavor in a travel size) was well worth every inch.

crowded sites like museums. I rely heavily on Purell, especially if I'm concerned about the purity of the water or the cleanliness of the bathrooms. Make it fun by having contests to see who can get his blob of gel to disappear fastest. Kids who are finger-suckers or eye-rubbers should wash extra frequently, as should anyone who has been playing or swimming in freshwater sources, which tend to have more bacteria than saltwater ones.

Play 'n' Wash

How do you lure kids into the tub at home? With toys, of course! If you haven't packed your rubber ducky armada, you'll need to improvise. Fortunately, between the trash can and those cute little bottles the hotel supplies, you can probably generate an impressive supply of novel bath toys. For example, sport water bottles are great for pouring or squirting, and Styrofoam fast food trays make perfect boats. (Use coin or natural object "passengers.") Once, we let one of the kids "play" with a frog he captured for his most memorable and cooperative bath ever, but I don't recommend that if you're remotely squeamish—it escaped and was tough to recapture.

You can also improvise sensory pleasures. Try adding a drop of mouthwash to the water for an invigorating scent and a touch of color. Floating "wildflowers" (i.e., parking lot weeds) add glamour for little girls. For boys, make "bubble bath" by adding a small amount of kid shampoo to the running water. (Avoid this for girls, who may get irritation or urinary tract infections from the bubble bath.)

Alfresco Showers

Bathing kids while you're camping takes a little more ingenuity—but is usually a necessity, since kids attract vast quantities of mud and may have had encounters of the poison ivy kind. I strongly recommend buying a "camp shower" (or even better a "sun shower," which is often sold with boating supplies). Young kids, who get chilled more easily than adults, will cooperate better if the water's warm. Combine water heated over the campfire with cold water (taking care to check that the resulting mix isn't too hot) or set out jugs of water to warm in the sun. Finally, even if you're using special environmentally safe soaps, scrub with Fels Naptha soap, Tecnu, or something similar if you suspect the kids have been in the poison ivy—the other stuff won't wash the oil off, and the resulting rash can mar the camping experience dramatically.

Forgotten Toothbrushes

Probably you think my solution of just sharing them is too gross. Sigh— another of my maternal failings. Call the desk if you're at a hotel—chains may have freebies available, or they can tell you the nearest place to get one. If that doesn't work, put a dab of toothpaste on the corner of a wash-cloth and use that to scrub teeth. Have the kid lick the cloth at the end, puppy-style, to remove junk from his tongue too. Finish up by rinsing well—with warmish water, which encourages better swishing.

"I've Peed in Pennsylvania!"
FLUSHING AWAY TRAVELING POTTY ISSUES

When I was contemplating parenthood, no one warned me that I'd spend an astronomical number of hours thinking about toilets and related topics. Oh sure, like most prospective parents, I knew that diapers and potty training were bound to be significant and time-consuming concerns, but I didn't realize I'd be devoting *years* of my thinking life to plumbing issues. Nor did I guess that deciding to travel with my kids would at least triple or quadruple my total hours of potty thoughts. So maybe you will benefit from some of my hard-won toileting-on-the-road experience, and save yourself a few hours to think about more pleasant topics, like moonlit strolls on the beach. With your honey. Or at least without any kids who are doing the pee dance.

Fear of the Unknown Potty

This is a surprisingly common problem in young kids. Things that bother young kids about potties that aren't their own include the following:

- *Smell* Talking about it and/or pinching their noses usually solves the problem; if not, have them tote lavender potpourri bags or something similar to breathe into.
- *Size/shape/appearance* Again, just talk about it and reassure your child that it will work anyhow. Also, provide a portable seat cover like the one made by Graco to adjust the fit.
- *Flushing differences* Warn your child about automatic flushers, recognizable by the lack of handle, especially since little kids often trigger the auto-flush before dismount. If loud sounds alarm him, let your child leave the stall before you flush.

SAFETY ZONE

I know this sounds like a joke, but it's not. Beware of unfamiliar toilet seats if you have a little boy! Once when we were visiting a friend, I helped my three year old push up right against the bowl (to improve his accuracy as a polite visitor should), lifted the seat for him, and let go—only to have the whole thing come crashing down, nearly decapitating—if you get my meaning —a tender part of his anatomy. I have since read about several similar accidents that had unhappier endings.

I've Peed in Pennsylvania!

Here's another strategy to get your child enthusiastic about using unfamiliar potties—and this one appeals to four-year-old boys especially. Get a travel-size map and laminate it. Instead of marking the places you've visited with little flags, get some toilet stickers (I've seen them at Toys "R" Us and in the potty-training supply aisle at other kid stores.) and let your child put one over the appropriate location each time he uses a potty someplace new. Now that's a childhood memento not everyone will have!

Coping With Potties That Really Are Different

First-time campers often develop constipation because of a reluctance or inability to go in Port-a-Johns, outhouse-style potties, or, most challenging of all, a hole in the woods. Schedule a time to try daily, let your child watch you, and make sure your child's feet and bum are supported. (In the wild, have him sit with his bum overhanging a low fallen branch or limb.) Also, see the constipation suggestions that follow on page 190.

If you'll be traveling abroad, you may encounter some truly *different* potty arrangements. For one thing, they may cost, so make sure you get coins before you need them. In many of the public toilets in Paris, *the whole room flushes!* (I imagine that's to counteract the problems created by the fact that every Parisian pedestrian has shoes caked with dog poo.) This can be alarming to many young children, as well as their parents, so let the kid leave before you flush. In parts of Asia, potties may be "squatters," requiring an approach to going that is unfamiliar to most Westerners. Help prepare your child for these differences. And remember that McDonald's restaurants can now be found almost everywhere—and they all seem to have clean, roomy Western-style bathrooms.

Drawing a Line in the Dirt and Other Outdoor Fun

Outdoorsy vacations are the perfect time to improve your son's aim by letting him practice his "dexterity" in the woods. This is another guy thing, like nonstop driving, and will probably happen whether or not you encourage it, so mostly I'm mentioning it so you female sorts don't get unnecessarily worked up when you notice it happening. (Just teach your guys to beware of the poison ivy. Oh, and if they offer to help douse the campfire—say no.)

The other outdoor peeing issue is what to tell your child to do when she's swimming and notices that she suddenly has to go. Our rule of thumb is that if you're in a pool and need to go, you *must* get out and find a potty. And if you need to poop, you have to head to the potty, even if you're splashing about in a lake or ocean. But if you're in said lake or ocean and you just need to *pee*, go right ahead!. (If that grosses you out, just think about all the fish pee in there with you. Just think about the *whale* pee! Or, maybe you better not. Just forget I said anything. I'm sure the water's nice and clean and nothing has ever peed or pooped in it.)

How Dry I'm Not: Accident Prevention and Intervention

Just to make traveling with young children extra "challenging" (a euphemism for "a pain in the boo-tay"), *you should expect more accidents when you are away from home,* because of general stress, changes in diet and schedules, lack of quick access to toilets, and so on. Schedule frequent potty stops and—this is the important part—make everyone try, even if they don't have to go! Always carry a change of clothes and a plastic bag for the wet ones when you're out and about. Be matter of fact and reassuring to your child, who may also be extra embarrassed. Tell a funny story about having an accident yourself when you were little and traveling. (Jeez, go ahead and make it up if you have to—you probably did have at least one and just don't remember it. This is not the time to be all high-minded and honest.)

Expect night-wetting too, *even if it isn't usually a problem.* If you took my earlier advice and packed a lap mat, you can put that under your child at night, or bring a waterproof sheet or tablecloth to protect the bed. Hotel managers, friends, and relatives will all thank you for this courtesy. Air out peed sleeping bags promptly, blotting as much moisture as possible. There's no easy way to get rid of the smell short of washing, but I know people who claim that baking soda sprinkled on and shaken off after a few hours will help. I also know one family that tried a pet odor-removing spray (Why the heck were they traveling with it?), but check with your doctor beforehand about whether it's safe for kids.

"But I Can't Poop in Poughkeepsie!"
FLUSHING AWAY PLUMBING CLOGS AND LEAKS

What's worse than a kid who's gotta go? One who can't! Or one who goes and goes and goes. Hope these ideas help.

Poop Pointers

To stave off or treat kiddy constipation, keep the following points in mind:

- *Diet* Water, water, and more water will help prevent constipation. En route, many parents limit drinks to decrease pee stops; just make sure to resume usual consumption at your destination. Eating fruit several times a day, especially dried ones like raisins and apricots (as well as the better-known prunes) will usually keep your child going. Other high fiber foods, like oatmeal (Go ahead and pile on the brown sugar.), bran cereal mixed with the sweet junk, or, if you're already feeling desperate, prune juice mixed 50/50 with Coke, will also do the trick in most cases.

- *Schedule* At home, your child probably has a time of day when he usually likes to go. When you're traveling, you need to block off that time for him too, preferably where he can hang at a relatively comfortable, familiar potty. My middle son, for one, was never able to accomplish the task in under fifteen minutes, and if we didn't just accept that, everyone was standing around impatiently harrumphing while he took longer than ever.

- *Exercise* Long travel days with few breaks for exercise can disrupt a young child's digestive process. Schedule daily vigorous running and climbing to keep your child—and his bowels—moving.

- *Desperate Measures* If your child is already badly constipated, you'll know it since he'll quickly make you as miserable as he is. I recommend giving a kid-safe stool softener (Use this remedy on a one-time basis—it can become a problem if used repeatedly.), applying warmth to his belly in the form of compresses or warm baths, and using aloe wet wipes on his sore bum. Lots of sympathy and the measures above should get him back on track fairly quickly. If not, consult a doctor.

Diarrhea Matters

To everyone involved. To prevent or treat it, try these measures:

- *A Good Diet* Bringing familiar foods from home is not only comforting to young children, but may also help prevent diarrhea caused by too many sudden changes. Avoid drastic increases in fruits and veggies unless your child is already struggling with constipation. Watch out, also, for too many treat foods, which can cause upset tummies on the road, just as they do at home. If your child does develop diarrhea, switch promptly to the BRAT diet (bananas, rice, applesauce, toast) until his tummy has had a chance to recover.

- *Being Cautious* If you're camping or traveling abroad, be careful about water. If it's not safe to drink, don't use it to brush teeth or wash hands and faces, since the bacteria can then enter through eyes and noses, and avoid ice. Just say no to uncooked foods, drinks with water in them, and fruits that don't require peeling. When camping, boil or treat all drinking and washing water. In countries with questionable water, stick to bottled water and soft drinks, making sure both are served to you with their seals intact.

- *Minimizing Stress* If your child is prone to stomach upsets, be extra careful to make sure he gets enough sleep and regular meals. Also, increase touching (extra hugs, holding, pats, massage), reassurance, and talking about feelings.

- *Medical Treatment* Before you leave, get your doctor to recommend an anti-diarrhea medicine for your kid—and one for you too. (I see Pepto-Bismol recommended most frequently for kids, and Imodium AD for adults.) If your child does have ongoing diarrhea, take care to avoid dehydration by replacing fluids with water or electrolyte solutions. (Pedialyte is ideal, or try clear broth.) If your child is still sick after twenty-four hours or has other symptoms such as fever, consult a doctor.

- *Comforting Sore Bottoms and Hurty Bellies* Warmth is soothing for kids with cramps. Avoid "diarrhea rash" by coating your kid's bottom with petroleum jelly at the first sign of diarrhea and using medicated wet wipes or at least dampened toilet paper to wipe his bottom. You can also rinse his bottom with warm water or have him soak it briefly in a shallow tub.

- *Wash Everyone's Hands! A Lot!*

Keep in mind that constipation is actually an overlooked cause of some cases of diarrhea. Stool can become liquid and leak around an impaction if your child has been constipated for several days. If you're unsure what's going on with your child's digestive troubles, contact a doctor.

Accommodating Roommates
AND OTHER SLEEPING ARRANGEMENT SOLUTIONS

Shared sleeping quarters may be a necessity on trips. Truthfully, preschoolers often love this arrangement—you've probably already noticed how much they love to sleep with you at home. But it can create frustration for adults who'd like to stay up past 8:30 (and sleep through the early "Rugrats" show), and it can cause excessive fatigue and grumpiness in small fry kept awake past their bedtimes. Here are some strategies for restful compromises.

Separate Quarters

The best solution for everyone is usually separate rooms. If you can't afford the suite solution, you'll have to be creative. Try one of the following suggestions:

- *Tents* Either fashion them from extra bedding or bring them with you. We used to tote a kids' play tent with us whenever possible, and bed the youngest kids in it in sleeping bags.

- *The Little Room, Just for Kids* Also known as the closet. Seriously. One of my kids used to sleep in hotel closets routinely, snuggled up in his sleeping bag. (Sometimes at home, he also slept in an emptied closet that he called his "hidey hole.") Be sure to prop the door open, so that your child can't get stuck inside. A family I know used to tuck their preschooler in on a pile of blankets in the bathtub. Once he was asleep, they'd transfer him to a regular bed. He *loved* this special treat, and was allowed to do it at home too, on special occasions like his birthday. Never underestimate a preschooler's delight in the ridiculous or the cozy!

- *The Sitting-Bathroom* We'd pile cushions, reading material, snacks, and maybe a bottle of wine for us in the bathroom, so we had a space where we could hang out semi-comfortably while the kids fell asleep. Then we'd return to the main room to sleep. (I recommend letting at least one adult take a soaking tubby during this time, which is also good for the vacation love-life.) Another option, though not so private, is to hang out in the hallway, while the kids doze off. Take chairs from the room with you and it's not so bad. A balcony is even better, if you have one; make sure to lock up and block the door for safety before you go to bed. Finally, a baby monitor may give you the flexibility to hang out a little farther away. (Just test the system in advance, and keep in mind that others may be able to tune in, too.)

- *Divide and Conquer* Let one adult go off and do something grown-up and fun, while the other stays behind. And be sure to take turns. This strategy rarely worked well in our family— it made the kids anxious to have someone off alone.

Sunrise: The Other Side of the Rooming-In Problem

Set guidelines and make arrangements to help your preschooler either sleep in, or at least not jump on your stomach at the crack of dawn. Try one or more of these ideas:

- *Use the Room-Darkening Shades* Many hotel rooms have them (and often another more sheer set); be sure to pull them closed. (Use a little of your duct tape to secure them, if they keep parting in the middle.) And then set the alarm, so you don't snooze half the morning away.

- *Tape the Clock* Use a piece of tape to hide the minute numerals on a digital alarm clock. Tell your child she can get up when the hour number says 8, or whatever time you choose.

- *Play Place* Before bed, set up a quiet play zone on the floor *as far from your bed as possible.* To gain a few extra minutes

MORE TO KNOW

When reserving rooms for you and your children, make sure you know the difference between *adjoining* rooms (side by side) and *connecting* rooms (door between them). Confirm the arrangements before departure—we've had problems with last-minute unavailability. Also, if you'll be staying a week in one place, you may be able to rent an apartment by the week, especially abroad, or even home-swap. Family travel guides and websites can usually direct you to services that arrange these accommodations in the area you're planning to visit.

of shut-eye for yourself, include a breakfast snack for the early risers. You'll wake up, of course, but you may be able to lie there in a half-dozing stupor and feel like you're getting some rest.

Snuggy Buggy Rubbies and Humpty Dumpty Habit-Breakers
SETTLE DOWN STRATEGIES TO GO

Most young children have a harder-than-usual time going to sleep while traveling. (I do too.) Time—and exhaustion—may solve the problem before it's time to go home, but meanwhile, try these ideas to help everyone close his peepers before dawn.

Bedtime Twins

This seems obvious, but I know I've overlooked it on trips: *You want bedtime on the road to be as much like bedtime at home as possible.* Arrange the props you've brought, like stuffed animals, blankets, and pillows, just the way they'd be in your kid's room. (I'm reminding you again about pillows, because smell seems to matter very much in helping kids settle down at night. If you didn't bring a pillow or at least a case, consider tucking in a shirt you've worn near the kid's head.) Even more important than props, though, is following your usual routine as exactly as possible.

Snuggy Buggy Rubbies

Overstimulated children have more tension than usual to discharge before they can fall asleep. Vigorous exercise during the day helps, as will a soothing bath. Also try massage and other touching techniques. To give a Snuggy Buggy Rubby, first gently cocoon your child in your arms while you hum a nice bug song like "Inchworm" (or some other lullaby-ish song). Next roll your child gently onto the bed, on her belly. With your fingertips, draw circles on her back. Then, rub or scritch her back vigorously.

Roll her over and squeeze her arms from shoulders to fingertips. Finish up with a gentle face massage and butterfly kisses.

Humpty Dumpty Habit-Breakers

Traveling preschoolers seem more prone to falling out of bed. These tactics may help keep away those things-that-go-bump-in-the-night-and-then-crawl-in-bed-with-you-to-kick-you-in-the-kidneys-till-the-alarm-goes-off:

- Push one side of the bed against a wall, if possible. (Be courteous and push it back before you go home.)
- Rearrange the covers so that your children sleep across the width. This gives them extra rolling room. Or tuck the bedclothes in extra tightly.
- Play "Roll Around" before bed. Have your child roll around the bed, middle to edges, until she has a good physical memory of its dimensions.
- Put the kid on the floor. A sleeping bag is great, but blankets will do. Kids' bones don't mind the hard floor like yours do.
- Cushion the fall. Pile extra pillows or chair cushions next to the bed. If you're lucky, the kid will sleep right through a tumble.

Night Noise Masks

The different sounds of a new place—whether they're street noises or unfamiliar quiet—will keep many preschoolers bright-eyed and bushy-tailed. Use fans, a radio tuned to static, or even your low humming to create some sleep-inducing white noise. You can also buy tapes or machines that play nature sounds. Tapes of children's songs or stories work well as bedtime soothers at home or on the road, but try to stick with familiar ones. I know one energetic mom who even taped the sounds of her daughter's city bedroom to play on country vacations.

Travels with Ted-Ted
TAKING CARE OF LOVEYS AND OTHER VALUABLES

The thought of losing a treasured lovey, whether it's a stuffed animal, a favorite blanket, or your wife's old satin teddy, is so horrible to contemplate that many families opt for leaving it at home. But, as you've probably realized if your child is attached to a lovey, that strategy means your kid is deprived of his special thing during a stressful time when he needs it more than ever. And, most significantly, that means that *no one gets any sleep at night*. Fortunately, it is possible to bring your lovey and keep it too! Here are tips from a parent who has successfully toted Ted-Ted—the bear, not the ladies' undergarment—over more than a dozen states, four countries, and two continents.

Stunt Double

This works for some kids (not mine). Acquire a special Travel Lovey (of which you will naturally have multiples). Aim for something small—a travel-sized lovey, like travel-sized toothpaste. Pretending play may help your child feel comfortable with Main Lovey's decision to stay behind, as will sending postcards to him. Before you leave home, ask your child if he'd like to leave Lovey in a special spot or maybe position him in a window or other prominent spot to watch for the family's safe return.

Head Count

Your child's lovey probably feels like a member of the family—so go ahead and include him officially. If you have more than one kid, you probably do a quick head count every time you leave some place. Just increase your mental checklist by one. I demanded to actually *see* Ted-Ted, just as I wanted visual confirmation that each kid had made it into the car. A ritual in which your child has her lovey wave good-bye to every place you leave will shift at least some of the burden of remembering to her. At a minimum, make a pack-up list of all the items you should have on departure (a good idea anyhow), and list Lovey prominently. Or, do what one friend of mine does with loveys and other "don't forget" items: store them with your car keys or plane tickets.

Temporary Storage

On arrival, when you help your child get settled in "her place," make sure you help Lovey get settled in his too. Someplace *visible* or *safely locked up* is good, but *not* on a bed, where he could get mixed in with linens or lost beneath bedding. (I know people who have spent some tense moments and much cash negotiating with hotel laundry staff to search mountains of linens.) I recommend making a special "bed" or seat of honor *inside a suitcase* for Lovey to rest in by day.

Take care especially that Lovey will be safe from pets and other potential assassins. We once left our oldest child's beloved Pooh Bear on a low chair when we were visiting relatives. When we all went out to lunch, the host's puppy "got" Pooh. Pooh's surgery included a stuff and fluff brain transplant, an impressive number of stitches, a false eye—and lots of lollipops for his distraught owner. Fortunately, everyone survived this experience—you might not be so lucky.

Lovey Leashes

You're probably safer discouraging your child from toting his lovey down to build sandcastles, but many kids will be determined to show Lovey the view from the Statue of Liberty or will need him for the courage to shake hands with a giant Donald Duck. *Don't count on a preschooler to hold on tightly to her lovey* at all times, no matter how precious he is to her. Either fasten a collar around the lovey's neck (The cat-sized ones will fit many stuffed animals.) and put it on strangulation-tight, or sew on a loop. Then attach the lovey securely to something you're unlikely to lose (purse, clothing) with a "leash" of some sort. Try safety pin chains, Velcro straps, or key leashes (the kind that hook onto keys and belt loops). For safety, the leash should be too short to get wrapped around a neck. Carrying Lovey in a zippered pack is another good alternative—you can get ones with clear or mesh pockets if your child needs him to be able to "see" out. My daughter liked to carry her loveys, of which she had a succession, in a doll baby carrier that she wore (and sometimes I got stuck wearing—try to look sophisticated and untouristy in that getup). Naturally, your child's lovey will be wearing his dog tags at all times, won't he? And those waterproof, indestructible dog tags or other labels will be firmly attached, won't they?

Looking for the Wiggle Room
WHERE AND HOW TO PLAY WHEN YOU'RE AWAY

Preschoolers need to play wherever they are. The mess, destruction, and/or frustration that result if you fail to anticipate and structure this need will drive you insane. Possibly it will also drive everyone within hearing distance insane. Try these ideas:

Create a Play Zone

Designate an area of your accommodations for kid play. Make sure the boundaries are clear and that the area is safe. Tie up long cords from drapes or blinds, push furniture with sharp corners or hard parts out of the way, and state rules for acceptable play (usually, no running, no wrestling, etc.) Don't assume that kids will know the rules automatically. Set out toys you've brought from home, keeping in mind that rotating

LITERATURE LINKS

Stories about loveys who go astray may convince your child to leave hers at home, help her think up a creative way to take it along, or give her hope for reunion if the worst happens. Some to read: *Where Are You, Blue Kangaroo?* by Emma Chichester Clark, about a little girl who is always forgetting her stuffed friend; *Owen* by Kevin Henkes, about a family who helps think up a way for a boy to have his blanket and "leave" it too; and *Jamaica's Find* by Juanita Havill, which examines the problem of a lost lovey from the point of view of the finder.

them works on the road as well as at home. Also—and this part is very important—designate a container or dresser drawer to be the toy corral, and help with a cleanup before leaving in the morning and at bedtime. If you're staying with friends and relatives, be assertive about asking where it's okay for the kids to play, and make sure you tidy up frequently.

Let Them Jump on the Bed and Run Down the Hall

Really—but have them do it in ways that are safe and respectful of property and other guests (and only at motels/hotels, not the homes of friends or relatives). Kids who run down the hallway (without screaming or banging) during the middle of the day are not going to disturb people excessively, and it's simply too tempting to avoid. We also allow small children to play the following jump-on-the-bed games (well before bedtime):

- ***The Flop Toss*** Kids line up. Dad tosses them, floppy style, into the middle of the big bed (preferably the one that the kids are sleeping in). They hop off and run around to get in line again. Continue until Dad is tired.
- ***The Big Sit-Down*** Kid stands in middle of bed. Jumps three times in place, then flops onto his bottom. Tries to bounce back up into standing position. Usually fails. Gets off and races around to try again. Not for kids over fifty pounds.
- ***Roll-Over, Roll-Over*** Position kid at foot of bed. Have him roll up to the headboard and back into your arms. Don't forget to catch him.

Playground Sightseeing

Investigating how the rest of the world plays is one of the most appealing sightseeing adventures for young kids. We always search for public parks and school playgrounds to try out. Teach your kids how to make temporary playmates, and you can have some of those nice world-shrinking cultural moments too. (Kids should introduce themselves by name, age, and where they're from and ask the same of other children. They should then say, "Want to play on the _____?") To find playgrounds, which are not always listed in guide-books, ask your hosts or the hotel desk clerk, stop families on the street (Really—usually they're happy to help, even in big cities.), and look up school addresses in the phone book (keeping in mind that some urban schoolyards are locked).

Add a Dose of Imagination Whenever You Can

It's easy to get grumpy and serious while traveling, but remember that the same imagination strategies that keep kids cooperative with routines (and ordeals) at home will ease the way when you're away.

Danger Ranger, Jr.
SAFETY TIPS FOR HOME-AWAY-FROM-HOME DANGERS

TALES FROM THE TRENCHES

Once when we checked into a hotel room that was more spacious than our usual accommodations, I sighed with satisfaction and said to my husband, "I'm so glad this place has a little wiggle room." One of my kids then spent longer than usual investigating the place, opening closet doors, peering in the bathroom, and so on. Finally I asked him what was up. "I'm just looking for the wiggle room," he explained. "I want to see what it looks like."

You'll be much happier if you teach your child "Leaves of three, let them be" *before* he finds that patch of poison ivy. And he'll feel much braver if he knows that sharks *cannot* live in the lake at your cabin. Here are some tips on keeping your child safe from new dangers in an unfamiliar place, and helping him feel brave and happy in the face of new scary things.

Environment-Proof Your Kid

What you want to do is find the delicate balance between alerting your child to possible dangers and making him crazy-fearful. Do a scan of possible risks in your new environment and talk to your child about them, emphasizing what he can do to keep himself safe. But keep in mind that he probably won't remember any of the lessons after just one discussion, and that you'll need to be active in helping him keep safe. Preschool children bear careful watching in new places.

A Handful of Safety Rules for Small Kids to Know

This list is hardly comprehensive, but it should cover many of the major risks that may be new to your child on a trip. Introduce a few at a time, as appropriate.

- *"Never go in the water without an adult.* **Ever.***"* Drowning is still a much bigger threat to young kids than sharks or strangers. Even in a guarded pool or when wearing a life jacket, a preschool child is *not* drown-proof.
- *"Always tell Mommy or Daddy before you go anywhere."* Make sure your young child knows not to venture onto balconies or into cupboards, vehicles, caves, or other places where he could get trapped unless you are with him. Review stranger rules too.
- *"Leaves of three, let them be."* There are safe plants with three leaves, but being overcautious will still keep your kid out of the poison ivy or poison oak.
- *"Stay on paths and out of tall weeds, especially if you aren't wearing long pants and bug spray."* Ticks, chiggers, and other bite-y guys live in those kinds of places. Light-colored clothing attracts fewer bugs (bees, mosquitoes, etc.). If you are in tick country, do a check nightly. (The deer ones are minute—look carefully.)
- *"Keep your distance from wild animals—never touch one without checking with an adult."* Help your child learn which bugs and little critters he can handle safely. He should be especially careful around wild animals that seem

sick or aren't afraid of him. If you'll be in areas with populations of dangerous animals, like alligators or bears, learn how to stay safe and share the information with your child.

- *"Do not eat any plants, berries, or mushrooms you find without checking with an adult."* Someday, your child may be able to identify wild blackberries or blueberries and nibble without double-checking, but preschoolers are prone to making mistakes.

- *"Don't drink 'wild' water—it might have germs that can make you sick."* Water from lakes, ponds, streams, and puddles needs to be boiled or treated before being consumed. And drinking salty ocean water can cause severe dehydration.

- *"Stay on the curb, and hold hands to cross the street."* This probably isn't a new danger, but it bears reviewing. Preschool children cannot safely cross *any* street alone. Their judgment of speed and distance is poor, and it's hard for drivers to see them.

- *"Look before you leap."* With preschoolers, the literal meaning of this is important. Encourage them to check out the height of their perch and the landing area before jumping off something. New playground equipment, bunk beds, and big rocks all pose danger to reckless young kids.

- *"When in doubt, check it out."* Encourage your child to trust his instincts. If something is giving him a funny feeling or worrying him, he should check it out with you.

Busting Unreasonable Fears

This three-pronged approach will resolve most fears:
- Reassurance and information
- Gradual approach or desensitization
- Time

The tricky part, of course, is time, because a preschooler may need a *lot* of time, in some cases *years*, until development gives him the thinking skills and experience he needs to understand and feel capable of handling a particular frightening situation. But meanwhile, your reassurance and support can help him keep his fear in bounds. Don't forget to bust your unreasonable fears, too, so that you don't inadvertently pass them along to your child.

If You're Traveling with the Crocodile Hunter Clone

Some children are just naturally more curious and less fearful. *These kids will require extra vigilance in new environments,* because they will discover dangers you never even imagine. Assign partners to kids like this, trade duties frequently with your spouse (because watching them will wear you out), and search out or arrange safe places for them to play and explore.

CHAPTER EIGHT

Because You Didn't Go All That Way Just to Listen to Incessant Whining, Did You?

A few years ago, I drove my three kids to Cleveland for the day while my husband stayed home to catch up on some work. We normally have a great time in Cleveland (Really, and yes, I already know all the jokes about the burning river and all that other stuff.) where my folks and two of my siblings live. But that weekend, things were just off. My kids had colds and missed their dad, Lucy's Pastry Shop was closed, and it rained so hard we had to skip the outing we'd planned with my parents. On Sunday evening when we started home in the driving rain, we were all feeling a bit down and bedraggled. I snapped rather fiercely at the kids whining in the backseat as we headed into a twenty-mile construction zone where orange barrels narrowed the turnpike to a single lane with no shoulder.

And then it happened. The windshield wipers, which were turned to their highest setting, froze and wouldn't start again. (If you ever have to drive a carload of small kids through a construction zone on the freeway in the pouring rain in the dark without windshield wipers, here's how you do it: lean your head out the window and peer at the car ahead of you.)

Fortunately, we made it to the next exit and even found our way to the nearest (and apparently only) service station in the area. It was closed. In the end, none of the fussing I did with fuses or knobs or wiping got the blades working. So we drove to the seedy motel down the street and took a room. We called my husband to let him know of our circumstances, ordered a pizza, and settled in to spend the evening without pajamas, toothbrushes, or so much as a book for a bedtime story. We played charades, wiped our teeth with the washcloths, and then I read the story of Noah and the flood from the Gideon's Bible in the nightstand. All night I listened to the *thwish, thwish* of cars on the freeway behind the motel and tossed and turned while my daughter beside me did her best impression of a giant squid attacking its prey.

In the morning, the rain had stopped. We bought cereal and milk at a convenience store and had breakfast in the room while watching "Scooby-Doo," which would normally be a no-no on a school morning. Then we piled in the car and drove home, singing songs and playing games. That night when the kids told their dad about our unexpected "vacation," they sighed and said, "We were soooo lucky. That was a great trip!"

I tell that story, because if my kids can turn a day-trip to Cleveland—complete with rain, disappointment, and car troubles—into a "great trip," your kid can have fun on his vacations to Disney World or the beach or wherever. Just look at what made this trip wonderful in the kids' eyes: a few normally forbidden treats and an unexpected adventure. That's a pretty simple formula that you should be able to replicate wherever you go.

Having said that, I know that having fun on a trip with little kids can be harder than you'd think. That's why this chapter has ideas for avoiding or dealing with the common whine-makers, like sand in the toilet paper, relatives who play favorites, and tired tootsies. There are also tips for threading your way through vacation minefields like buying souvenirs or taking photographs. There's a mini-section on helping young children enjoy big (and pricey) amusement parks. But most importantly, there are ideas for adopting a vacation have-fun attitude and a list of simple, inexpensive pleasures that can turn even the most miserable vacation into a great trip. Take Joy!

Wee-Minders
THE RULES OF PLEASURE

You'd think that having fun on vacation would come automatically, but often it doesn't. It may be particularly hard to click into pleasure mode when you have young kids, because the hard work of maintaining small fry doesn't take a vacation when you do. Although the bother of childcare won't completely disappear, there are ways to shift from the Business as Usual to the Isn't This Great! Channel.

How to Have Fun

Location, location, location may work for real estate, but attitude, attitude, attitude is what makes a good—or lousy—vacation. Try these ideas to help your child get and stay in the travel adventure spirit:

- *Monitor Your Own Attitude—It's Catching* If you're relaxed, your kids are more likely, but not guaranteed, to be too. But, if you're unhappy or angry, your kids *definitely* will be too.
- *Eat Enough Ice Cream* I've personally always considered that to be the main point of vacation. Make a point of doing *something* that seems decadent and special to your child, whether it's buying five balloons when one is really plenty, or eating normally forbidden Chocolate Frosted Sugar Bombs for breakfast. (My kids' favorite vacation ritual is that each gets to choose a box of his favorite cereal, even if it's outrageously expensive and sugary and I don't have a coupon.) Certainly you don't want to do anything that will harm your child's health or put you in debt, but vacations are a time to briefly relax many of the rules that govern everyday lives and put pleasure at the forefront.
- *Remember: The Best Part Is Being Together* For many young children, simply being together *really* is the best part. Share group hugs, hold hands and skip, and sing songs like

the traditional kids' song, "The More We Get Together" (sung to the tune of "Did You Ever See a Lassie?").

The more we get together, together, together,
The more we get together, the happier we'll be!

Top Choice Awards

It's a *family* vacation, right? That means *everyone* gets to have fun. List possible activities (editing out those you can't afford, can't do, or can't stand), and let everyone pick his top three choices. Then, make a big effort to do everyone's top choice (and preferably two of the top three), even if the rest of you think the activity is dorky or boring. (And those who think it's dorky or boring still have to act halfway enthusiastic and patient during it. No more than three deep sighs and five eye rolls per person per outing.)

If someone's top choice is inappropriate for others (e.g., an older sibling wants to go on a roller coaster that the preschooler is too short—or scared—for), don't forget the divide and conquer strategy. Yes, I know that places like Disney will let you stand in line and trade off riding turns while someone waits with a younger child, *but would you want to wait in line for an hour and a half and then not even get to go on the ride?* Add to that imaginary scenario that you're four years old and have tired feet and a low frustration tolerance. Okay, then! You can be mature and take the little guy on It's a Small World yet again while the others ride Space Mountain. And later your spouse can take your place while you and the big kid go on the waterslides.

Look Out! Don't Fall in the Tourist Traps!
BEWARE THE EVIL HAVE-TOS

Tourist traps are not just those places advertised on seventy-eight billboards between Exits 14 and 19 that turn out to have a dozen sickly goats, a bloated pig, and a three-acre gift shop. They're also all those vacation have-tos, whether it's an ingrained belief from your childhood that you must wear heels and a suit on an airplane (only true if you're the pilot or flight attendant) or the list of places that you *can't* miss (according to the travel agent who doesn't even own any shoes as young as your kids). Here's an alert of common pitfalls and ideas for skirting the edge of them without falling in.

Visiting Relatives

Not necessarily bad, of course—but then I've got great relatives. Still, dragging a reluctant, rambunctious preschooler to spend the afternoon at the antique-studded home of your childless second cousin is not mandatory just because you're related and in the same town. Ease the stress on your child (and yourself) by doing one of the following: visit briefly on the phone, promise yourself you'll send a long newsy letter when you get home while being careful never to mention that you were in town, or meet your relative at a park or other place where your child can play freely while you visit.

Hitting Hot Spots—All of Them

Whirlwind tours aren't that much fun even when you're twenty and childfree—and they're definitely not fun when you're forcing small whiny children to come with you. Pick the places you must see, the activities you must do—and then cut that number in half. You'll probably still have too many plans, but you can be flexible and eliminate a few more as you go. At a minimum, plan for last-second detours to something that looks like more fun than what you were going to do—and for repeats of things the kids discover they *love!* Remember, you're dealing with preschoolers—those short guys whose motto is "Do it again!"

Spending Lots of Money

I know—I've already advised you to splurge. The trick is to splurge within a budget so you don't go home to months of skimping or anxiety. Young kids are easily satisfied with simple pleasures—my kids got a bigger kick out of catching lizards at the hotel than they did out of breakfast with Mickey Mouse. (Actually, I can't swear to that, because we decided to skip the expensive Mickey meal since everyone was having so much fun catching lizards.) See "Sooth-enirs" page 213 and "Cheap and Easy Smile-Finder List" on page 218 for ideas on cutting corners while still having a great time. And set a firm budget for extras beyond your basic expenses (food, lodging, and travel). Let everyone vote on how to spend it.

Dumping

There is no law that you must hire an outrageously expensive babysitter who gives your child separation anxiety and nightmares—and makes you pay in lost sleep for the rest of your vacation. If it makes your kid (or you) significantly uncomfortable to have an unfamiliar caregiver, consider saving your cash for a dinner out when you're home again and can hire the high school kid down the street whom your kid adores. On the other hand, if you can persuade your kid that your alone time is also a treat for him, (because he loves the on-site child care center and staff, or the videos and goodies you've offered have him jumping for joy), there's no law that says you have to be together every minute of a family vacation. Look, too, for less obvious arrangements, like trading off (and *trading* is the key word) with relatives (especially ones who have similar-aged children) or taking turns with your spouse for alone time.

"I Said 'Smile and Look Happy,' Dang Nabbit!"
SURVIVING PHOTO OPS

Some of the grumpiest moments in our family travels have come when—and because—I've been trying to record for posterity how happy we were. Kids chafe at the interruptions caused by photography, as well as the need to hold still or do something they just don't feel like doing. I can't give you tips on taking prizewinning photos or videos (main advice: make sure there's really film in the camera), but I can give you ideas that might help you capture some grins, or at least keep the kids from hating your guts while you're trying.

Candid Camera

Instead of interrupting your child and getting him to smile at the camera, discreetly take pictures of him in action. This will work better if someone else is supervising the kid. You probably won't get many full-face head shots, but you won't annoy the heck out of your child either. Plus, the pictures will reflect reality better and they'll probably be more interesting.

Okay, You Still Want the Smile Shot—
Here Are Some Better Ways Than "Say Cheese!" to Coax One

- "Quick! Frown!"
- "Isn't That Steve from 'Blue's Clues'?"
- "Everyone say 'Diarrhea!'"
- "Make your silliest face!" (Click—you really have to take that photograph for the next one to work.) "Now your biggest smile."
- The method acting approach: "You've just found out I'm buying you a whole mountain of cotton candy. Show me how you'd look. Lights, camera, *action!*"
- Or, my favorite: "Smile and look happy, dang nabbit!"

Group Shots Where Most of the Kids Aren't Crying

The big group shot is especially challenging with young kids, and you might as well resign yourself that some of them will be crying. Or picking their noses. But to minimize the number of criers try

- Arranging all the adults and older kids, getting the camera focused and set, and then popping the little guys in at the last second;
- Taking the picture upside down. You can either have the kids all bend over to look at the camera upside down—surprisingly effective and interesting—or *you* can bend over to take the picture, which usually surprises everyone enough that they smile briefly through their tears and take their fingers out of their nostrils. Other silly approaches can work too.

Think up one of your own and make it a tradition! And that brings me to…

The Traditional, Yet Wacky, Shot

Your child will probably stand still for a traditional shot that you take on every vacation—provided it's a goofy one instead of a boring pose standing in front of your hotel. For example, my oldest once fell in a fountain when my sister was watching him. Since then, we regularly take pictures to send to her in which he appears to be falling into yet another fountain. Kyle always cooperates for those photos, even though he's now a cool thirteen year old. One of my editors contributed another great idea— her family always takes a few *Where's Waldo?* shots. Later it's fun trying to spot the kid who is barely visible behind a statue. Also see the Klutz book *Tricky Pix: Do-It-Yourself Trick Photography* by Paula Weed. The book is intended for kids, but is simple enough for technologically challenged adults to use, and it includes great how-to information on taking fun shots in which your child will appear to be headless or holding a tiny parent in her hand. And it comes with a real reusable 35mm camera that might actually have film in it.

Come Out from Behind the Lens

Just give up at the outset. (Figure you'll have forgotten to load film in the camera anyway.) At any rate, don't get so caught up recording your vacation that you forget to "be there" with your child. You won't have pictures of the moments you're interacting with him, but those times are the ones your child is most likely to remember fondly years from now. Talk with your child about taking "mental snapshots" by focusing on a certain moment in a way that he'll be able to remember vividly later. Call his attention to the feel of the wind on his face, the smell of the salt spray, the way the sand pulls away from under his feet as the wave recedes, the warm moist feeling of your clasped hands. Make sure to pull out the mental photo album from time to time, too, so you can both enjoy revisiting those moments you've captured.

Sooth-enirs
COMFORTING MEMORIES TO TAKE AWAY

"Souvenirs." Does that word conjure up T-shirts and little knickknacks that bring a rush of happy memories? Or does it make you shudder as you remember trying to quell a major tantrum caused by your refusal to buy your child the $49.99 shark's head that sang "Under the Sea" in six languages? The only way to avoid the latter memory is to stay out of the traditional tacky souvenir shop with anyone under twenty-eight. Fortunately, the following souvenirs can usually be obtained without setting foot in one of those unpleasant places—and they may even bring a rush of happy memories! Maybe!

A Disposable Camera

For your kid, not you. The resulting pictures will be horrendous, because they'll have been taken by a little kid who puts his finger over the lens, looks over the viewfinder instead of through it, and jerks the camera violently every time he pushes the shutter release. But you'll get them developed anyhow, and your child will be delighted with the results. And maybe since you let him take a nice smiling picture of you, he'll let you take one of him.

A Taste of Vacation and Other Comforting Memories

Next February, a bottle of maple syrup will help you recall that delicious pancake breakfast in the Vermont cabin much more effectively than a fake Native American drum purchased at the resort's gift shop will. And the syrup will soon be used up and not cluttering every spare inch of shelf space in your kid's room. Plus, it will be quiet. Most kids readily acquire edible souvenirs—just make them wait to consume them until you're at least on the way home. Other "comfort souvenirs" include: blankets or pillows (good for the trip home if you forgot to bring any), a tape of relevant music or nature sounds (You might even get away with having your kid record five minutes or so of sounds regularly and considering that his souvenir.), or anything you find your child needs but you didn't bring. (That's why we have lots of souvenir sweatshirts.)

Ephemera

That's a fancy word for "stuff most people have the sense to throw away." It includes items like ticket stubs, paper placemats, brochures, amusement park wristbands, and all the other junk piled up in my "Put in Scrapbook" boxes. Be smart, and make your child attach these goodies to stiff paper as he acquires them. Or save them in sheet protectors or zipper seal bags (which you can punch holes in for saving in a binder). I also include little kid collectibles, like broken seashells, "foreign" pinecones, and ratty-looking feathers in this category. At the holidays, you and your child can glue his collectibles around wooden picture frames and give them to the relatives. And they'll have to accept them. Other people have their kids collect rocks, then use a Sharpie marker to record place, date, and a memory to save.

ON THE WEB

The picture frame idea is making me think you might be the crafty sort—and if you are, you can also *make* craft-souvenirs, like sand-cast plaster-of-Paris footprints, nature print T-shirts, or sand and seashell mold candles. The website www.family.go.com has some good directions for making these and other good vacation memory crafts—just click on "Craft Finder" and enter the craft you'd like to try.

Toys You Could Buy at Home That Have Nothing to Do with Your Vacation

I resisted this category mightily for years, and was surprised to discover when I finally gave in that: 1) They were usually less expensive but higher quality and better play value than the things designated as genuine souvenirs; and 2) Years later, the kids still pick them up and say, "Remember when I got this when we went to the ranch and I loved to play with it in the pine needles?" Go figure.

MORE TO KNOW

If you're taking an international trip, there are some great, inexpensive souvenirs for young kids that you can collect in ordinary stores: Band-Aids (a Best Bet), school or art supplies like markers and notebooks, the foreign version of some at-home favorite like Pokemon cards, spare coins or stamps, and kid's books in a foreign language.

It's All Relative
GETTING ALONG WHEN GETTING TOGETHER

Whether the whole extended clan is getting together or you're just spending a weekend with grandparents, reunions are one of the most common reasons that families with young children travel. And when get-togethers go wrong, they can be dramatically painful. These ideas won't help with severe dysfunction, but they may help your child (and you) cope with some of the usual problems and embrace the special love that relatives have in abundance.

Spoilers

Here's the rule: Grandparents are allowed to spoil their grandkids. Even if that means breaking some of your rules, *as long as it does not pose harm to your child's long-term health or safety.* Thus, they may not let your child ride in the car unbuckled, but they can say yes to an extra dessert, especially if visits together are infrequent. The same thing, in a little more moderation, goes for aunts and uncles. The following problems, though, require intervention:

- *One Child is Favored or Disfavored* You have to act—and make sure it stops. Over time, the imbalance will spread unhappiness like ripples in a pond. Assume the best, though—

often grandparents just know one child better or less. Help them out by describing interests, giving them one-on-one time with whoever is neglected, encouraging the left-out guys to express affection. If measures like these don't work, say something (gently and tactfully, of course—but firmly.)

- *They Aren't in Tune with Your Child* And it's leading to tears, bratty behavior, or other fusses. Step in and advocate gently for your child. Say things that help your child cope or save face, while not undermining an important bond. "We had a long trip, Mom, and he's tired. He'll be ready to go to the park with you after he settles in and gets some rest." Talk with your child and give him reassurance and information. "Grandma has been waiting so long to see you that it's hard for her to keep waiting now that we're here. But she understands. You can cuddle with me for a bit until you're used to it here and ready to play."

Cheek-Pincher Pointers

Preschoolers can go suddenly shy (or worse, rude) when they meet overly friendly relations. If your child chronically has a problem with this, forewarn adults to go slow and give her time to warm up to them. Prepare your child, too, by showing her photos of the people she'll be meeting, talking about why they love her, and role-playing a greeting. If that strategy doesn't work—or you didn't get a chance to put it in place in advance—try these approaches:

- *Getting Your Child on the Same Level* You'd feel a bit taken aback too, if a giant you didn't recognize grabbed you up in a bear hug. Lift your child up, stand her on a chair, or encourage the swoopy adult to sit on the floor with her.
- *Teaching Your Child to Shake Hands* Adults usually find it charming when a small child extends her hand in greeting, and I've noticed it makes most of them tone the greeting down. Worth a try.

- **Supporting Your Child** If she's balking at kissing the cheek of a relative she doesn't remember, don't make her. Tell the other adult that, for safety, you're teaching your child to decide when someone can touch her. If a relative is too rough or rambunctious and you can see that your child is uncomfortable, step in and gently redirect the interaction. Be firm in stopping it, if necessary, but keep in mind that kids often tolerate and enjoy roughhousing with exciting uncles, fun grandpas, and big cousins.

Cousin Magic

My sister-in-law, Karen Baicker, coined this term to describe both the special relationship that cousins have and the positive influence they can have on each other's behavior. Cousins have the "we're family" comfort level of siblings, but without the rivalry and too-much-togetherness baggage of actual brothers and sisters. Encourage younger cousins to look up to and admire the big ones, find opportunities for the older ones to teach or help the little guys, and make time for the same-age ones to play uninterrupted. Other techniques for building the magical cousin bond:

LITERATURE LINKS

Books can help prepare your child for what it's like to get together with relatives and give her a positive attitude. Try *The Relatives Came* and *Henry and Mudge in the Family Trees*, both by Cynthia Rylant.

- **The Cousin Sleepover** Mix and match kids in sleeping quarters. If everyone's too excited to sleep, try an all-but sleepover. Put the kids in pajamas and beds for pillow fights and pillow talk, but then separate them for sleep.
- **Cousins versus Grown-ups** The old us-versus-them trick cements friendships quickly. Try simple board or card games (On vacation, play with candy markers that winners get to

eat when the game is done.) or handicapped races, games of tag, or swimming pool contests.

- *After-Glue* Maintain cousin magic after the vacation by sharing "handy-downs" as my kids call their favored used-to-be-my-cousin's outfits—or even the occasional handy-up, when a small child receives a too-big gift. Arrange for the kids to chat on the phone, send just-for-fun small gifts, and keep track of big life events like lost teeth or first days of school.

Cheap and Easy Smile-Finder List
TOP TEN IDEAS FOR ALMOST ANYWHERE

Just as my preschoolers usually preferred the big box to the big present, they often enjoyed the cheap or freebie activities more than the expensive excursions on vacation. Here are some of our favorite don't-break-the-bank vacation delights.

Throwing Rocks in Water

They don't get any cheaper than this. The advanced version is skipping rocks (challenging for most preschoolers), but simply dropping pebbles, tossing stones, or lugging small (okay, very small) boulders to heave into water ranging from puddles to oceans will occupy the average preschooler happily for a half hour or more. My middle kid would have skipped pretty much any amusement park ride to do this. We also got one of those giant slingshot launchers, and the kids get a kick out of helping launch broken shells or "sandballs" into the deep (when there aren't any bathers).

Sweet Stuff

Ice cream, candy, lemonade, and other junk become more than just tasty treats when you weave them into an outing, or better yet, a ritual. Develop traditions, like skipping to the candy shop for saltwater taffy on the last day at the beach, or guzzling lemonade with Granny in the hammock each afternoon.

Animal Adventures

What kid doesn't love chasing pigeons or tossing bread crumbs to ducks or seagulls? (Just take care the kid doesn't get attacked and over-whelmed—I still remember my terror at being chased by a hissing swan when I was about four.) My kids also devote hours to pursuing frogs, toads, and small lizards. Trips to any animal-related venue will be a hit too (though of course more expensive). Hands-on places like petting zoos, pony rides, and please-touch aquarium tanks are especially entertaining.

Messy Play

Water or sand play are obvious choices at the beach or a hotel with a pool, but you can improve on the usual if you keep your mind open. For example, a simple addition like a *real* shovel completely transforms the digging in the sand experience. (Look for the narrow shovel that gar-deners call a "poaching spade"—it's small and light enough for many kids.) Many botanical gardens and some urban parks have really inter-esting interactive fountains that kids can play in. And keep your eyes open for *small* streams and creeks, but supervise play very carefully—there may be unexpected deep places. Even the fort your child builds with sticks, stones, pine needles, and moss in the dirt pile at your picnic site may be his favorite vacation memory.

Balloons, Bubbles, Balls, and More

Traditional playthings may take on added meaning when they are shared with the whole family in a new locale. Bubbles really zip and dart in a sea breeze, and a balloon bobbing along behind may bring magic to an other-wise long and tiring walk. Intergenerational flag football games, especially where no one tries to win, tend to dissolve in rolling-around laughter. (Remember to let the tiniest guys try a center sneak—they're really good at it.) And you can't go wrong with a kite—which doesn't need to be a real one. Experiment to find things that will "fly" when you tie a string to them and run along the beach. (No, you may not use your sister's underpants. Oh, all right, just this once, because it's vacation. But just the old holey pair.)

Treasure Maps

When we went to visit one of the houses my father lived in as a child, he took us to nearby "Penny Hill." He then produced a map that he said he'd made as a kid, marking the spot where he'd buried a bunch of pennies. He gave us each a trowel and we spent a great afternoon hopefully unearthing various mounds. Finally found the cache too! Funny, wasn't it, how some pennies from the 1960s found their way into his 1930s treasure trove? You can make a map and bury a treasure if you don't have a pre-planted one—and come back another time to see if it's still there.

Watch Street Performers

Most big cities have a square where you can find regular performances of a bewildering variety. Your kids will enjoy the magic of fire-eaters, the silliness of mimes (even if you don't), the drama of a puppet show—and the chance to put some money in when the performers pass the hat.

Go for a Ride

These may range from cheap to pricey, but there's nearly always one to be found. Try boats of every size, shape, and kind, from rowboats to steam paddle replicas (Just be sure your child is wearing an approved PFD on small ones.). Go for a horse and buggy tour or choose a carnival ride. Or take a ride on a trolley, bus, train (steam, commuter), incline or tram, cable car, or subway. Kids love them all.

Fishing

Young kids can fish without a license, but unlucky grown-ups need them unless they're fishing in the surf. In my experience, even pretend fishing with a string tied on a stick (maybe with a paper clip hook) will work for fifteen or twenty minutes, provided there are minnows to watch. But the real thing, with bait and success, will be a highlight of almost any preschooler's trip, unless you're my daughter who suddenly realized that the worms *die* when the fish swallow them. We (meaning my husband Steve) recommend using an inexpensive but name brand rod with a spinning reel (the kind released with a button). Ask other fisher folk in the area what they're using for bait. For more tips on gear and strategy, see the book, *Fishing with Small Fry: How to Hook Your Kids on Fishing* by Bob Ellsberg.

Working Together

Make sure to include the kids in the "work" of vacation, too, whether it's husking fresh corn for dinner, packing suitcases, or hunting for bait. Having your undivided attention and feeling important to the family may make these moments their favorite of all. (Okay, probably not, especially if they have older siblings who have taught them the art of work avoidance—but it *could* happen, and I haven't been able to think up anything else for my tenth idea.)

Hey! There's Nothing Here But Sand and Water!
SANDING DOWN ROUGH BEACH ISSUES

I love the beach. So much so that I'll endure two eight-hour drives with three cranky preschoolers and a week of dumping sand out of the sheets, crunching sand-laced cereal for breakfast, snuggling sand-encrusted bodies, and even shaking stray grains out of the toilet paper (not to mention the whole packing/unpacking/packing/unpacking ordeal, the sunscreen battles, the squabbles over whose turn it is to use the big shovel, and so on) to get my annual fix. In the process, I *have* noticed that there are a few tactics that can help keep fears and sand-in-the-toilet paper to a minimum. Here they are:

Fear of the Big Water

There's no getting around it—the ocean is huge and the waves loud, enormous, and surprising. Especially when you're not much more than three feet tall. Yours will not be the first preschooler to shift from gleeful anticipation to stark terror and a desire to stay in the beach house 24-7 after his first glimpse of the real thing. Most kids come around and enjoy dabbling their toes in the surf after a few days, but you can speed the process through gradual approach and education. Set up your towels, umbrella, etc., well back from the waves, using something to screen the wind (and ocean view if necessary). Be sure to keep an eye on the tide, so that you maintain a safe cushion between you and the water. Each day, move a few feet closer to water. An inflatable kiddy pool is easily packed up, and lets you bring a pint-sized ocean to your child. Let her lick some of the salty water from her skin to get used to the taste. And demonstrate some of the cool properties of ocean water by dropping eggs into glasses of tap and ocean water—the egg will float easily in the ocean water. Be sure to hold her at first when you take her down near the surf. Before long, she'll be ready to play wave tag (where she tries not to let the incoming foam even touch her toes)—but for goodness sakes, don't let her get knocked over by a wave (like we did with our phobic daughter).

No Fear of the Big Water

This one is actually worse. Keep a seagull eye on this child every second (which you would be doing anyhow, of course—no beach reading for parents of preschoolers, sorry). Naturally, you don't want to terrify your child with tales of riptides, sharks, and man-o-war stings—but you will need to talk with him about the fact that the waves can be dangerous *so he must have a grown-up partner even to play near the water.* These kids, incidentally, are *not* phased by getting bowled over by a big wave. The only safe solution is *unflagging* vigilance. Then go ahead and enjoy your mer-child and his delight in the sea!

Creepy-Swimmies and Pinchy-Scuttlies

All those little creatures in the sand and water are a little too much like the ever-fearsome buzzy bees for some kids to relax and enjoy the beach scene. Distraction may give your child some temporary relief; get her zipping through a sand obstacle course (castles to leap over, holes to jump in, mounds to hop off) or playing a little run-down with the cousins. Then introduce her gradually to some of the more benign guys, like sand fiddlers. At first, you'll probably need to handle them for her, but after a while, you'll be too tired or busy to dig up more and more for her to watch scurry along and burrow back into the sand, so she'll have to do it herself. Let your child chase ghost crabs (the ones who live in holes well up on the beach) and she'll soon realize they're more frightened of her than the other way around. And stay out of the water on days when it's filled with jellyfish.

Sand-Off Strategies

Everyone will be less itchy and cranky if you remove sand before kids come inside or hop in the car. Keep jugs of water (filled at your destination) in the hot car, and you'll have nice warm water for the task. (Also, leave a clean towel in the car, so you'll have a sand-free one for drying.) Or set a dish tub or similar container outside your door, with a mat to step on, followed by a towel or bathmat just inside. If possible, make kids shower outside, but at a minimum, have them remove their suits and brush off their bodies—an amazing amount of sand can get trapped in girls' tight suits or boys' pockets. If necessary, make a changing room from a huge towel (either form a cylinder or hold the corners at kid-head level against the car or a wall). Have the kids use a hand towel to brush off inside it and slip on something clean. Finally, cornstarch is a good sand-removal alternative to water. (Wet skin quickly reattracts sand grains.) Just sprinkle some over the sandy places and brush off—a good idea *before* the kids put their hands in the cereal box. Oh—and for sand-free toilet paper, hide a roll for yourself in a tightly sealed freezer bag under the vanity.

No-Scream Sunscreen
ALMOST

My husband thinks the whole sunscreen thing is just a plot by the manufacturers of the stuff to drum up business. This is because he, like most of us of that generation, spent whole summers running around protected by little more than Bermuda shorts or poofy little "sunsuits" (the sunsuits were on me, not him) and *maybe* a smear of Sea 'N' Ski (probably SPF negative ten, since the point of suntan lotion then was to make you tan *more*). What he forgets is that lots of us now pay visits to the dermatologist to have "suspicious growths" excised. Plus, the sun—or rather the ozone, I think—has changed, and it really is easier to get fried these days. So, sorry, no choice: the sunscreen battle, like the booster seat one, is a fight you must wage and win.

Applications Not Accepted

That's what it should read on your child's squirmy uncooperative little body. Especially if you're trying to rub ice cold stuff on his wet, sandy body and rubbing off half his skin in the process. (And don't you hate the way sunscreen on wet skin makes those globby, waxy smears that will never rub in?) For comfort, thoroughness, and better protection, try these tips:

- Apply sunscreen well *before* your child heads out to the beach, pool, or any other place in the sun. It takes time to soak in and have maximum effectiveness.
- If you're the calm, organized sort, you can float the bottle or tube in warm water, so that it feels nice and warm and spreads more easily when you apply it. But if you're like me and scrambling around yelling at people about leaving their wet towels on the floor, making Kool-Aid, hunting for the sunglasses that are on the top of your head, and generally being a rushy morning mess, take a deep breath, pour a big blob in your palms, and rub your hands together well before applying the stuff.
- Make putting on sunscreen a pleasant sensory experience for your child *and* you. Slow your breathing, talk to your child in a soothing voice, and move your hands slowly and firmly, like you're massaging him. And talk about what you're doing and how nice it feels in a clear voice that your hus-

band can hear easily, so maybe he'll take a hint and not man-handle you when he does your back.

- Aim for *thorough* coverage, even if that means you use so much lotion that your child has white blotches all over—kids really don't care about that, and they *will* care about a bad sunburn. Don't forget those easy-to-miss places, like ears, lips, tops of feet, and right along the tan line.

- Try different applicators, like sprays, sticks, and wipes to see if any work better for you and your child. I've found the sprays disappointing—it's hard to tell if you got every spot, and you can't use them on faces, ears, etc.—and the over-spray gets, well, all over. But the sticks are great for lips and reapplications to shoulders or tops of feet. The wipes are too danged expensive for anything but emergencies. And I *hate* that stuff that goes on purple so you can see where you've missed, because I still can't tell, and it's always the only stuff left when it's my turn to put some on, and it doesn't seem to fade to invisible like it's supposed to, so I have to lie around on the beach looking like a *slightly* slimmer Barney.

- Remember, your child *can* get burned under his clothes, especially if they're wet. HA, HA, HA, HA! That's my hus-band's response—he says it's ridiculous, that he's never had so much as a slight change in hue under his clothes, and I have to admit that's been my experience too. But wearing a hat and maybe a T-shirt is a good idea, as is coming inside during the middle of the day to play Candy Bingo.

- Don't let your kid put sunscreen on your back. You'll end up with a large pale handprint right in the middle and painful red patches all over. Make your husband do it. Oh, never mind. Just give up and wear a shirt.

Happy Trails
WALKING WITH LESS WHINING

Wherever you travel, chances are good that your child will be expected to do more walking than usual. For many kids, this translates into also doing more complaining than usual. If you prefer not to trek down the long and whining road, it'll take some effort—but your preparation and support will pay off every step of the way.

Not-So-Cross Training

It is definitely a good idea to prepare for the extra physical demands of traveling before you ever leave home. Make your training walks fun and purposeful by setting them up as a personal best contest. For example, pick a distant-ish destination that your child can't yet walk to. Each day, walk a block or section of trail nearer to it. Celebrate big time when you reach it, perhaps planting a little cocktail toothpick flag to claim it—and be sure to take a photo of the achievement. My favorite training method from my childhood, though, was the "Evening Hike to Baskin-Robbins." To build endurance, we took increasingly longer routes home, which none of us minded (and indeed hardly noticed) because we were busy licking our cones and arguing about who got more pieces of gum in our bubble gum flavor scoops. If your child will be lugging some of her own baggage on your trip, build up those muscles in the process by loading up Puppy Pee-Pee and some other buddies for her to tote in a backpack or push in a doll stroller.

Good Gear = Good Cheer

I'm going to remind you *again* to make sure your child is outfitted with shoes *and* socks comparable to what you'd find comfortable—and be sure to pretest them before you leave. Moleskin is good for easing blisters that may develop and for preventing them in the first place. And (I know, nag, nag, nag) dress your child in layers that can be stripped or added to as needed. Another problem for small kids is toting backpacks that don't fit properly. Buy a good quality one in the smallest possible size and adjust the straps so that it rides tightly against your child's body and above her hips.

"The Aunts Go Marching One by One"

I always giggle when I hear that song because I think about the time one of the preschoolers I taught thought the song was about the uncle's wife kind of ants, and wanted to know why they were all going down in that hole. At any rate, a marching song or just about any song—can revive the troops' spirits when they're flagging, or help them pick up the pace. Try classics like "When the Saints Go Marching In" (letting kids pick another word to substitute for "Saints" like "Boogers" even though it throws off the meter).

Don't Walk

I mean that seriously. Options: shell out bucks for transportation more often than you normally would, or push the kid in a jogging stroller, or pull him in a wagon even though he's really too big for that sort of thing. Carry him piggyback for a block and then let him walk a few, then carry him like a sack of potatoes, and so on. Or—and this works amazingly well—run for one block, skip for the next, gallop down the third, and so on, changing frequently. This method will work even better if you make the effort to weave in a pretending theme, like riding mustangs on the range or blasting off in your spaceship, or being frogs hopping across a lily pad pursued by a sharp-toothed crocodile.

The Prep Step
WHAT TO DO *BEFORE* YOU HEAD TO THE AMUSEMENT PARK

Some preschoolers *adore* amusement parks, and some *detest* them. If your preschooler turns out to be of the latter persuasion, you'll probably be philosophical about the $6.95 you spent for her junior ticket at a nearby park. But I'm going to guess that you won't be so understanding when you discover she'll only go on the same ride over and over after you've shelled out big bucks for airfare, transfers, pricey hotel rooms, and multi-day passports to the Mouse Place. And, even when an amusement park visit is just a short stop on your itinerary, everyone's probably going to feel a mite disappointed if your child fails to enjoy the treat arranged specially with her in mind. And that's why preparation is essential. Try these ideas to get your child ready to be amused, or at least not terrified.

LITERATURE LINKS

There are about a zillion books and other references on visiting Disney. Probably they all have their good points, but if you want to narrow your search, I suggest *The Unofficial Guide to Walt Disney World With Kids* by Bob Sehlinger, which is updated regularly. There is also a picture-heavy guide directed at kids (though ones older than the preschool years) called *Birnbaum's Walt Disney World for Kids, By Kids* edited by Jill Safro that will give your child a taste of what's to come.

Info-Gathering

"Destination" parks will usually be written up in guidebooks for nearby cities. There are multiple guides on the really big parks, like Disney World, that feed you every detail you need to know from the locations of all the rest rooms to ratings of attractions to where to stay. The internet is also an increasingly useful source for investigating theme parks before you go. Many have websites that give operating information, directions, and descriptions of attractions, including restrictions. Recommendations from friends and neighbors may give you particularly useful personal perspectives.

One thing to keep in mind is that more and more amusement parks devote the majority of their amusing toward older audiences. This is true even for attractions that seem like they would be for little kids, so be sure to evaluate carefully if you want to take the park trip now or wait a few years until the kids will appreciate all it has to offer. If you do decide to go, look for parks pitched to the younger crowd, like Sesame Place in

Langhorne, Pennsylvania, or ones that have a variety of activities for the youngest visitors, such as shows, animal exhibits, and water park play.

Prepping Your Child

How you get your child ready for an amusement park trip can make all the difference between a disastrous visit and a delightful one. Some tips:

- Make sure she understands that the costumed characters are *big*, as in bigger than her mommy and daddy. And that they don't *talk*, so they can't answer her questions. And that she might go all that way and *not see* the one she's hoping to find (though consult the guidebooks for tips on finding the ones you need).

- Get her dizzy. And used to being bumped, jostled, rocked, jerked, and everything else. Play amusement park rides at the playground, adding in your own pretend special effects and loud noises.

- Learn about special effects. Get out the Halloween decorations and books on scary themes. Practice coping skills, like closing her eyes and covering her ears, or telling herself, "It's just make-believe."

- Discuss money matters in kid terms. Talk about not getting everything she wants or doing everything she'd like.

- Hang out in crowds and stand in lines. See how she does. Play some waiting games and build up your repertoire. Talk to her about the not-so-fun parts to expect in the visit, but reassure her that she'll be able to manage them.

- Take a test run at a small carnival or county fair before you attempt one of the biggies. (But keep in mind that even if she loves the little kiddy land at the church fair, a major amusement park may still overwhelm her.)

- Look at choices of attractions and get her thinking about what she'd like to try and what she'd definitely prefer to avoid. Remember she'll change her mind.

- Keep her as healthy as possible as the trip approaches. Beg off play visits with friends with the sniffles or suspicious rashes.
- Line up possible motion sickness remedies and try them out close to home.

Looking for Wheeeee!
THE PSYCHOLOGY AND PHYSICS OF FUN

How do you tell what will make your child giggle with glee and beg for more from what will turn her green and quivering? Well, sometimes you just have to find out the hard way—like the time we took our son on the Tilt-a-Whirl ride since he loved spinning on the tire swing at the park, only to have him stagger around pale and headachy the rest of the day. But, there are clues about what will probably work and what definitely won't, based on the developmental interests and abilities of young kids, their temperaments and tendencies, their current passions, and their reactions to similar experiences. Hope these ideas help you find what makes your kid say, "Wheeeee!"

What's Fun?

- *Motion* Look for carnival-style rides that mimic motions and experiences that your child enjoys on the playground or at home. For example, the Ferris wheel is a possible choice for kids who are constantly scaling the jungle gym to perch at the top (but don't even consider it for a kid who can't go down the slide at the park because he gets paralyzed at the top of the steps). Remember that the experience on any ride is likely to be *more* intense than similar ones he has encountered (our problem on the Tilt-A-Whirl), so if she doesn't like the tame version, forget the ride. And if your child is generally physically timid, stick to the kiddy rides, and avoid the ones that are aimed at older audiences, even if your child meets the height requirement. Similarly, intense, active kids are likely to pronounce the cute mini-versions of big rides in Playland "dumb" and "dorky."

- **Imagination and Familiar Character-Based Attractions** Rides and shows that fit with one of your child's current passions may be positively magical to her—and may even give her the courage to ignore features that would otherwise distress her. But be wary when your child has scary theme interests like dinosaurs; the realness of special effects can turn fun to terror, as the parents of many four-year-old pirate aficionados have discovered on "Pirates of the Caribbean" at Disney.

- **Cars You Can Drive Yourself** The only problem with these rides is that they often have height restrictions, which frustrates the heck out of wannabe-drivers. Try letting your child steer while you reach your leg across to push the accelerator. Other pretend-to-be-big rides are also popular.

- **Scary—But Not Too Scary** In general, this aspect is the hardest part for me to judge. I've taken some kids on rides with such poorly done effects I expected the kids to be disappointed—only to have them hiding their heads in my armpits in terror after the first cheesecloth ghost dangled from a string near the car.

- **Kid-Sized Things** For several years, my daughter named the miniature porcelain toilets and sinks in the rest room in Kiddy Land at Kennywood (our local amusement park) as her favorite thing there. Fairy or nursery rhyme lands, small houses to visit, and other "little" things please kids very much. So can big things—many kids like the "Honey, I Shrunk the Kids" attraction at Disney—but some big things, like costumed characters, may frighten kids who expected them to be smaller.

- *Giving Tickets to the Taker* All-day passes have mostly eliminated this pleasure, but don't discount its pleasure when it's available. But expect your child to lose the tickets unless you give them to him at the last second.

- *The Extras—the Food, Playground Opportunities, Splash Play* Sometimes the shows, too, but so often they have such long waits that kids have exhausted their patience before they even begin. And midway games are way too difficult and frustrating for most kids. The souped-up playground experiences, like Cookie Mountain at Sesame Place, generally get highest fun ratings by little guys. Water attractions specifically aimed at young kids are a close second, provided your child doesn't mind being splashed and squirted. And eating traditions, like sharing french fries while waiting in line to drive the little cars, combine the magic of ritual with the satisfaction of a treat.

What's Not a Bit Fun?

The content of many rides and attractions frequently scares the preschool set. Watch out for these effects that may be too frightening:

- witches/ghosts/monsters
- skeletons/bones/coffins
- fire
- fierce animals/bugs/snakes
- things breaking or going wrong
- guns/cannons/bombs

Even poorly done special effects usually seem way more real to young kids than you can believe, which is one of the problems with Disney since theirs are so *good*. Types of effects designed to scare and which tend to be excessively successful with young kids:

- things which appear to loom/advance/attack
- the dark, eerie music, laughter (especially if it seems mismatched, like laughter during something scary)

- optical illusions (like spinning spirals, holograms)
- surprise sensations (like jets of water or puffs of air)
- loud noises and flashing lights.

Strategies for Success

Start small and sure, and work your way up to more "challenging" attractions, even though this usually defeats all those avoid-the-crowd strategies. Skip anything borderline frightening when your child is tired, hungry, full, or simply overstimulated. Forewarn your child about scary things before you get on the ride, at least until you've had a chance to gauge her tolerance. You can talk with her about special effects and how everything is just make-believe and how everyone else is smiling and having fun—but when she's in the midst of the stuff, she won't believe a word of it. Preschoolers trust their eyes, which are blind to all the wires and projectors.

Whistle While You Wait
LINE GAMES

My moment of shining success as a parent-entertainer came when we were waiting in a ridiculously long line at an amusement park with our three kids who ranged in age from three to six. I trotted out one waiting game after another to keep my guys amused, and pretty soon the little kids in front of us and behind us joined in. When *finally* it was time for the kids in front to ride, they actually *groaned!* Now, I'm not saying these games will be *that* successful every time—that was pretty much a one-time thing for me—but they will make waiting significantly less painful most of the time.

Well, Can You Do This?

We routinely use waiting time to practice or learn new skills.
- Snapping fingers (Try having him wet his fingertips if he's having trouble.)
- Winking (first one eye and then the other)

- Twiddling thumbs (forward and backward, then while he sticks his tongue in and out)
- Whistling (Try different kinds, like inhaling or using two fingers.)
- Tongue clicking and other mouth noises (like the one where you squeeze air out of your cheeks along your upper gums and it sounds a little like Donald Duck—know what I'm talking about?)
- Finger-in-cheek "popping" (The trick is to have your finger barely in your cheek and running along the part in your lips to seal it while you puff out your cheeks.)
- Balancing on one foot or hopping (We do these as contests of some sort.)
- High fives and fancy handshakes
- Jumping jacks, toe touches, and other calisthenics
- Looking cross-eyed or rolling eyes up in your head
- Wiggling your ears, raising one eyebrow
- Clicking heels together (difficult)
- Dance steps (like line dances, the grapevine folk dance step, the Macarena)
- Running in place (Vary the pace.)

Puppy and Master

This is basically just very silly Simon Says. Try really hard to be the master instead of the puppy if you have any sense of dignity. The master has the puppy do a series of tricks that can be done standing in line, but aren't necessarily traditional dog tricks. We might have the doggie do the twist, for instance, or try to convince us to give him a bone using only his eyebrows to "talk." But if the master laughs, then the puppy gets to be master. And it is very, very, very hard not to laugh.

More Things to Do

Many of the time-filler games elsewhere in the book will work in line too. Try these kinds of activities:

- *Clapping Games* Simple ones like "Pease Porridge Hot" and "Miss Mary Mack" are best with young children. Just clap your hands together and then against your child's hands while you say the rhymes.

- *Language Games* Teach your child to say his name backwards and in pig latin. See if he can learn everyone else's names those ways too. New Nursery Rhymes is fun for silly kids. Say the first line of a nursery rhyme and have your child make up a new second line that fits the rhyme, more or less, like "Humpty Dumpty sat on a wall, Wasn't it dumb of him to pretend he was tall?"

- *Counting Out Rhymes* Like "One potato" and "Engine, engine number nine." This activity will last a very long time.

- *I'm Thinking of a Number* Between one and whatever. The other player guesses and the thinker gives feedback saying "higher" or "lower." Play with increasingly big numbers and teach your child the strategy of always guessing the middle number between the two. Count how many guesses it takes the guesser to come up with the right number.

- *Odd and Evens* One player picks odd or even. Then the two players wave their fists saying, "One, two, three, shoot!" and thrusting out one or two fingers on shoot. The total of both players' fingers is added. If it matches the guesser's choice (three—odd, two or four—even), he gets to guess again. Otherwise the other player gets a turn. This game is more successful if you take a moment to have the players decide how many fingers to shoot before they count. Paper, Scissors, Rock is a similar game that can be played with more people.

We Are Not Amused
DEALING WITH PROBLEMS

I'm sure I won't manage to hit all the problems you might encounter. I know my own children are remarkably resourceful in coming up with difficulties I never anticipated in my wildest imagination, and I'm sure yours are too. But maybe I'll have thought up some of the worst ordeals—and I hope some workable solutions to them.

You've Taken Her on a Ride or to an Attraction You Shouldn't Have

Generally by the time you realize this, it's too late to get off. Pull your child close against your body and talk to her in a calm voice. Have her close her eyes and cover her ears. Counting or reciting the alphabet helps many kids to focus and feel calmer. Help your child anticipate changes in motion or lighting if possible. After you get off, debrief—praise her good coping, apologize for the mistake, and move quickly to distract her with something much easier for her.

You Can't Please Everyone

If you have kids of varying ages, amusement parks can be especially frustrating. Consider dividing up; two-way radios can make it reasonably easy to keep in touch. Or take turns, not ride by ride probably, but chunk of time by chunk of time. Give the left-out ones an alternate pleasure during their down time (junk food comes to mind or special toys like Game Boy). Search out shows or active play areas that everyone can enjoy for occasional compromises.

The Pee Dance. Near The Front Of The Line
You've Been Waiting In For Ninety Minutes

Oh man, why do I put myself in the position of trying to think of solutions to impossible problems like this? Okay, okay—here goes.

1. Don't get in that position. Schedule potty stops immediately before you get in long lines. And consider putting your child

in Pull-Ups while at the park if she's even halfway agreeable, so at least it won't be a disaster if she doesn't make it.

2. Beg the attendant to let you step out and return to the front of the line. Won't work in many parks, but sometimes people take pity on folks with young children (though not usually ride operators who tend to be in their pre-child years).

3. Help your child hold it. Have her squeeze her legs and say the alphabet. Take three slow, deep breaths. Check to see if she feels better. Let her hold herself while riding, even if that's not technically polite in public. And when you get on, ask the attendant for the location of the nearest potty so you'll be ready to dash there afterwards.

4. Give up, go to the potty, realizing that nobody would have enjoyed the ride if your poor kid had peed all over just as the ride got going.

Tired, Overwhelmed, Miserable

Tell her, "We spent a lot of money and went to a ton of trouble to bring you here, so you will have fun! I mean it!" I've seen lots of people try that technique, but frankly, it never seemed to work. Instead, take a chill-out break. If you can, go back to your lodgings and go for a swim or take a nap. Failing that, search for someplace shady and quiet. (Sometimes the far side of the rest rooms is deserted.) Let your child throw crumbs to the sparrows or chase the pigeons. Take off everyone's shoes and let toes air out for a few minutes. Rub weary tootsies to restore them. Hug your child. Splash water on your faces. And drink some. Laugh. Pretend to take a magic carpet ride to a fluffy cloud. Eat an ice cream cone. Skip instead of walking. Go to a show, especially one that's not popular.

**You Suddenly Notice That Your Child Who Is in Line
for a Kiddy Ride without You Is Sucking on the Railing
That 6.3 Million Children Have Rubbed Their Snotty, Germy Hands—
and Who Knows What Else—All Over**

That happened to me once. Here's what you do. Feel like barfing. Try to get your child's attention. See him smile at you without removing his mouth from the railing. Try to get his brother to make him stop. See him misunderstand and lick the railing too. After the ride, make them wash out their mouths with Coke. Give them vitamin C and keep your fingers crossed. Two days later, you get sick while the lickers stay remarkably healthy. Wonder what possessed you to have kids.

CHAPTER NINE

Minor
Disaster
Management

Once when I was kid, my family stayed in a cabin at a state park for a few nights. One morning when my little brother woke up, he noticed something sticky in his eyelashes that he couldn't pull out. It turned out to be a tick, firmly affixed to the *inside* of his eyelid and completely tangled in his lashes. Not even my normally unflappable and resourceful mother could remove it. We all trooped over to the nearest emergency room where they sprayed numbing stuff in Evan's eye and used a hot thingy to convince the tick to release its grip. And my sister was so grossed out she fainted. We all felt a bit jumpy and skin-crawly the rest of the trip, but we had fun canoeing and hiking and stuff anyhow.

More recently, my husband and I spent a night in New York City, while our three kids stayed with my wonderful sister-in-law and her family. And we were all enjoying our little mini-vacations until my oldest managed to whack the youngest in the mouth with the seesaw and knock out two of her baby teeth. My daughter was hysterical because she was convinced the Tooth Fairy wouldn't find her and she wouldn't even get the money she was due after her trauma. But Karen, who taught me all I need to know about "Tooth Fairy Finders" (page 248), saved the day. And it worked out for the best, since it turns out that Tooth Fairies in New Jersey have way bigger budgets than the Pennsylvania ones.

In addition to these problems, we've had our share of lost children, pools closed for renovation, hurricanes, blizzards, bee stings, ear infections, jellyfish stings, crab pinches, sunburn, drought, floods, missed birthday parties and soccer camps, and assorted other disappointments and frustrations. So far though, no leeches, famines, or plagues of locusts.

As you may have noticed, minor vacation disasters come in all shapes and sizes. While many have the potential to ruin a trip, usually some prompt and appropriate intervention can put the vacation right back on track. Maybe a *different* track, but at least one that will enable everything to keep moving forward. And that's what this chapter is all about—ideas to keep Trouble with a capital *T* from ruining your vacation to River City or wherever it is you've decided to go. You'll find ideas for preventing serious health problems like heat stroke and dehydration (and staying more comfortable in the process), coping with illness and homesickness, and finding ways to keep your kids where they're supposed to be—near you. There are even ideas on handling those potentially disastrous occasions like weddings your child is in. But most importantly, there are tips on keeping a stiff upper lip or at least a belly that shakes like a bowl full of jelly when you laugh. So on your next vacation, may the wind be at your back and the germs somewhere else—or may you at least keep the ability to put everything in perspective. Bon voyage!

Separation Anxieties
STICKING TOGETHER STRATEGIES AND EMERGENCY RESPONSES

My parents' slapstick description of their hours-long struggle to get our whole family back together again at the New York World's Fair still cracks me up even though I keenly remember how scared I was at the time. Separations can happen despite your best efforts. But with luck, these ideas will speed happy reunions. Remember to discuss the issue before every outing. Small children have short memories, and having the reminders be routine and matter-of-fact can also reduce the scare factor.

Being Prepared When Visiting a Public Place

- Pick a meeting spot that's easy to find. (If there's an official place for lost children, use that.) If someone gets separated from the group, everyone will know where to go to get reunited. A young child should not go to the meeting place alone, unless he can see it. If he can't, he should ask a helper to take him there.

- Label your child with information that will enable helpers to reunite him with you promptly, *including the family's designated meeting place*, your names, and your cell phone number. (See the suggestions in "Red Shirting" on page 89 for dressing and labeling your child effectively). You may also want to make sure that every child has a laminated family photo tucked in his pocket or in a locket. The photograph may not only aid helpers in finding you, but may also provide comfort to your child.

- Point out what helper people (uniformed employees or guards, other families with young children) look like. Remind your child briefly that he is never to leave with a stranger.

- Assign buddies in crowds, hold hands crossing streets or boarding transportation, and stop every time you leave an area to do a head count.

- If your family is splitting up, designate a meeting place and time. Cell phones, beepers, and two-way radios can all make it easier to stay in touch. I understand that some attractions now rent beepers and two-way radios. Consider buying family radios to make staying in touch easier.

Being Prepared When Visiting Outdoor Areas

- Have everyone wear a whistle to blow in case of emergencies. Make sure your child is dressed for the weather (including weather expected later in the day) and has a trash bag to use as an emergency poncho.
- Make a footprint record of each child, to help searchers follow a trail. There are several ways to do this, but the easiest is probably to have your child step lightly in mud and then on a piece of paper to make a print of the soles of his shoes. I know my kids *never* seem to have any trouble finding mud, but if yours can't, spray or pour some water on the bottoms of their shoes before having them step in the dirt. Be sure to save your prints where they won't get too mangled, or the marks will wear off.

Teaching Your Child How to Cope with Separation in a Public Place

- Tell your child to stop where he is. Then look all around (turning slowly in a circle) to see if he can find you, or at least see the meeting place. He can call your name (*your first or whole name*, not Mommy or Daddy) and wait a minute to see if you come.
- Instruct him to approach a helper and say that he needs help finding his mommy and daddy if he can't find you or the meeting place. He can share the information on his label and state that he would like to go to the meeting place.
- Remind him to stay calm. Someone *will* find him. He shouldn't hide—you promise he won't be in trouble or punished.

Teaching Your Child How to Cope with Separation in Outdoor Areas

- Tell him to stop and hug a tree. Staying put will make it easier for someone to find him.
- Have him blow his whistle (three blasts) and listen for an answer.

- Teach him to stay calm and make noise. Sing songs. After each song, he should blow his whistle three times again.
- If he hears people or an airplane, he should blow his whistle and wave (preferably with a piece of bright clothing).
- Remind him not to hide. Remember that someone *will* find him. Don't hide. He won't be in trouble.
- If he isn't found quickly, he should find protection nearby. A hole or cave is ideal, but leaves or even mud will help him keep warm. He should try to find water too.

Finding A Lost Child

- One adult (and any other children) should go quickly to the designated meeting place and stay there. The other should initiate a search, notify authorities, and check in at the meeting place frequently.
- Remain calm. You *will* find your child.
- Check back where you last saw your child. Turn in a full circle, looking carefully.
- Call your child by his full name, or out of doors, blow your whistle. Listen for replies.
- Provide other searchers with as much information as possible, such as what your child was wearing, including shoes; a photograph or physical description; and what had interested him so far during your visit. (He may have gone back to something he liked.)

TRY THIS!

Talk to your child about getting "separated," or not being able to find you, instead of getting lost. Some kids have wandered around for a long time, not asking for help because they knew where they were and didn't consider themselves "lost." The word "lost" also sounds scarier to many kids and may cause them to panic.

- Make sure your cell phone is turned on.
- Remember to check bathrooms, food areas, and gift shops.
- When your child is found, do not scold or punish him—you don't want him to hide next time. Praise him for any of the coping skills he used, and offer suggestions for what he might do if you get separated again. Hug him, and give him lots of opportunities to talk about the experience. And don't forget to notify other searchers!

LITERATURE LINKS

Books about getting lost are useful in helping prepare your child in the event that he gets separated from you. They also help reassure kids after a scary experience, and give them openings to talk about it again. One of my favorites is *Angus Lost* by Marjorie Flack (about a dog who wanders out in search of adventure and has a hard time finding his way home again). It's old and probably out of print—look for it at the library. My kids, though, love the multi-strip episode from the comic strip *Calvin and Hobbes* where Calvin accidentally follows the wrong mom's legs at the zoo (in the *Weirdos from Another Planet* Collection).

Cooler Heads Prevailing
TEMPERATURE CONTROL TACTICS

Kids who are overheated or chilled are not only crabby, they're also at risk of serious health problems, like heat exhaustion/stroke and dehydration, or hypothermia and frostbite. These tips will help keep your child's temper from boiling over in uncomfortable weather and enable you to aid her if a dangerous situation develops.

Keeping a Cool Head—and Body

In hot weather, use the following methods to keep your child cool:

- Make sure she drinks plenty of fluids, especially water. Fluid can also be obtained from foods like ice pops, Jell-O, and watermelon.
- Dress her appropriately in light colors, breathable fabrics like cotton, and a hat. Make sure she wears sunscreen and encourage her to wear sunglasses.
- Take frequent air conditioning and/or splash-in-the-water breaks.
- Use a spray mister. A perfume-size atomizer will fit in a purse or pocket and can be refilled frequently. Portable fans also improve comfort but won't lower body temperature.
- Wrap ice cubes in a cloth or paper towel. Your child can wear them under a hat. As they melt, the drips will further cool him.
- Wash faces with cool water every time you use the rest room. Splash water on her arms and torso as well. Let it evaporate to cool her.
- Take care during extremely humid or unusually hot weather. Stay inside during the middle of the day (10:00 AM to 2:00 or 3:00 PM). Move slowly and don't rush.
- *Never leave a child in an unmoving vehicle.* The temperature can become dangerously hot quickly and kill a small child in a short period of time.
- Remember that a young child sweats less efficiently and can tolerate much less heat than an adult.

Warming-Up

In cold weather, use the following techniques to keep your child warm and cozy:

- Make sure she consumes enough calories and fat. People burn more energy when they're keeping their bodies warm.

- Dress your child appropriately in layers (They're better at trapping heat.) and dark colors that absorb warmth from the sun.
- Have your child wear a hat. It's really true that heat is lost rapidly through the head. And have her wear mittens rather than gloves, because they keep fingers warmer. Always protect extremities like the tips of noses and ears, fingers, and toes.
- Take regular inside warm-up breaks from outdoor play.
- Stay dry. If your child does become wet, get her inside and into dry clothing quickly.
- If it's windy or unusually cold, cover faces and other exposed skin with ski masks or gaiter face shields. (Try to avoid scarves, which can pose a strangulation hazard.)
- Teach your child to warm her chilly fingers by tucking them under her armpits. Blowing into a face gaiter or her mittens generates a little warmth too. Friction, created by rubbing hands on body parts, will warm skin But don't do this if you suspect frostbite—it can permanently damage tissues. Or, share your body heat by holding her against you.
- Encourage her to exercise, like jumping or jogging in place to help her raise her body temperature.
- Carry a good supply of chemical hand warmers. (Look for them in ski supply stores and most general sporting goods stores during the winter.) They can be used for keeping fingers and toes comfortable or for helping rapid rewarming during an emergency.
- If you're trapped outside in the cold unprepared, find shelter, even if it's just a windbreak. Use leaves, pine needles, or even mud as insulation. Have your child curl into a ball and tuck her hands into her armpits. Snuggle tightly against her.
- Remember that children get dangerously overchilled much faster than adults. Be especially careful when you are exercising and your child is not (for example, because you're pushing her in a stroller or pulling her in a bike carrier or wagon).

SAFETY ZONE

Know the warning signs of heat exhaustion, hypothermia, and frost bite—and seek professional help as soon as you see them.

- Early signs of being overheated include sweating and cramps in the lower abdomen. If your child has ceased sweating and has red skin, a fever, and a rapid pulse, he may be suffering from heatstroke. In later stages, the skin becomes cold and clammy and the child may feel dizzy. This is a life-threatening emergency, and you should take steps to cool your child by giving him fluids, getting him wet, removing his clothing, and seeking cool shelter while you summon help.

- Hypothermia is marked by a drop in body temperature (below 95 degrees Fahrenheit), drowsiness, confusion, and slurred speech. Advanced hypothermia may lead to loss of consciousness; the victim may even appear dead, but don't give up hope. Wrap the child in warm blankets, cover her face, and warm her gradually while moving her as little as possible until help arrives.

- Frostbite first shows up as red skin and a stinging or burning sensation. Second-degree frostbite will produce mottled gray skin and a sensation of numbness or pins-and-needles. If the skin is hard to the touch and waxy white, third-degree frostbite has occurred. Gradually warm affected areas in warm, not hot, water or under your armpit, and seek medical help for second- or third-degree frostbite.

Tooth Fairy Finders
AND OTHER TIPS FOR SPECIAL OCCASION PROBLEMS

Celebrating a special occasion on vacation, whether planned, like having a birthday at Grandma's house, or unexpected, like a visit from the Tooth Fairy, often provokes concerns for young children. They may be disappointed if traditions are handled differently, or worried about whether the Tooth Fairy or Santa will find them. They'll probably experience added stresses, too, like needing to have "company" manners, receiving more gifts than usual, or simply having more stimulation to endure. Try some of these tips to ensure that special occasions are times of celebration instead of tears.

Tooth Fairy Finders

If your child happens to lose a tooth on vacation, she need have no fear. Whichever Tooth Fairy covers the region you're visiting is authorized to take the tooth *and* leave money (or an I.O.U. if she was unprepared for the extra expense). Normally, the Tooth Fairy simply monitors every bed and discovers teeth beneath any pillow. If your child is worried, though, stick a note on the door advising "Lost Tooth Inside," and the fairy will stop in. A small flag made from a straw and a piece of paper embellished with a tooth (and hung out the window) also alerts the fairy of a need for a visit. Or, your child can save the tooth until she gets home, and her regular fairy will perform the duties belatedly.

Santa operates similarly. If you are planning to be away, your child can send him a note advising him of her whereabouts on December 24. Mark the lower left-hand corner of the envelope: "Notice of Temporary Change of Address." The post office usually gives Santa mail special handling, and if you've posted the letter early enough, your child *may* receive a reply assuring her that Santa knows where she'll be on Christmas. If, however, you have forgotten to notify him in time, simply sprinkle reindeer food (a mixture of oats and glitter is good) outside where you're staying. The reindeer will find it, and then Santa will be certain not to miss your child. You can even leave a note, asking Santa to split gifts between home and your away place.

When Traditions Aren't Traditional

The thing about traditions that's so great—their predictability—can become a problem if you're celebrating away from home and your hosts do things differently. These ideas should help with the "But that's not what we do!" complaints:

- ***When in Rome...*** The usual polite approach of following your hosts' ways may be too much for young kids on special occasions. Prepare your child for how things will be done, if you know, and play up the differences as special and wonderful too. But if your child seems stressed, take along one or more of your own traditions—a gift to open the night before, a favorite decoration to put up in your child's room, or a favorite special food to share with your hosts.

- ***Have Multiple Celebrations*** I remember my third birthday well despite my young age because of the excitement of having *three* birthday parties—one at my great-aunt's home in New York, one a week later at home with my family, and another with my friends. When our kids have special occasions on the road, we often leave some or all of our own celebration at home to have before or after the trip. It saves lugging lots of presents and lets the child enjoy the occasion with less stress. And the birthday kid feels lucky to celebrate repeatedly, even if the at-home celebration is a bit lower key than usual.

- ***Take One, Please*** Have your child identify some new ritual she enjoyed and incorporate it into your future celebrations at home. This weaving of customs will promote a closer bond with family and friends and help make your child flexible enough to accept more differences the next time she encounters them.

Pomp and Special Circumstances
HELPING YOUR CHILD MANAGE CEREMONIAL OBLIGATIONS

Preschoolers are left out of many ceremonies and adult occasions, which is usually fine with them. But if they are included in ways that are respectful of their needs and limitations, they can benefit from witnessing the big events of life—and they may contribute, too, by bringing added joy or giving innocent comfort. If you'll be going out of town to attend these special events, though, remember to factor in the additional stress of traveling and its likely effects on your child's behavior when deciding how much or even whether to include her. The following points for weddings and funerals also apply to many other ritual occasions, from commencements to Bar Mitzvahs.

Weddings...

Preschoolers generally enjoy weddings and other happy events, so long as the ceremony and speeches don't drag on too long. But there are some snags, besides long fancy dresses, that can trip them up. Perhaps these tips will help:

- *Preparation* Put on a dress rehearsal at home beforehand; it's well worth the investment of time (especially if it's complete with cake and dancing). Arrive at the wedding site early enough to reserve a center aisle seat so your child will be able to see well, but then go play outside until just before the ceremony. See chapter 2 for ideas on keeping her quiet and occupied if her attention flags.
- *Clothing* Bring a change of clothes if your child will be staying for the reception. Then if she's uncomfortable or too active for her special outfit, you can switch to something more suitable. If your child is in the wedding and is expected to wear something that itches or bothers her, play around well *before* the wedding to find ways, like wearing an undershirt or leaving off the slip, to help her feel better.

- *Cold Feet* They're not just for the bride and groom. Many flower girls and ring bearers who pranced cheerfully down the aisle at rehearsal balk when they see all the people. Have a Plan B ready, such as having a parent or bridesmaid accompany your child (or even carry her). Also position a parent near the front of the church for her to focus on as she makes her way there (and to keep her company during the ceremony). And if that parent happens to be holding a small wrapped gift out as bait...

- *Adults Only Reception* Try to arrange for your child to preview her arrangements for during the reception, especially if they're to be in an unfamiliar place and with an unfamiliar caregiver. Most children are happier if they have siblings, cousins, or other kids with them, so it's a good time to double up on a sitter if you can. Promise to bring a favor or a bit of cake to dream on if she's disappointed to be missing out, and be sure to prepare some special kid entertainment too.

...And Funerals

Definitely a harder call than weddings. Things to consider:

- *To Take Your Child or Not?* The sadness of the occasion will probably be less of a problem for a preschooler than the trouble of keeping still and quiet. Viewings, though, can frighten or confuse some children—and you may not be able to predict in advance which kids will have a hard time. I wouldn't force a young child to come—and probably wouldn't even encourage her to. If you do decide to take your child, prepare her for what will happen and how the dead person will look if the casket will be open. Also, be ready to step out if your child is frightened or behaves inappropriately. Expect that she'll prefer you or someone else she's comfortable with to provide this support. Preschoolers can usually attend after-funeral luncheons or receptions without difficulty, and may bring comfort and distraction to other mourners.

- *What to Tell a Child* Use the words "die" and "death." Euphemisms, like "gone away" or "sleeping forever," only confuse young children and may make them unnecessarily angry or worried. Explain that death is permanent and that the person will not be able to breathe, talk, play, or eat anymore. It doesn't hurt once you are dead. Answer your child's questions, which may be surprisingly blunt and graphic in their curiosity ("What does a dead person smell like?" and "Can he poop?" or "Who will live in his house now?") as clearly and honestly as you can. With luck, your child will reserve them for before or after the funeral, but if not, sit near the back and whisper answers; death questions need prompt answers.

- *Substitute Care* This is one of those between a rock and a hard place issues. Funerals may frighten young kids—but so may being separated from their parents, especially in a strange place, with a strange caregiver, at a time when their sensitivities to loss are heightened. Consider having one parent miss the funeral and join the other mourners afterward.

- *The Faces and Phases of Grief* Preschoolers may show little or no sadness, even if someone they've loved very much dies. Some may be angry or annoyed at the dead person. These are all normal reactions. The problem is that young kids really do not understand the permanence or implications of death. Your sadness is more likely to have an impact on them, and may worry some kids a good deal. Reassure your child that it's okay for you to be sad, and that you will feel a bit better before long. Accept graciously their attempts at comforting you, but don't be cross if they simply act indifferent. Children this age don't have a script for the situation. Don't be surprised either, if your child wants to sleep with you during this trip (and after

you get back home, too), and expect other upsets, from illness
to motion sickness to bedwetting.

A Pox on Your Vacation
WHEN ILLNESS STRIKES

My brother came down with chicken pox on Day 2 of a trip to Canada.
Talk about a bummer. It's not like you could just load him up with Tylenol
and trot him around with us—one glance and anyone could see he had
some horrible disease. And naturally, Evan felt miserable and wanted to be
home in his own bed. My parents took turns sitting with him in the
motel room (which means mostly my mom sat around, because Evan, like
most kids, had a preferred parent for comforting duties). The rest of us
went off and did fun things and brought back treats, toys, and calamine
lotion. I think I even felt vaguely sympathetic! If your kid gets sick, you're
probably going to be stuck with a similar scenario. (But if you're the one
who's sick, everyone will expect you just to soldier on.) These ideas,
though, may make it a little bit easier on your sick puppy.

Get Medical Help

Ask for help a little sooner on a vacation than you might at home. Ear
or sinus infections, strep throat, and assorted other bacterial maladies may
improve quickly (and cease being contagious) within twenty-four hours
of starting antibiotics. Some viral infections can also be minimized by
taking antiviral medications if they're started within the first day or two.
When you're traveling with small children, it's wise to check on medical
arrangements (like what your insurance will cover and where the nearest
hospital/urgent care facility will be) *before* you leave home. Even if you
didn't, you can muddle through with help from the Yellow Pages or front
desk. Don't forget to try your doctor at home. Sometimes they can call in a
prescription to a pharmacy near you or at least provide advice and maybe
a referral. Treatment may end up costing more than at home, but a lousy
vacation is expensive too.

Cuddle and Coddle

What works at home, works on the road. Warm blankies, tempting beverages, a parent's lap, and unlimited cartoon-watching will soothe most young children. And go buy some of the super-soft tissues if gross noses are involved, since hotel tissues are usually cheap and scratchy. Keep in mind that fresh air won't hurt your child, so go ahead and spend some time outside if possible, as long as your child is properly dressed and not exposing large crowds to his germs. Sick kids will probably be very disappointed *plus* miss the comforts of home, so be extra-tolerant of tears and tantrums, and extra-generous with your attention.

The rest of the family should go on about the vacation, because there's no point sitting around just sharing germs. And make sure the healthy guys drink plenty of fluids, eat well, and get lots of rest, because immune systems compromised by the stress of travel are already vulnerable. Finally, don't forget to take good care of the nursemaid parent—take her lots of ice cream to keep her spirits up.

Bring the Vacation to the Invalid

Naturally you'll bring back goodies to comfort the left-behinds. When possible, bringing a bit of the vacation experience to the sick guy will be particularly cheering. For example, a large bin of sand, some shells, and a trowel will be a welcome (if somewhat messy) distraction at the beach, or try items like a balloon, a toy taxi, and a museum souvenir for a city vacation.

When The Show Must Go On

If circumstances force you to keep going, slow your pace and push fluids big time; sick kids are at increased risk of dehydration, and plenty of liquids really do seem to hasten recovery. Keep your child as comfortable as possible with appropriate over-the-counter medications, and be tolerant of her excessive whininess—she really can't help it. And make sure she sneezes into her elbow instead of people's faces.

Have the Sense to Get Out in the Rain!
WEATHERING BAD WEATHER

Our family has had its share of bad weather trips—like the beach trip where there were red flags *every single day* and we never got to play in the surf even once—and I'd be lying if I said it didn't make some of us a wee bit unhappy. But there were bright spots in the week, such as stunt kite flying, seine-netting interesting creatures in the bay, and daily photo shoots of scowling kids next to the red flag, that we might not have tried during a good weather week. Plus, we ate lots of extra ice cream to make ourselves feel better. That last idea works pretty well, but if you need something more, try some of these ideas:

The Clothes Make the Can

Having the right clothes can make all the difference between having fun despite—or even because of—the weather. A chilly day at the beach can be an opportunity for kites and nature walks if you remembered to bring sweatshirts and long pants, and a raincoat enables your child to have a blast stomping in all the puddles instead of digging in the sand. If you didn't come prepared, improvise—layer clothing, wear garbage bag ponchos, or buy something new as a combo souvenir and outfit. So get dressed, and keep going!

Take a Walk on the Bright Side

Search out activities that are just right for the weather you have—like taking big sheets of cardboard down to the beach on a blustery day and letting the wind blow you along, or going toad hunting under the carport on a wet and gloomy day (That's one of my daughter's favorites.). If the day is too warm for good skiing, it may still be okay for making slightly slushy snowmen. It's a lot easier to enjoy these options, though, if you've made a point of thinking about them *before* the bad weather strikes. Plus, then you can kind of wish for the bad weather, and the weather gods of course won't cooperate, and then you'll have to do what you really came for anyway. Right?

Plan B, I Mean Plan *C*

On a rainy day at the beach, everyone will be at the movies or shopping at the outlet malls, and on a bad weather city day, folks will crowd the major museums. *You* should go to the less usual places, like smaller specialty museums, the public library or bookstore (which may even have special programs your child can catch), the ice cream parlor, or a nature walk (which may have different things to see in bad weather). We've occasionally had good luck with places like bowling alleys and ice rinks, especially if we went early. Bad weather days are also good times to do souvenir and gift shopping if you don't mind the crowds.

Any time that you're taking a weather-dependent vacation, like a week at a ski resort, you should go prepared with games, arts and crafts materials, and other typical distractions, because it's rare to have good weather every single day of a vacation. We particularly like playing old-fashioned parlor games like Charades (scaled down for the young players).

The Rainbow Effect

One of my favorite memories from the year that I worked in Boston is of a day when I got stuck waiting for my trolley for about forty minutes in freezing rain. When I finally got off the trolley, I was soaked and shivering and miserable, so I splurged (this will give you some idea of how little daycare teachers earn) and bought myself an English muffin and a cup of hot chocolate at the corner diner before walking the rest of the way to my apartment. I don't think anything has ever tasted so good, and I was thoroughly cheerful by the time I arrived home. That's the

SAFETY ZONE

Heed warnings for genuinely severe weather, even if that means evacuating when you suspect the National Weather Service is simply being alarmist. Even if you are in fact physically safe, the experience of cowering in an interior closet as a hurricane passes overhead will terrify your child—and you still won't manage to salvage your vacation.

rainbow effect—how much you appreciate a little beauty or comfort after a hard time. (A love of the rainbow effect is my personal theory of why people like backwoods camping.) The point, anyhow, is to tell you to help your child look for ways to create or notice the rainbow effect when the weather goes wrong on you.

Feel Betters
TLC AFTER SUNBURNS, BITES, STINGS, AND BLEEDIES

Encounters with unfriendly creatures and other environmental hazards may be disproportionately upsetting to a traveling preschooler. Small kids often overreact to bites, stings, and blood in general, and when you add the stress of being in an unfamiliar environment away from their usual soothers, you have the makings of a kiddy catastrophe. These ideas, and the ones in "Scared Tactics" on page 259 can soothe hurties and help shrink big reactions.

Oh, Mr. Sun?

Even a kid slathered in sunscreen may wind up with a bad sunburn— on the tops of her feet where you forgot to put any lotion or on that pale, pale skin where her bathing suit strap didn't stay put. Soothe sunburns inside and out. Over-the-counter pain relievers will reduce pain and swelling, and plenty of fluids are important too. Cool skin with a tepid bath and/or cool compresses. To keep the compresses in place, wrap a little girl up to prance around in a wet towel sari or stole, cloak a boy in a dampened toga, or offer wet towel capes to junior super heroes. Just don't let them sit on *your* bed, unless you like your sheets on the clammy side. Follow up with a moisturizer like Eucerin, or one with vitamin E or aloe. At bedtime, try spraying the bottom sheet and pillowcase lightly with a mister and giving a cooling tuck-in blow-all-over. If your kid complains that the bedclothes hurt, let him fall asleep uncovered and put a light sheet over later. Or sometimes we can get this trick to work: direct a fan right at bed height and gently lift the top sheet until it gets caught in the breeze and hovers an inch or so over the sleepy-head guy. Just be absolutely certain your child knows not to get up and stick his fingers in the fan.

Itchy, Itchy, Scratchy, Scratchy

Bug bites can cause intense itching, which is often worse at bedtime or first thing in the morning. I find that a product called After Bite is especially effective in reducing itching, especially if applied right after the bite occurs. If you don't have access to pharmacy products, ice cubes and cool compresses sometimes help. Another "cure" I've seen several times but keep forgetting to try, is very *warm* compresses. Other home remedies include slapping, pinching, or rubbing the skin around the bite without touching the itchy spot, or playing a vigorous game of "Run Around and Tickle" so the kid is too distracted to notice the itching. Spider bites can get huge, and tick bites can be followed by illnesses like Lyme disease; these require a check-in with your pediatrician.

Bloodcurdling Sting Scream!

You'll know if your child gets stung, whether it's a bee, wasp, or jellyfish. Unless your child has multiple stings or severe allergies to the venom, this is less of a medical emergency than a psychological one. Hold your child tightly and reassure her that you are there and you'll take care of her. Remove the stinger from a bee sting by scraping it with a credit card. Various substances will ease the pain of a sting if you don't have an appropriate commercial product. A paste made from Adolph's Meat Tenderizer, baking soda, or Old Bay Seasoning usually does the trick. Papaya slices are supposed to do the trick too, but I rarely have those handy. (Old Bay, on the other hand, I have in abundance, since every year I forget to take it with me to the beach for our annual shrimp dinner, and I have to buy yet another tin of it.) The big problem is that now your child is going to be more freaked than ever by bugs or sea creatures. Talk about ways to avoid stings, like standing still around bees and keeping an eye out in the water, and follow up with the suggestions in the next section, "Scared Tactics," to help her find her courage again.

Blood

Major cuts require a trip to the emergency room, but everything else just needs to be cleaned with soap and water, dabbed with antibiotic ointment, and plastered with as many Band-Aids as possible. Hugs, smooches, and sometimes an ice pack or bag of frozen peas on the boo-boo, are almost as healing as Band-Aids. Remind your child, because she may have forgotten, that her body can make new blood, and that skin has the nearly magic ability to grow back together again. Check the boo-boo daily and notice the new baby skin growing in.

Lions! And Tigers! And—What Do You Mean It Was Just a Mosquito?

Once a child has had a bad experience, which can be anything from a disgusting tick sucking her blood to a big crop of mosquito bites, she may be inordinately and easily frightened. Be sympathetic and reassuring, saying things like, "Lots of people feel nervous outside for a while after they've been bitten, but you're okay." Be sure to discuss her bravery and how remarkably strong and fast-healing her body is. You want to give her the confidence that she could handle another bad experience, and not falsely reassure her that it will never happen again.

Scared Tactics
HOW TO UN-FRIGHTEN AND RE-ENCOURAGE

Preschoolers who have gone to pieces after a scary experience usually need help reassembling the bits and cementing them back in place. In time, though, if you keep assisting them and teaching about it, they'll be able to handle the repairs themselves. Try this approach to calming and shoring up courage.

Breathing Lessons

For some crazy reason, people were designed with a tendency to either hold their breath or hyperventilate when they get hurt or scared—but it's deep, full breaths that make you feel better. Giving a frightened child a firm bear hug will often force her to exhale and resume more normal breathing. Hysterically crying kids may hyperventilate—that is, get too much oxygen because they're not exhaling enough—and a hug won't usually help them as much as a drink of water will. Breathing into a paper bag or cupped hands restores the proper oxygen balance. Wiping cold water on kids' faces seems to help them return to normal breathing patterns, too, as will your own calm, deep breathing.

Reassurance 101

Even if your child doesn't show her relief at first, and even if you don't *do* anything, just being with your child and touching her is tremendously calming—that's a response hardwired into people. People are also programmed to fear the dark, including the "being in the dark" kind of dark, so information you give your child improves her ability to cope with the problem. (Think about how many times you've heard people say, "It's the not-knowing that's the worst.") So, tell your child what happened ("You got stung by a bee and that really hurts.") and what you're doing to help, and outline what will happen later. Finally, hope is what gets people back on track, so let your child know of your confidence in her abilities to cope and your certainty that everything will be better soon.

Tell Me About It Later

Research has shown that people who are resilient in the face of catastrophe have several things in common, including a sense of optimism—and a tendency to talk and talk and talk about what happened. Give your child openings to discuss a traumatic event. Some kids will want to discuss the experience immediately, but more commonly, young children need to hear from you first. They often lack the verbal abilities to express their feelings about what happened, so you should label their likely reactions for them. They also lack the experience to put the incident in perspective. You can help by telling them stories about people who've had similar problems, and linking this recovery to how they've gotten over other problems.

And Even Later We'll Laugh About It!

Some kids benefit from humor right away—"I know that monster scared you, but I'll bet your scream frightened the boogers right out of him!"—but more often, young children need even more distance before they can laugh about bad experiences. Still, there's nothing like laughing in the face of fear to make you feel more powerful than your boogeymen—so help your child find that ability.

It's About Time

The great healer—for real. Your child's fear and distress will fade with time, and that can comfort you when you're holding a child who's been sobbing for the last fifteen minutes and will not be soothed.

Home Remedies for Homesickness
WHAT TO DO WHEN YOUR KID FEELS BLUE

Homesickness is less common when your child is with you, since family, not a house or apartment, is the real home for most people. But young children see many objects as almost alive, and they may consider your house—and definitely your pets—to be legitimate family members. And they may miss them terribly, to the point of crying or at least irritability, when they're away. Fortunately, homesickness is generally short-lived, if for no other reason than few parents with young children have the stamina to take extended trips. But if your child is nonetheless singing the homesick blues, these techniques can change his tune.

Perspective-Giving

The main thing you may need to do is reassure your child that you *will* be going home, even if you were wise and told her before you left, because she may have forgotten or become confused. It also helps most kids to have a concrete representation of the length of vacation. So make another one of those stupid—I mean helpful—paper chains with a link for each day until you return. (During the preschool years, you may develop an urge to invest in companies that make stuff like construction paper, safety scissors, and glue, since they must be selling those products like hotcakes.)

Connections

Checking in on the home front may reassure you as well as your child, since it gives you a chance to ease your worry that you might have left the garage door open (as we did once—we were gone for a whole week, too, but luckily nothing happened). When you phone the neighbor on Tuesday to check on the garage door thing once and for all so you'll be able to sleep, your child can say "hi" and ask how his swing set and pumpkin plant are doing. I also read about a family that wrote daily postcards to their cat as a way to chronicle their journey. I'll bet it was comforting to their young child as well, since it helped her feel connected to the loved one left behind. Buying small gifts for your kid's closest friends will also reassure him that they won't forget him before he returns.

Bonds and Securities

Sometimes a child's complaints of homesickness are simply a longing for the predictability and familiarity of his usual daily life. When that's the case, slow your pace and take a quieter day. Touch him more, feed him familiar foods at usual times, and tuck him in bed early and with the full works bedtime routine.

Moon Beamers

Sing reassuring songs, like "It's a Small World" (which you will know by heart if you've taken a preschooler to any of the Disney parks). Then, when it's dark, take him outside to look at the moon. Even if it's not full, you can probably squint and make out the smiling face of the man in the moon. Then talk to your child about how this moon, this very same moon, is looking down at him right now—and it's looking down at his house too! (Pul-eeze! Skip the arguments about time zones and total honesty—your child needs this!) Then sing:

I see the moon, the moon sees me.
The moon sees somebody I'd like to see.
God bless the moon, and God bless me.
And God bless somebody I'd like to see.

Finish up by blowing a kiss to the moon for it to beam down to your home for you.

The Best Disappointments in Life Aren't Free
COPING WHEN THINGS DON'T TURN OUT AS EXPECTED

This last one is for you instead of your child. I know I've been blathering on nonstop about how to make your child happy, but I really do want you to be happy too. And that's why I wish I could make all your family travels turn out the way they look in the brochures and the movies, but I can't. The best I can do is teach you the alchemy of turning vacation disasters into amusing stories to tell at cocktail parties and give you permission to throw an extravagant pity party for yourself. Sorry! Be happy! Here's how!

Stepping Stones

"This experience will build character." "What does not break me, makes me stronger." Those are the things you tell yourself so you can keep your chin up when you get a flat on the way to your vacation, the car gets towed because the "No Parking" sign was stolen, you have to spend most of your cash to retrieve your car, you have another flat on the way home (There's no spare, of course, because it's already on the front left wheel.), the tow truck from the auto club doesn't show up for almost three hours, and then—because you must have some really bad karma or a brain turned to mush by too many hours of listening to Barney singing "I love you, you love me, we're a happy family" while waiting for the tow truck—you leave your wallet on the roof of the car after paying the service station the rest of your cash to fix your flat tire. That really happened to us once (Only with even more bad things and without the Barney tape excuse. But get this—we found the wallet! With the credit cards still in it!), and we are all still alive and smiling and only need strong sedatives occasionally.

Humor

Okay, so that was the last idea too. But it's a good one, especially if you have lots of vacation disappointments to turn into stories, because folks at the cocktail party will enjoy your description of your vacation woes much more if it makes them laugh. One warning: your spouse will think the stories are much funnier if they're about the knuckle-headed things you did in the face of disaster instead of the stupid things she did. If you can't think of any funny bits on your own, watch movies like *National Lampoon's Vacation* or *Planes, Trains and Automobiles* and adapt a few of their good parts. But not the one about the pillows in the latter movie. Shudder.

Silver Linings

Every cloud has one, and besides, it's an ill wind that blows no good. Those adages haven't been around for ages for nothing—they're good for helping you deceive yourself into thinking that your vacation wasn't *all* bad. And probably it wasn't, and if you can just stop crying for a few minutes, you'll think of why it was a good thing that the beach was closed because of all the shark attacks after they lifted the evacuation orders from the hurricane.

Wallow in It

Sometimes the best thing you can do is just to let yourselves feel totally, utterly, completely miserable and sorry for yourselves. You might even want to exaggerate a teeny bit and make things sound even worse than they really were. Then have an extra large bowl of ice cream, because what's a pity party without refreshments?

It's Only Money

Okay and maybe a lot of trouble, not to mention your only time off for the next year. But really and truly, lots of people have things much worse. And the more you can remember that and be grateful for your many blessings without being *really* smacked upside the head like we all were on September 11, 2001, the better off you'll be. And the better an example you'll set for your child and all the other good people of this world.